George W. Bush and the
Redemptive Dream

Inner Lives

Series Editor
William Todd Schultz

Forthcoming books in the series:

William Todd Schultz on Truman Capote
Alan C. Elms on Sigmund Freud
Tim Kasser on John Lennon
Kyle Arnold on Philip K. Dick

George W. Bush and the Redemptive Dream

A Psychological Portrait

Dan P. McAdams

OXFORD
UNIVERSITY PRESS

2011

OXFORD
UNIVERSITY PRESS

Oxford University Press, Inc., publishes works that further Oxford University's objective
of excellence in research, scholarship, and education.

Oxford   New York

Auckland   Cape Town   Dar es Salaam   Hong Kong   Karachi

Kuala Lumpur   Madrid   Melbourne   Mexico City   Nairobi

New Delhi   Shanghai   Taipei   Toronto

With offices in

Argentina   Austria   Brazil   Chile   Czech Republic   France   Greece

Guatemala   Hungary   Italy   Japan   Poland   Portugal   Singapore

South Korea   Switzerland   Thailand   Turkey   Ukraine   Vietnam

Published by Oxford University Press, Inc.

198 Madison Avenue, New York, New York 10016

www.oup.com

Oxford is a registered trademark of Oxford University Press, Inc.

Library of Congress Cataloging-in-Publication Data
McAdams, Dan P.
  George W. Bush and the redemptive dream : a psychological portrait /
Dan P. McAdams.
       p. cm.
  Includes bibliographical references.
  ISBN-13: 978-0-19-975208-9 (alk. paper)
  ISBN-10: 0-19-975208-7 (alk. paper)
  1. Bush, George W. (George Walker), 1946—Psychology. 2. Decision
making—Psychological aspects. 3. Redemption—Psychology I. Title.
  E903.3.M43 2011
  973.928092—dc22
  [B]

                                                          2010026601

9 8 7 6 5 4 3 2 1

Printed in the United States of America on acid-free paper

For Ruth and Amanda

Contents

Acknowledgments

Many good friends and colleagues provided support, advice, and critique during the period I worked on the Bush project. My biggest thank you goes to my wife, Rebecca Pallmeyer, who read and carefully considered every word of every draft. She provided invaluable editorial assistance throughout, to say nothing of the unconditional love. Next in line for my sincere gratitude stand Brad Olson, Jon Adler, Jim Anderson, and Todd Schultz. Brad worked with me early on to gather sources and think through aspects of the book's arguments, and he gave me good advice for every chapter. Jon sent me wonderfully astute suggestions for all the chapters via email. Jim also provided written critiques, and he gave me further advice and strong encouragement at our weekly tennis outings. In addition to providing thoughtful editorial advice on all the chapters, it was Todd's brilliant idea to launch a book series with Oxford University Press on "Inner Lives," for which this book is the inaugural volume.

Let me also express my gratitude to the many people who read various chapters and responded with good advice, words of wisdom, and the like. They include: Michelle Albaugh, Bob Arkin, Keith Cox, Joe Dadabo, Renee Engeln-Maddox, Hal Ersner-Hershfield, Jonathan Haidt, Kathrin Hanek, Walter Hanek, Brady Jones, Mike Kaufman, Miriam Klevan, Gina Logan, Hank Neuberger, Bill Peterson, Tasha Richardson, Rick Robins, Jim

Spillane, Keegan Walden, and Josh Wilt. And special thanks to Lori Handelman at Oxford University Press for her strong editorial support.

The research that went into the making of this book was supported by a grant from the Foley Family Foundation of Milwaukee, Wisconsin, to establish the Foley Center for the Study of Lives at Northwestern University.

George W. Bush and the
Redemptive Dream

Introduction: Why Did President George W. Bush Invade Iraq?

When it comes to the psychology of George W. Bush, there are two prevailing views. The first is that he was an idiot. The second is that he was a saint.

"Idiot" is not the technical term, of course. Those who revile the 43rd president have accused him of many psychological shortcomings. Some have claimed, for example, that he suffered from a serious case of Attention Deficit Hyperactivity Disorder, or that his general intelligence was simply too low to be an effective president of the United States. One Washington psychoanalyst has written that the first 2 years of life rendered George W. Bush an "undernurtured and emotionally hobbled infant, terrified of confronting the dangers within his own psyche."[1] Whether the critics, then, are talking about his powers of cognition or his basic emotional makeup, George W. Bush just didn't have the necessities.

Arguments for sainthood, or something like that, come from those who admire what they see as his rock-solid convictions and his steadfast commitment to protecting America from terrorism. Relentlessly optimistic and deeply principled, George W. Bush was a paragon of robust mental health and social engagement, his defenders have asserted. And don't forget that he stood strong against evil. Called to a higher purpose, he rallied the nation in a time of crisis. Affable, dynamic, and inspiring, he was a man of action who championed freedom for the world. You watch: he will be vindicated in the end!

Both sides agree on one thing, though: George W. Bush was a big deal, even by the exalted standards of American presidents. No Chester Arthur was he. This guy had a huge impact. He was a transformational president, an extraordinarily consequential actor on the world stage, perhaps *the* most consequential actor to date in this young century.

Arguably the most consequential aspect of the Bush presidency—the biggest decision he ever made—was the American invasion of Iraq, which began in the spring of 2003. The decision was controversial from the beginning. In contrast, for example, to the near-unanimous support from Congress that President Lyndon B. Johnson enjoyed in the first 1 to 2 years of the American build-up in the Vietnam War, politicians and many Americans spoke out against the Bush administration's plan to invade Iraq long before the invasion was launched. In the wake of 9/11 and in the midst of the administration's all-out persuasion campaign to convince Americans that Saddam Hussein must be eliminated, a total of 133 congressional representatives and 23 senators voted, in October 2002, *against* authorizing the president to use armed forces in Iraq. An obscure politician in Illinois—destined to become Bush's successor in the White House—called it a "dumb" war. As the Iraq War dragged on, an increasing number of critics moved well beyond words like "dumb" to "debacle," "quagmire," and "senseless tragedy." But others, by contrast, never gave up on their support. When the 2007 "surge" of additional troops occasioned some decline in hostilities and improvement in the political situation in Iraq, the war's supporters were jubilant, while its detractors were unimpressed. All in all, the Iraq War may be the most polarizing legacy of the Bush presidency.

Let us recall, albeit briefly, how it all happened back then:

- *September 11, 2001*: Terrorists attack the World Trade Center and the Pentagon, killing approximately 3,000 Americans. The administration quickly realizes that Osama bin Laden and the Al Qaeda network are responsible for the attacks. Within days, the president and his national security team begin planning a military response for Afghanistan, the terrorists' presumed refuge.
- *Fall of 2001:* Letters containing deadly anthrax spores are mailed to two U.S. senators and various news media offices, killing five people and infecting 17 others. The prospect that terrorists might unleash chemical and biological weapons of mass destruction causes further anxiety among Americans. The likelihood that the Iraqi dictator Saddam Hussein possesses such weapons gains considerable traction in the public mind.
- *December 2001:* American military and intelligence operations in Afghanistan enjoy some success, although Osama bin Laden escapes capture in the Afghan mountains of Tora Bora. Hamid Karzai is installed as Afghan president.
- *January 29, 2002:* In his State of the Union address, President Bush groups Iraq with Iran and North Korea as comprising an "axis of evil." "By seeking weapons of mass destruction," the president says, "these regimes pose a grave and gathering danger." Over time, many Americans come to see Saddam as an enemy in the president's overall "war on terror," even though the Iraqi dictator was not involved in the original impetus for that war—the 9/11 attacks.

- *June 1, 2002:* President Bush outlines his new doctrine of pre-emptive war in a commencement speech at the U.S. Military Academy at West Point.
- *August 22, 2002:* In a speech to the Veterans of Foreign Wars in Nashville, TN, Vice President Dick Cheney asserts that there is no doubt Saddam Hussein possesses weapons of mass destruction to be used against America and her allies.
- *October 2002:* As United Nations inspectors plan to search for weapons of mass destruction in Iraq, Congress votes to authorize the president's deployment of armed forces against Saddam Hussein, as the president "deems to be necessary and appropriate." The vote is 296 to 133 in the House and 77 to 23 in the Senate.
- *November 2002:* The U.N. Security Council votes 15 to 0 that Saddam Hussein must face serious consequences if he is indeed harboring weapons of mass destruction. (No such weapons are ever found.)
- *February 5, 2003:* In a speech to the United Nations, Secretary of State Colin Powell (who was initially opposed to military involvement in Iraq) makes a forceful case for an American-led invasion.
- *March 19, 2003:* President Bush orders the invasion of Iraq: "For the peace of the world and the benefit and freedom of the Iraqi people, I hereby give the order to execute Operation Iraqi Freedom. May God bless the troops." After ordering military operations, the president goes for a walk outside the Oval Office, by himself. Recalling the moment later, he said: "It was emotional for me. I prayed as I walked around the circle."[2]

Why did President Bush invade Iraq? On one level, the answer to the question seems easy. He invaded Iraq to rid the world of a murderous dictator. He invaded Iraq to protect the United States and its allies. He invaded Iraq to set the Iraqi people free. But the answer is easy only if we believe that most U.S. presidents under the same circumstances would have done the same thing. There is strong reason to suppose, however, that many others, had they found themselves in the same situation, would *not* have done what George W. Bush did. Case in point: His own *father,* President George H. W. Bush, had a grand opportunity to send American troops all the way into Baghdad during the 1991 Gulf War, and he chose not to do so. Reflecting the elder Bush's overall view, the venerable Republican advisor Brent Scowcroft warned, in August 2002, that invading Iraq would turn the entire Middle East into a "cauldron and thus destroy the war on terrorism."[3] Most Democrats assume that if Al Gore had won the presidential election in 2000, he would not have ordered an invasion of Iraq 3 years later. We can only guess, of course, but it seems unlikely that Presidents Nixon or Carter would have invaded Iraq in the wake of 9/11. Probably not Clinton either. Reagan? Maybe, maybe not. It is impossible to know, of course. But it certainly seems reasonable to conclude that more than a few Americans, whom we might imagine as president in 2003, would not have launched a preemptive invasion of Iraq.

When it seems that many others might *not* have done what George W. Bush did, one is motivated to search harder for the reasons behind his decision. Those reasons probably encompass political, economic, and ideological concerns. They might also include *psychological* factors. Psychological accounts do not trump other kinds of explanations. At most, they are only part of the story. But sometimes the psychological part is crucial and thereby helps to shed light on things previously shrouded in darkness. To the extent psychological explanations for Bush's decision have been offered to date, they have tended to focus on George W. Bush's assumedly conflicted relationship with his father. Stripped to its essentials, one common explanation goes like this: *throughout his life, George W. Bush tried to be like his father, but he always failed; by invading Iraq, the frustrated son sought to prove that he was the better man.* Those who buy into the "idiot" theory when it comes to the psychology of George W. Bush revel in the idea that Oedipal dynamics turned the son into a stubborn and simple-minded narcissist who invaded Iraq in order to play out an emotionally fraught family drama. Those who buy into the "saint" version either dismiss these kinds of explanations or put a positive spin on them—suggesting, for example, that George W. Bush courageously finished the job his father started.

In this book, I have a more psychologically compelling explanation to offer. My explanation flows from a full interpretation of George W. Bush's life and his personality, a psychological portrait of the man who famously called himself "The Decider," with a focus on the key decision of his presidency. In order to understand the fateful decision, therefore, we must develop a broad and nuanced psychological understanding of the decision-maker and the development of his personality over the course of life.

In a nutshell, my explanation goes like this:

George W. Bush's decision to invade Iraq was partly determined by a set of personal factors that came together, at a particular historical and biographical moment, to form a perfect psychological storm. The factors include: (1) strong dispositional traits in his personality that can be traced all the way back to his childhood years; (2) a set of motivational goals passed down from one generation to the next in the Bush family, including the desire to defeat his beloved father's greatest enemies; (3) a collection of values that eventually formed a coherent but unique brand of political conservatism; and (4) a personal story of redemption that George W. Bush developed and internalized for his own life at midlife, and then projected onto the world after the terrorist attacks of 9/11.

The dispositional traits set him up, psychologically speaking, to act boldly and with tremendous confidence on the world stage. The personal goals directed his boundless energy toward Iraq. The value system he internalized and articulated further, even up through his midlife years, provided him with an ideological framework within which to comprehend an invasion of Iraq. The redemptive story he developed for his own life around the time of his 40th birthday—a personal narrative about moving from sin to salvation, and about recovery through self-discipline—gave him the most powerful justification for the war and reinforced his confidence that he and America would emerge victorious in the end. The key feature of that story was George W. Bush's dream, the redemptive dream, to restore the kind of small-town goodness and freedom that he experienced growing up in Midland, Texas. It is the same goodness and freedom that he imagined America herself to have experienced, once upon a time.

What makes my psychological explanation of Bush's decision and my psychological portrait of his life any better than anybody else's? One thing that makes my account (much) better is its reliance on psychological *science*. In today's world, psychological talk is too often cheap and easy. Just about anybody can explain just about any piece of human behavior by invoking unsubstantiated folk notions or clinical anecdotes. With few exceptions, these pronouncements fail to draw upon, or even acknowledge, scientific research and theory in psychology and related fields. If there is a psychological analysis of George W. Bush's life that calls broadly and systematically upon psychological science, I have not seen it.

In *George W. Bush and the Redemptive Dream*, I draw upon the best-validated scientific concepts and theories in contemporary personality, social, developmental, and cognitive psychology, as well as relevant findings from psychological neuroscience. Over the past decade, psychological scientists in these subfields have made significant progress in understanding the cognitive, emotional, and motivational underpinnings of human behavior and experience. In making sense of why George W. Bush decided to invade Iraq, I have made liberal use of some of the best and brightest concepts to be found in psychological science today. These come from the burgeoning psychological literature on temperament traits of

personality, research on personal goals and strivings, social-psycho-
logical studies of political conservatism, new findings on moral
intuitions and people's gut feelings about right and wrong, studies
of autobiographical memory, the interdisciplinary study of life narratives and how people make sense of themselves through stories,
research on culture and personality, and perspectives on group life
and human development that come from evolutionary psychology.

For material on the life and presidency of George W. Bush,
I have relied exclusively on information that is widely available in
the public domain—books and articles, mainly. I have no new
secret fact or incident to reveal about Bush, no dramatic, game-
changing, now-to-be-disclosed-for-the-first-time revelation that
gives us "the key" to understanding the personality of the 43rd
president. The press and many others have examined every nook
and cranny of Bush's presidency, and just about everything that
can be discerned regarding his life. There are not likely to be many
new bombshell facts about Bush just waiting to be discovered.
Furthermore, the psychology of a person rarely, if ever, hinges on
a single "key" moment or event, despite popular conceptions to
the contrary. Psychological science shows that human personality
is complexly determined by many different factors that develop
and interact over time and across many, many situations. When it
comes to what happened in George W. Bush's life, we already have
more than enough information.

What we have not had until now, however, is any sensible and
scientifically grounded framework for putting it all together into an
illuminating psychological portrait. My interpretation of George W.
Bush's life and his decision, as president, to invade Iraq develops out
of a conception of human personality that has recently gained
broad acceptance and acclaim in the field of personality psychology.[4]
This new framework provides a powerful organization for scientific

research findings on personality that have accumulated over the past few decades. It also provides a compelling way to think psychologically about a single human life as it develops over time—any life, yours, mine, or George W. Bush's. In other words, the scientific framework I apply to George W. Bush's life in this book might be used to analyze nearly any biography. The framework is simple. It says that personality develops over time *in layers*, and each layer corresponds to a particular way of seeing the self. There are three layers: the self as actor, the self as agent, and the self as author.

We begin life as social *actors*. Even in infancy, we perform behaviors in the midst of other human beings, an actor on a social stage. How we enact our performances is strongly driven by our basic *dispositional traits*. Infants come into the world with very different temperament tendencies. Some babies are more energetic than other babies; some are more inhibited; some are consistently more cheerful. Over time and with experience, these differences morph into fundamental personality traits, expressed as differences in extraversion, agreeableness, conscientiousness, and so on. Our traits continue to develop and influence our social performances until our dying day. As we will see in Chapter 1, George W. Bush entered life with strong predispositions toward sky-high extraversion and rock-bottom openness to experience. These two traits strongly influenced his social performances from childhood onward, and both played major roles in setting him up, psychologically speaking, for *something like* an Iraq invasion. The dramatic events of 9/11 provided President George W. Bush with an ideal stage for the performance of a lifetime, and a standing-room-only audience ready to applaud.

Sometime in middle childhood, a second layer of personality starts to form. As children begin to generate personal goals and plans for their social performances, they effectively become motivated *agents*. To be an agent is to act according to self-chosen goals and values. Layered over basic traits, personal goals and values are strongly shaped by family experiences, schooling, religious influences, and other environmental factors. In Chapter 2, we will see how the 7-year-old George W. Bush developed his first personal goals in response to the death of his younger sister, Robin. Later, he internalized a set of goals passed down from one generation to the next in the Bush family, culminating in the goal to defeat his beloved father's greatest enemies. In Chapter 3, we will see how these goals connected up with his conservative values. Despite his unalloyed love for his father, George W. Bush developed a very different kind of conservative ideology than the one generally espoused by his father. A unique mixture of what George W. Bush named "compassionate conservatism" and the neonconservatism that he learned from Paul Wolfowitz and other advisors became an important aspect of his personality as president, and it helped to provide an ideological justification for his decision to invade Iraq.

As we move into late adolescence and early adulthood, our traits (self as actor) and our goals and values (self as agent) continue to develop and to influence our behavior and experience. But a third layer typically begins to form, as we seek to *author* a meaningful and unifying story for our lives. Contemporary research in psychological science documents the integrative power of people's *life stories*—internalized and evolving narratives of the reconstructed past and imagined future. Our stories function as personal myths, rather than objective accounts. Their relation to reality is sometimes tenuous. Nonetheless, our inner stories about who we are, who we have been, and where we are going provide meaning and ultimate purpose for our lives. At the same time, our stories say as much about the culture wherein we live as they do about the lives we are living. In a sense, each of us authors his or her own story with the strong assistance of the culture within which that story makes sense, more like co-authorship, if truth be told. If we were ever able to partition credit for the narrative, culture should share in some of the royalties and some of the blame.

Throughout his 20s and 30s, George W. Bush suffered from a kind of writer's block, psychologically speaking. Put simply, he could not find a story for his life. But around the age of 40 years, things turned rather dramatically. He experienced a religious conversion, gave up drinking for good, and finally authored a satisfying and purpose-driving story of the self, as we will see in Chapters 4 and 5. It is that story, a powerfully *redemptive* narrative about the restoration of goodness through self-discipline, that ultimately convinced George W. Bush that his fateful choice to launch a war against Iraq and Saddam Hussein was the right one, and that everything would work out for the good in the end. George W. Bush's self-defining life story is a quintessentially American story, a way of narrating the self whose roots go back hundreds of years in American history and heritage. In the life and presidency of George W. Bush, then, his redemptive life story linked up with his traits, his goals, and his values to provide the finishing psychological touch for his decision to invade Iraq.

Like most Americans, I have strong opinions about the Iraq War, and about the American president who launched it. But in writing this book, I have tried to put those opinions aside, as best I can, to provide a fair-minded psychological analysis of the decision and the man. As frustrating as this may be for some readers, this book takes no moral or political position on the Iraq War. It is not my purpose here to proclaim that President Bush's decision to invade Iraq was right or wrong. Instead, I seek to examine the psychological factors that may have gone into the decision, factors that reflect on the personality of the decision maker himself. In focusing mainly on this particular decision, furthermore, the book does not consider a number of other important and highly controversial aspects of the Bush presidency: his faith-based approach to social services, for example, or the administration's education policy, tax cuts, response to Hurricane Katrina, the interrogation of enemy combatants at Guantanamo and other detention centers, or the response to the economic crisis of 2008. It is likely that the psychological factors I identify in this book had impacts in other areas of the Bush presidency. The traits, goals, values, and stories that comprise George W. Bush's personality played themselves out in many different areas of his life. Nonetheless, I have set forth a specific task in this book. Whereas I draw widely from Bush's life in my analysis, I aim to shine the brightest light on one specific spot in his presidency. It may be the most important spot.

Finally, a word about names. George W. Bush was famous for giving nicknames to other people. Over the course of his life, moreover, he collected many nicknames for himself. At various times he was called "Little George," "Georgie," "Bushtail," "the Bombastic Bushkin," "Bushie," and "Dubya" (for "W"), among others. Apparently, nicknames run in the Bush family. His father, George H. W. Bush, was known by many family members and close friends as "Poppy." In order to distinguish George W. Bush from his father George H. W. Bush, I will often refer to the former as "George W." and to the latter, occasionally, as "Poppy." When referring to George W. Bush as a boy and young teenager, I will often use the nickname "Georgie," which was a family favorite and a term of endearment. Therefore, my occasional usage of the name "Georgie" to denote George W. Bush as a child should not be read as a derisive put-down. It is simply a name that was often used for him when he was young. And I kind of like the name, by the way. For me, it helps to convey a sense of youth, innocence, and possibility—and it helps me solve the problem of having too many "Georges" in this book.

ONE

The Actor's Traits

George W. Bush never decided to be a rambunctious 1-year-old. Born to George Herbert Walker Bush and Barbara (Pierce) Bush on July 6, 1946 in New Haven, Connecticut, little Georgie (as he was often called by the family) burst onto the stage with a tremendous amount of positive social energy. In a letter to a friend, his father described his firstborn, just 13 months old, in this way: "Whenever I come home he greets me and talks a blue streak, sentences disjointed, of course, by enthusiasm and spirit boundless." "He tries to say everything and the results are often hilarious."[1] Of course, babies often do and say funny things. But from the beginning, Georgie seemed to be blessed with a special ability to make an audience laugh, to stimulate in other people positive emotions like joy and excitement, to spread good cheer. In later years, his brother Marvin described George W. as the "family clown."[2] It was largely a compliment. People appreciated the comic role and the enthusiastic way he played it.

Like all of us, George W. Bush began life as an actor on a social stage, without choice or awareness. Long before we know what our roles are to be, we perform them in our own unique ways, expressing a characteristic style that we were never able to choose—perhaps a smiley disposition, a tendency to recoil in the face of novelty, a coyness that never fails to endear, a confident swagger. Shakespeare was surely right when he said that all the world's a stage and each of us a player.[3] But Shakespeare failed to emphasize how little control each of us has over *how* we enact the performances that, strung together over many years, come to comprise a life. Like Georgie, each of us gets our first roles from the *temperament dispositions* we have been assigned—those characteristic and consistent ways of acting on the social stage, instantly recognizable to our fellow performers, audiences, and critics. Even in the first months of life, we express our God-given—well, really DNA-driven—dispositional traits. "Mewling and puking" infants we all may be, as Shakespeare described the opening act, but some of us are relentlessly cheerful about it all; others whine and moan. By the time we become conscious of ourselves as social actors on stage (around age 4 years), it may already be too late in the play to change certain features of our characteristic behavioral style.[4] Our traits get a head start on us; for the rest of life, we have to play catch-up.

For Georgie the actor, his first big role was that of the exuberant family clown. Think about the role of a clown. What is the role's main purpose? It is to make you laugh, to lift your spirits. How does the clown do it? By coming at you, with jokes and outrageous behavior. There is no room in this role for shyness or subtlety. The clown is outgoing, gregarious, over-the-top, in-your-face. There is something aggressive about him, and something very physical, how he pushes and prods to get an emotional response.

Biographers of the Bush family single out Georgie's "innate aggressiveness" as a key temperament trait, by which they mean to suggest an exuberant social dominance.[5] In his campaign autobiography, published in 1999, George W. attributes the very same traits to himself: "I am restless"; "I am impatient"; "I am outgoing"; "I've always invaded other people's spaces, leaning into them, touching, hugging, getting close"; "[I] am perpetual motion"; "I provoke people, confront them in a teasing way"; "I will tease."[6] As one journalist puts it, George W. Bush "moves toward conviviality like a heat-seeking missile."[7]

When Georgie was 2 years old, his father packed up the new red Studebaker and moved the family to Texas, where George Senior would begin a highly successful career in the energy business. After short stints in Odessa, Texas, and in California, the Bushes settled in Midland, Texas, a middle-class community that housed many young, upwardly mobile couples from the East Coast who were hoping to strike it rich in oil. For the next 10 years, Georgie enjoyed what he later described as a "happy blur" of baseball, bike riding, friendships, and mischief.[8] A sister, Robin, was born in 1949, followed by brothers John Ellis (known as "Jeb," born in 1953), Neil (1955), and Marvin (1956) and sister Dorothy (known as "Doro," born in 1959). Georgie loved cowboys. In a letter to his own father back in Connecticut, George Senior wrote of his wonderful Texas family: "Robin is now walking around, and Georgie has grown to be a near-man, talks dirty once in awhile and occasionally swears, aged four and a half. He lives in his cowboy clothes."[9]

Armed with their BB guns, the neighborhood's little cowboys took potshots at the frogs who populated a gully behind the Bush property. Georgie was the ringleader. On at least one occasion, they lit firecrackers and inserted them into frogs' mouths, hurling them in the air as exploding grenades. "We were terrible to animals," admits one childhood friend. "Terrible."[10] As gruesome as it all seems, this kind of behavior was apparently not all that aberrant among little West Texan boys at the time. Clinical psychologists suggest that cruelty to animals can be an early predictor of delinquency, criminality, and other social disorders. But an ominous diagnostic scenario seems far-fetched in the Bush case. Georgie may have been no angel, but he was no sociopath-in-the-making either. He was a cowboy, a roughneck, a tough guy, full of swagger even at age 10 years, and always one for clowning around. To his classmates' delight, Georgie played the clown in the schoolroom. You remember boys like him—the ones who made rude noises with their armpits, farted when the teacher left the room and then blamed the little girl sitting across the row, or mimicked the teacher when her back was turned. The other kids said, "Good morning, Mrs. Weatherspoon," when they greeted their Sunday school teacher. Georgie, on the other hand, would shout, "Hiya, little lady. Lookin' sexy!"[11]

Throughout his school years and even into college, George W. Bush was always one of the most popular guys in the class. He was seventh-grade class president at San Jacinto Junior High School. Years later, a female classmate admitted that she voted for Georgie in that particular election because he was "cuter" than the other candidate.[12] (He no doubt also won votes for his personality.) In 1959, the Bush family moved to Houston, where Georgie attended the Kinkaid Preparatory School. Even as the proverbial small-town boy new to the big city, his good looks and high energy won Georgie many friends in Houston. It was at Kinkaid that he began to bestow nicknames on his friends and classmates, a practice that would follow him all the way to the White House. One hulking classmate became "Rodan," after a monster in a Japanese horror film. A lanky student became "Stretch." The smartest kid in the class was "Brain." (Georgie himself acquired a series of nicknames over the years—from "Bushtail" and "Bombastic Bushkin" to "Dubya" and, his future wife's pet name for him, "Bushie.") It was also at Kinkaid that Georgie began to exhibit an uncanny ability to remember people's names (even when he did not bestow nicknames on them). Years later in college, he would study the school register to learn his classmates' names.

When the time for high school arrived, Georgie assumed that he was headed for the local public school or one of Houston's private prep schools that his Kinkaid classmates would be attending. But his parents had other ideas. They decided that he should follow George Senior's educational path and attend Phillips Andover Academy, an exclusive, private boarding school for young men, twenty miles north of Boston. Four years later, his parents would encourage their son to apply for Yale University, George Senior's college alma mater. And so it all came to pass, without too much dissent from their firstborn.

The transition from Houston to Andover, however, was difficult. The cold New England winter chilled George W.'s spirits, and the school's regimented formality threatened to crush the brash Texan's impulses. Andover men were required to wear jackets and ties to class and to attend chapel 5 days a week. From early morning to the 10:00 p.m. curfew, the school day was mapped out with military precision. George W. also struggled with the schoolwork, receiving distressingly low marks for the first time in his academic career. Still, he managed to flourish, largely by dint of his overwhelming gregariousness, his good spirits, his uncanny proclivity to find new ways to make fun mischief, and his ability to forge relationships with different groups of students from different backgrounds and social classes. As one biographer put it:

> "young Bush's particular genius—the facility for wiping out in milliseconds the distance separating himself from total strangers—would more than compensate [for the difficulties he faced at Andover]. What drew the other boys to him was that instant familiarity: remembering their names (or, if one's surname twisted the tongue, assigning a nickname), flipping arms around shoulders, acute eye contact, a gruff yet seductive whisper."[13]

Poking fun at the Andover sports establishment, George W. set up an intramural stickball league. Games were to be played with broomsticks and an old tennis ball. He appointed himself the stickball league's "high commissioner." He organized teams and gave them mildly scandalous names, like "the Beavers" and the "Nads" (their cheer: "Go-Nads!"). The absurd thing became wildly popular at Andover. Nearly the entire student body showed up for the championship match. Designating himself to be the umpire for the final contest, the high commissioner was carried onto the field on the shoulders of his classmates. The Steamers beat the Beavers, 3 to 0.

When it comes to the personality of George W. Bush, the predominant theme that seems to run through the first act in his life's drama is the rambunctiousness and social exuberance about which his father wrote when the boy was only 13 months of age. Through his high school years, this enthusiastic actor played the clown role as well as anybody you or I might have encountered back then, had we followed him around to those various social stages upon which George W. performed from 1946 to 1964, from Midland to Houston to Andover. He played the role with such skill and fidelity that he became a Big Man on Campus at an elite, private high school that valued duty, scholarship, and sports above all else—all this from a guy who was mediocre in both schoolwork and sports, and who scoffed at the school's traditions.

Giving a unique shape and vital energy to the clown role was a set of personality dispositions that encompassed enthusiasm, gregariousness, social dominance, optimism, a tendency toward frivolity, and the ability to spread positive emotion in others. These action tendencies won him many friends and brought him popularity wherever he went. And they continued to work for him in this way as he moved into adulthood, providing young George W. with a remarkable temperament resource for developing interpersonal relationships and building a broad social network. An incident at Yale exemplified this central tendency in the personality of George W. Bush. As part of a fraternity hazing ritual, the 54 pledges for Delta Kappa Epsilon (DKE) were paddled, verbally abused, and given a variety of distasteful tasks to perform. Sleep-deprived and disoriented, they were dragged into a room and told, one by one, to name all the other pledges in their class. The "DKEs" abused their pledges in this way every year. Going back as far as anybody knew, no victim had ever been able to provide full names for more than a handful of his fellow pledges. A typical score might be a 6 or 7. When it came George W.'s turn, he made history: He named all 54.

***

Over the past two decades, personality scientists have made important discoveries about the basic psychological traits that drive and shape human action. Relying on questionnaires and surveys, laboratory experiments, behavioral observations, family studies, twin studies, psychophysiological assessments, brain scans, sophisticated statistical analyses, and a range of other scientific methods, these investigators have charted the deep geography of psychological individuality. Their scientific studies have explored in detail what makes each of us a unique actor on the social stage of life.[14] The findings of their studies sometimes confirm common sense, but often they do not. Many scientific findings about personality are surprising and even unsettling, and they go against what many parents, therapists, and other self-proclaimed "experts" believe. In considering the personality of George W. Bush, let us cast our lot with science, over blind faith and folklore, and see what we can learn. Based on the broad scientific literature, here are four things that we now know about personality:

1. *A handful of dispositional traits provide the foundation upon which our character and our identity are built.* At the deepest layer of personality, we find five broad clusters or groupings of basic traits.[15] Personality scientists routinely call these the Big Five. For each of the five, I will use the popular names provided by Paul Costa and Jeff McCrae, two scientists who have conducted ground-breaking studies on the Big Five personality traits. The first grouping of basic traits is *extraversion* (E), or the tendency to behave in outgoing, gregarious, spontaneous, and socially dominant ways. The second is *neuroticism* (N), which subsumes tendencies toward anxiety, sadness, distress, and other negative emotional states. The third grouping is *conscientiousness* (C), which speaks to how disciplined, focused, organized, and hard-working a person may be. The fourth cluster goes by the name of *agreeableness* (A), and it encompasses altruism, humility, and being a very nice and

caring person. Finally, there is *openness to experience (O)*—a more cognitively-based trait that concerns the extent to which a person is comfortable with change, intellectually curious, and broad-minded.

If you rearrange the first letters of the five groupings, you have the word OCEAN. The Big Five are a vast ocean of personality traits, divided into five areas or seas. The five areas are statistically independent from each other, meaning that where you stand in one given area (say, agreeableness) has no predictive bearing on where you might stand in another area (say, neuroticism). Each of the five areas, furthermore, subsumes many smaller or narrower traits. For example, extraversion includes smaller traits of sociability, activity level, and the tendency to experience positive emotions. Some smaller traits, furthermore, may be seen as blends—fitting partly in one area and partly in another. For example, the trait of impulsiveness fits partly in extraversion (*E*) and neuroticism (*N*) and partly on the low end of conscientiousness (*C*). Just about any general behavioral disposition you can think of (and the English language gives you literally thousands of possibilities) fits somewhere in the OCEAN.[16]

2. *Individual differences in dispositional traits make a huge difference in our lives.* What are the things we care most about in life? Our families? Our work? Our happiness? Our health? Fundamental differences in personality traits impact all of these things. High levels of neuroticism, for example, tend to be associated with instability in relationships and with divorce. People high in conscientiousness attain much higher levels of job success than those scoring lower on measures of *C*. They also live longer. A landmark longitudinal study shows that being low in conscientiousness *at age 10 years* is a risk factor for an early

death down the road, about equal to the medical risk that comes from elevated levels of blood cholesterol.[17] Research shows that extraverts tend to be happier than introverts. Of course, these are simply statistical trends—as are the linkages, for example, between smoking cigarettes and lung cancer. You can always find somebody who smoked two packs a day and lived to be 100. There are always individual exceptions to empirical findings in the behavioral and health sciences. But the scientific trends are still clear. Personality traits matter.[18]

3. *Traits are surprisingly stable across much of the life course.* Signs of the emerging Big Five traits appear in early childhood.[19] Children's early performances in social situations give clues regarding the kinds of social actors they will eventually become. For example, kindergartners who show good impulse control and are able to delay immediate gratification to obtain long-term rewards tend to grow up to score high on adult measures of conscientiousness. Teacher ratings of how outgoing and how gentle their students are in grade school tend to correlate significantly with those students' adult scores on measures of extraversion and agreeableness, respectively. Stability in traits is especially high in the adult years. Although change can always occur, people tend to show consistent trait profiles from, say, age 30 to 50 years. In other words, a person high in neuroticism at 30 years of age will probably score relatively high on that same trait 20 years later, and this is likely true even if he or she gets psychotherapy at age 40. It is really hard to change your traits, especially as you move beyond young adulthood. I don't want to sound too fatalistic here. Some changes do surely occur. For example, many people tend to grow slightly more conscientious and more agreeable as they get older, reflecting a broad developmental trend from adolescence through midlife.

Still, dramatic shifts (though possible) are rare, and relative temporal stability in individual differences tends to be the norm.[20] If you don't believe me, be sure to attend your next high school reunion.

4. *Traits are substantially heritable.* Studies in behavior genetics show that at least half of the variance in adult personality traits results from genetic variability across people. What does this mean in English? It means that genes are a big deal when it comes to dispositional traits. Basic differences in our acting styles—how outgoing we tend to be, how anxious and prone to depression, how focused and organized, how friendly and caring we are in a very general sense—are substantially driven by the genotypes we are born with. This is partly why we never seem to catch up with our traits, as I suggested at the beginning of this chapter. Our genes get the party going long before we are even aware that we are there.

Now, don't take this line of argument too far. Scientists have yet to identify a particular gene that produces a particular personality trait, and they likely never will. It seems that *many* genes go into the making of any given trait, and that genes interact in complex ways with environmental inputs over the life course. Environments *do* matter. But probably not the environments that most people think of. For example, studies consistently show that, with a few extreme exceptions, the general ways that parents raise their children—how permissive or strict they are, for example—*have virtually no effect* on the development of the children's personality traits. If you are high in conscientiousness, it is probably not because your parents encouraged you to study, or to make your bed, or anything they did, really. Similarly, big or dramatic events in your life don't usually make your traits happen. If you are an introvert, it is not because your first girlfriend dumped you. If you think you are high in neuroticism because your parents divorced when you were five years old, you are making a causal explanation for which there is no scientific evidence. Translated: you are probably wrong. If you want to blame your parents, blame them for the genes.[21]

How might we know our trait scores? Personality scientists have traditionally used two simple and surprisingly valid methods. Either they ask the actor about traits, or they ask the audience. The first method is called self-report, and it is the more common, especially when measuring traits in adults. In self-report, a person answers a series of simple questions about the self. For extraversion, questions might include, "Do you enjoy yourself at lively parties?" and "Are you a carefree person?" And so on. The second method asks other people to rate the person on simple questions. The "other people" might be friends or spouses, or they might be researchers themselves who observe the actor's behavior under controlled laboratory conditions. Ratings of children's traits are often done by parents or by laboratory researchers.

The logic behind both methods of trait assessment—asking the actor and asking the audience—is the logic of social observation. Human beings are social animals who evolved to live in groups. Our brains are extraordinarily sensitive to social information, all of which comes to us through some form of observation. We cannot help but watch and listen to each other, check each other out, make judgments about each other's action tendencies. Similarly, we cannot help but observe *our own behavior* on the social stage. Each of us has a pretty good sense of where we stand on each of the Big Five traits because we have been observing our own behavior (and noting our own feelings and thoughts), and observing how other people react to our behavior and what they say about us, for almost as long as we have lived—technically, since about the age of 4 years. Roughly speaking, we know our traits, and other people who know us know our traits pretty well, too. Evidence for that last statement comes from years of research showing relatively high (though by no means perfect) correlations between actors' self-reports and ratings of those actors made by others who know them.[22]

Let us now return to the hero of our story. I do not have official results from a well-validated measure of Big Five traits completed by George W. Bush himself. Nor have I ever had the opportunity to ask his friends and acquaintances to rate him systematically on a series of trait dimensions. But I (and we) have the next best thing. What we all have is a copious public record that consists of countless trait attributions about George W. Bush made by people who know him (as well as by people who have never personally met him, but have observed him over the years). And we have Bush's self-reported attributions—things he has said about his own personality in interviews and speeches, and in his 1999 campaign autobiography, *A Charge to Keep.*

What do these different sources of "data" say? Despite the fact that the 43rd president continues to be a polarizing figure on the American scene, evoking wildly divergent opinions and feelings, there is near-universal consensus on at least one fundamental feature of his personality. *According to nearly everybody who has ever known him, George W. Bush is, and probably always has been, a blazing extravert.* Indeed, a team of researchers who systematically rated all of the U.S. presidents on the Big Five traits, going back to George Washington, ranked George W. Bush at the top on extraversion, essentially tied with Teddy Roosevelt and Bill Clinton. On a scale running from 0 to 100, Bush received a 99.6. At the bottom was Calvin Coolidge, with a score of 0.4.[23] (It has been reported that a woman seated next to Coolidge at dinner one evening said to him, "Mr. Coolidge, I've made a bet against a fellow who said it was impossible to get more than two words out of you." His famous reply: "You lose.")

The social exuberance, the swagger, the mischievous high jinks and merriment, the teasing, the nicknaming, the in-your-face gregariousness, the ability to make people laugh, the uncanny knack for remembering names and the sheer motivation to do so, the popularity he enjoyed on virtually every social stage where George W. Bush performed in the first two decades of his life—it is all largely about the actor's extraversion. Of course, there is always more than one trait at play in behavior. Behavior is always complexly shaped by a range of dispositions and by the social context wherein the behavior is performed. But let us keep it simple at first. There is simply no getting away from the trait of extraversion in the life of George W. Bush. It is where we have to start in thinking about the structure of his personality.

Scientific research shows that extraversion encompasses much more than merely being outgoing. Compared to those scoring toward the introversion end of the continuum, those high in extraversion are indeed described as more gregarious and sociable, more likely to associate with more people on a daily basis, more people-oriented. But they are also more spontaneous and (oftentimes) impulsive. They are more likely to take risks, especially in social interactions. They can be bold and brazen. They seek excitement. Their behavior is strongly energized by what neuroscientists call the brain's *Behavioral Approach System* (the *BAS*).

The BAS is responsible for motivating behavior aimed at approaching goals in the environment and obtaining positive emotional rewards. The BAS is made up of various pathways and structures in the brain that are implicated in the release of a chemical called *dopamine*. One of many substances responsible for conveying information from one nerve cell to another, dopamine is a neurotransmitter that is broadly associated with experiences of reward and pleasure, as well as the craving for reward and pleasure. The BAS is essential for human survival, for where would we be if we never approached goals and sought out rewards in the social environment? (We would be dead.) Indeed, everybody has a BAS, and dopamine works pretty much the same way in everybody's brain (and in the brains of monkeys, dogs, rats, and other mammals). However, it would seem that individual differences in extraversion track subtle differences in the way the BAS operates from one brain to the next. In simple terms, extreme extraverts like George W. Bush have a more active BAS than do the rest of us.[24]

Extraversion is a powerful resource for good in personality because of its tendency to recruit positive emotion. The research here is clear, albeit annoying to people like me, who must admit to a few introverted tendencies. People high in extraversion tend to be happier and to enjoy more positive emotion than people who score lower in extraversion.[25] And positive emotions like joy and excitement are almost always good—good for the happy person who experiences them, but also good for others around the happy person. Again and again, psychological studies show that when people enjoy positive emotions, they perform at higher levels, they expand their horizons and develop their best potentials, and they do good and helpful things for others. In the words of Barbara Fredrickson, a prominent emotions researcher, positive emotions "build and broaden" the self and enhance the world within which the self operates.[26]

High extraversion, however, is not always good. There can be downsides. When it comes to psychopathology, for example, high extraversion is associated with what psychologists call *externalizing disorders*, such as delinquency and substance abuse.[27] Extraverts can be quick to anger, as we see in both George W. Bush and Bill Clinton. In service of the BAS, the emotion of anger can generate an aggressive approach toward achieving social goals.[28] The challenge is to focus the anger in a constructive way. There is also some evidence to suggest that people high in extraversion tend not to learn as much as they should from punishment and from mistakes they make.[29]

Overall, however, the social and emotional positives tend to outweigh the negatives when it comes to extraversion. Optimistic, enthusiastic, confident, and fun-loving, extraverts seek out social rewards with gusto and charisma. They are movers and shakers on the social stage. We social actors all have different strengths and weaknesses. For the most part, extraversion is a formidable strength.

***

George W. Bush carried his extraversion with him through the next two decades of wanderlust and failure. As much as anything else (including even his famous father), extraversion helped to get him through.

When George W. graduated from Yale in the spring of 1968, over 536,000 American troops were fighting in Vietnam. Eligible now for the draft, he interviewed with Col. Walter "Buck" Staudt, commander of the 147th Fighter Wing of the Texas Air National Guard. The interview was made possible by a series of phone calls, initiated either by George Bush Senior or by a friend of his in Houston who contacted Ben Barnes, former speaker of the Texas House of Representatives, who in turn contacted Col. Staudt. George W. told Staudt that he wanted to be a fighter pilot like his father, who had served heroically in World War II. It was highly unlikely, however, that a pilot in the Texas Air National Guard would ever be called upon to bomb targets in Haiphong harbor. Obtaining a coveted spot in the Air Guard would most certainly keep the young man out of the Vietnam War.

George W. took the entrance exam and was accepted for pilot training. He became a competent pilot and remained on active Reserve duty from 1969 to 1973. During this time, he lived in seven different apartments in three different states, held at least three different dead-end jobs, and had many girlfriends. It was the beginning of what George W. later called his "nomadic period." "He was so lost and floating," his friend Doug Hannah recalled. "It was the first time he had kind of lost his anchor. He wasn't doing anything."[30] What Hannah meant was that he wasn't doing anything *productive*. In vintage extraversion form, George W. was doing an awful lot of drinking and partying, and a lot of driving around Houston in his sports car, on the prowl for pretty women and a good time.

Hoping he might find focus and a vocation in life, George W. attended Harvard Business School from 1973 to 1975. With his West Texan swagger, his penchant for country music, and his habit of chewing tobacco and spitting it into a cup, George W. cut an odd form in Cambridge, Massachusetts. Nonetheless, he managed to make friends here, too. Although he would later describe Harvard as a turning point, nothing especially dramatic seems to have happened during this time. He did well enough in his classes, and he learned to use some of the tools and vocabulary of the business world. It does not seem right to suggest that Harvard turned George W. in the direction of business, because he was modestly interested in business affairs long before he took classes in Cambridge. Harvard, and the simple passing of time, may have helped, however, to solidify these interests. Upon receipt of the

MBA, he decided to take his shot in the oil business, as his father had done almost three decades before.

George W. returned to Midland, Texas, in 1975. He started out as a "land man," searching court records for mineral rights and trying to put oil deals together. With financial assistance from his uncle, Johnny Bush, George W. started his own company, Arbusto Oil. The company's name was Spanish for "Bush," but the middle syllable proved to be more prophetic. Over the next 7 years and despite millions of dollars of investment, oil drilling turned out to be a bust. In 1984, Arbusto merged with the more successful Spectrum 7. In early 1986, however, world oil prices collapsed, and Spectrum 7 faced bankruptcy.

In the meantime, George W. threw his hat into Texas politics. But that was a failure, too. He lost the 1978 congressional race to Kent Hance, a tough, good-old-boy Texan who ridiculed George W.'s Ivy League pedigree. Andover, Yale, and Harvard turned out to be liabilities that the young, aspiring politician could not overcome. He would have been much better off with a degree from Texas Tech. After the crushing defeat, the losing candidate vowed never to be "out-Texaned" again. Throughout this period, George W. continued to drink heavily. Some family members worried that his drinking problem had shaded into outright alcoholism. On the positive side, George W. met Laura Welch in 1977, and married her a few months later. In November 1981, the couple gave birth to twins.

Things began to turn brighter for George W. around the time of his 40th birthday. Psychologically speaking, this period truly did mark a significant turning point. First, he developed a deeper Christian faith, which seemed to soften some of his rough edges and give him focus. Second, he swore off alcohol. Third, he became involved in his father's presidential campaign. Vice president under

Ronald Reagan from 1981 to 1989, George H. W. Bush began planning for his own run for the presidency early in Reagan's second term. Known as "The Enforcer" among the many aides who worked on his father's ultimately successful campaign, the firstborn son brought energy, discipline, and fierce loyalty to the effort. In the 1988 election, George W. was especially effective in helping his father relate to Christian evangelicals, who by then had become an indispensible part of the Republican political base.

Fourth, he became part owner of the Texas Rangers baseball team, fulfilling a lifelong dream to have a meaningful role in professional baseball. (Georgie had wanted to be like Willie Mays when he grew up; later he would express interest in becoming the commissioner of Major League Baseball.) George W. hobnobbed with the Rangers players and fans, and he was instrumental in raising funds to construct a new stadium for the team, which gave him very positive visibility throughout Texas in the late 1980s and early 1990s. In 1992, his father failed to win a second term as president, losing to Bill Clinton. Shortly after his father's defeat, George W. announced that he would run for governor of Texas, against the popular incumbent Ann Richards. To most people's amazement, including his parents', he defeated Richards in the 1994 race. On that fateful night, second-born son Jeb Bush (whose childhood dream was to become president) lost his initial bid to become governor of Florida.

Through the ups and downs of his 20s, 30s, and 40s, George W. remained the restless and energetic extravert who always managed to win friends, raise spirits, and attract a crowd. Despite many setbacks, he exuded supreme confidence that things would work out for him in the long run, to the point of cockiness. Of course, when your father is in the White House (as he was from 1981–1993, first as vice president), it is easy to be confident.

Doors tend to open. You get noticed. Still, George W.'s dispositional extraversion served him well during this time. He effectively brought people together in business deals, even if Arbusto drilled one dry hole after another. He assembled a vast network of friends and admirers in Midland and Houston. As part owner of the Rangers, he was a relentless booster and optimistic public face. Years later, when George W. Bush himself occupied the White House, a former Pentagon official compared his approach to the presidency to the way he ran the baseball team: "He served as a corporate master-of-ceremonies, attending to the morale of the management team."[31]

From San Jacinto Junior High to the governor's mansion in Austin, George W. excelled in boosting morale. Humor proved to be one of his best methods, as it had back when he played the role of the class clown. Of course, humor is always contextual. What might seem hilarious at a gathering of Texas politicos in the late 1990s might not bring so many laughs at, say, a Palo Alto dinner party in 2010.

Which brings us to the Bob Bullock story. Sometimes a single incident expresses a trait so clearly that a psychologist like me cannot let it go. Let us turn to a scene in George W.'s life where he is at his most outrageously extraverted best, or worst. It is 1997, and Governor Bush is attending a breakfast meeting with state political officials, including the bombastic, 250-pound Bob Bullock. The most powerful Democrat in Texas, Bullock is the state's lieutenant governor. Over scrambled eggs and toast and outside the purview of cameras, Bullock announces that he is planning to throw his weight behind a legislative bill that Governor Bush opposes.

"I'm sorry, Governor," Bullock says, "but I'm going to have to fuck you on this one." Everybody goes silent, nervous. It is an awkward moment. George W. gets up, walks over to Bullock, grabs him by the shoulders, and plants a huge, wet kiss on his lips.

"What the hell did you do that for?" Bullock blurts out, wiping his mouth in disgust.

Bush shoots back: "If you're going to fuck me, you'll have to kiss me first."

For a brief moment, everybody is stunned. Then, the room erupts in riotous laughter and applause.[32]

***

Two of the most extraverted presidents of all time were George W. Bush and Bill Clinton. Like Bush, Clinton was a social dynamo, famous for working every room he ever walked into. Both men were supremely gregarious, outgoing, upbeat, enthusiastic, and energetic—even more so than most other politicians we know and see, granting that to be a politician at all in this day and age requires no small minimum of people skills. Like extreme extraverts the world over, George W. Bush and Bill Clinton could be impulsive and prone to taking big risks. They were also both famous for sudden bursts of anger, another behavioral tendency that research has connected to extraversion.

Yet nobody has ever confused George W. Bush with Bill Clinton. Despite their similarities on the trait of extraversion, many people who have observed these two political actors over the past two decades would cast George W. and Clinton in sharp contrast. In many important ways, they seem very different from each other.

One ostensible difference that supporters of George W. Bush have often identified is *discipline*. As president, Clinton seemed to lose focus at times; he could be undisciplined with respect to his political agenda and, more famously, his personal life. By contrast,

George W. ran a much tighter ship, both professionally and personally. Whereas Clinton always had a difficult time keeping to a schedule, meetings began and ended at the precisely appointed minute in the Bush White House. Clinton stayed up late chatting with aides and eating donuts. George W. was in bed by 10:00 p.m. In a more general sense, Bush seemed better able to control the strong BAS impulses that accompany high extraversion, whereas Bill Clinton never got high marks on impulse control. Yet, George W. was scattered and undisciplined, nearly out of control at times, in his 20s and 30s. And Clinton could focus like a laser beam on an issue when it mattered deeply to him, as he showed in his determined effort, albeit unsuccessful, to forge a peace agreement between Israel and the Palestinians. Clinton often exhibited steely resolve in battling the Republican Congress during the last 6 years of his presidency.

Another potential difference between the two men, perennially identified by Clinton supporters, is intelligence. Clinton was much smarter, they will say. Throughout his presidency, critics and comedians lampooned Bush as an intellectual dolt. He wasn't smart enough to be the president of the United States, they said. Perhaps you remember this bumper sticker: "Somewhere in Texas, a village has lost its idiot."

Now, no American president to my knowledge has ever been dumb enough to take an IQ test, at least not while in office. But a few research psychologists have made educated guesses regarding the relative cognitive skills of those men who have held the highest office in the land. They have based their estimates on a careful reading of the historical record, including speeches given and letters composed by presidents, and on historians' reports regarding the presidents' reputations among their peers. Estimating the IQs of (mostly) dead presidents is an inexact science at best, and given how contentious the issue of intelligence is in our society, a risky one. Still, the remarks of research psychologist Dean Keith Simonton are instructive here. The world's leading scholar in the quantitative psychological study of historical figures, Simonton argues that most presidents have shown levels of general intelligence that are significantly above the average for the population at large. Near the top of the pack, according to Simonton, are John Quincy Adams and Thomas Jefferson. Jimmy Carter and Bill Clinton also receive very high marks on intelligence. But George W. Bush is no slouch. Simonton's estimates have him at about the same level as Lyndon Johnson and Harry Truman. The analyses suggest that if researchers could obtain a valid IQ measure for Bush, he would probably score in the top 10% of the distribution for adults in the United States. Simonton concludes: "Bush is definitely intelligent . . . He is certainly smart enough to be president of the United States."[33]

Most people who knew Bush well when he was governor of Texas or president of the United States seem to agree with Professor Simonton. White House Press Secretary Scott McClellan wrote, "Bush is plenty smart enough to be president."[34] *New York Times* reporter Frank Bruni followed Bush all over the country during the 2000 presidential campaign. He described the future president as funny, even silly at times, engaging, sensible—and plenty smart.[35] During that same campaign, Bill Clinton warned Democrats not to underestimate Bush's cognitive powers. Compared to his opponent Al Gore, Bush had much less background in domestic and foreign policy, Clinton argued, but that may say little about his intelligence. After Gore lost, Clinton said this about Bush: "He doesn't know anything; he doesn't want to know anything; but he is not dumb."[36]

The first statement in Clinton's pithy triptych is an exaggeration of course; the third makes Simonton's point. But the most

interesting statement is the middle one: Bush "doesn't *want to*
know anything." He is just not very *curious* about the world at
large, Clinton suggested. Many observers of the 43rd president
have said the same thing. Former Democratic Chairman Robert
Strauss put it this way: "I don't think he's curious enough to ask
about important things. That's his weakness—he's incurious."[37]
Arizona Senator John McCain said this: "As a matter of fact, he is
not intellectually curious."[38] Press Secretary McClellan claimed
that Bush *was* curious about some things, but "his intellectual curiosity tends to be centered on knowing what he needs in order to
effectively articulate, advocate, and defend his policies."[39] *New York
Times* columnist Nicholas Kristof said that George W. Bush
was "less interested in ideas than perhaps anybody I've ever
interviewed."[40]

Throughout much of his life, George W. Bush seemed surprisingly *uninterested* in the broader world around him. This lack
of curiosity dovetailed on occasion with his tendencies toward
extraversion, for at times it seemed as if he were simply having too
much fun to notice what was going on in society, culture, and the
world at large. In high school, he seemed blissfully unaware of
momentous world events from the early 1960s, such as the Bay of
Pigs disaster and America's nuclear showdown with the Soviets over
missiles in Cuba. A classmate at Andover remembers George W.
Bush this way:

> "[At Andover in 1961–1962] most of us were scared shit-
> less by the Cuban Missile Crisis. People were emptying
> out supermarkets and crawling into bomb shelters,
> everybody was so convinced there was going to be a
> nuclear war. But George just kept clowning around,

trying to raise everybody's spirits. Either he felt it was his
job to keep things upbeat, or he just didn't get it."[41]

*Either he felt it was his job to keep things upbeat, or he just didn't
get it.* From the standpoint of the psychology of dispositional
traits, this statement is priceless. It pits two very different psychological tendencies against each other. Either George W. was doing
his usual extraversion thing, or he was expressing some other
broad trait in his personality that kept him from "getting it." What
is that other trait? In the lexicon of the Big Five, the other broad
trait that is so central to the dispositional profile of George W.
Bush is *openness to experience*, defined as a tendency to explore new
thoughts, values, feelings, and experiences, to be intellectually
adventurous and expansive in one's consciousness, to question
convention and seek out complexity. People high in openness to
experience are described (by themselves and others) as imaginative, reflective, artistic, aesthetically sensitive, broad-minded, and
refined. It is important to note that openness to experience is not
the same thing as intelligence. You don't have to be smart to be
high in openness, and many people who are very intelligent do not
necessarily rank high on this personality trait.[42] Where might
George W. rank? *Very low.* The same team of psychologists who
rated Bush as one of the most extraverted presidents in history
ranked him dead last on openness to experience.[43]

People who are low on openness to experience are uncomfortable with change and ambiguity. They value routine, predict-
ability, and consistency. Their preferences can extend to daily
activities. George W. Bush was famous for sticking to a regular
routine and staying in his comfort zone. As governor, he had
the same fruit salad for breakfast every day and almost always

ordered simple, American, comfort food for dinner.[44] He stuck religiously to his jogging regimen. On weekends, the governor would retreat to his fishing lodge in East Texas and, in the words of one biographer, "gravitate to the same fishing holes, where he would inevitably catch and release the same bass, over and over, to the point where he had actually named the fish who were his constant prey: 'Let's see what ol' Henry's up to.'"[45] Later as president, he regularly retreated to his ranch in Crawford, Texas, even in the sweltering days of August, where he would ride his bike over the rough terrain, clear brush, and relax. When he traveled to foreign countries, he spent very little time taking in the sights or inquiring into local history, culture, and customs.

When it comes to considering personality's importance for the presidency, the most relevant features of openness to experience pertain to characteristic ways of thinking about the world. People low in openness tend to comprehend cultural, political, and moral issues as relatively straightforward matters of right and wrong. They stake out clear positions on complex issues and tend to allow for few exceptions to the rules. Their values are clear and simple. They may see the world as a matter of good versus evil, winners versus losers, us versus them, or those (like themselves) who know the truth versus everybody else. Things are black and white, with few shades of gray. "I don't do nuance," George W. Bush told reporters.[46] People low in openness often do not do nuance—not so much because they cannot but more because they find it distasteful or uncomfortable to do so. They hate ambiguity. When people high in openness look upon those low in openness they see narrow-mindedness, dogmatism, lack of sophistication, and a hopelessly parochial approach to life. When people low in openness look upon those high in openness, they see weakness, muddle-headedness, ambivalence, and a shameful lack of conviction. They see people who cannot make up their minds, or who change their minds when conditions change. They see a *flip-flopper*, which was the Bush campaign's favorite appellation for their 2004 Democratic opponent, Senator John Kerry.

Openness to experience is strongly related to a psychological characteristic called *integrative complexity*, which is the tendency to adopt multiple points of view in argument. A person shows high integrative complexity when he or she sees many different angles and perspectives on a complex and contested issue and is able to integrate those different perspectives into a coherent argument. A person shows low integrative complexity when he or she fails to comprehend other perspectives, making integration unnecessary.[47] Most people show different levels of integrative complexity for different issues. For example, you may understand and partially accept many different arguments on the controversial issue of gay marriage, but when it comes to gun ownership, you may see it one way and one way only. On the right to bear arms, you may refuse to consider or fail to understand other points of view, even though you are perfectly able and willing to entertain multiple positions regarding other cultural and moral issues. It is also the case that people's integrative complexity can change over time. For example, research suggests that when people are facing big threats in their lives, their integrative complexity tends to go down.[48] In our darkest moments, we may look for simple truths. Research also suggests that most presidents do the same thing— that is, they display high levels of integrative complexity for some issues and low levels for others, and their scores change with changing political conditions.

But, George W. Bush appears to have been an exception, according to researchers who have carefully coded his public statements for integrative complexity. Across virtually every issue studied, from school reform to the war in Iraq, George W. Bush adopted a simple argument line and stuck to it, showing very little appreciation for competing points of view. His speeches showed lower integrative complexity than any elected U.S. president of the twentieth century, and his scores did not vary from one issue to the next, and did not change over the course of his presidency.[49]

Bush's supporters have always interpreted this kind of consistency and certitude as strength. He is a man of conviction, they will say. You know where he stands. You can trust him to do the right thing. Bush's supporters make a very good point. Indeed, some research shows that being low in openness, and expressing low levels of integrative complexity, can be an advantage under certain circumstances. People low in openness are seen as more predictable and trustworthy, and they may find it easier to sustain their commitments.[50] They are rarely plagued by doubt. With respect to some controversies, a position rooted in low integrative complexity may end up being the most principled. In the years before the American Civil War, radical abolitionists showed significantly lower levels of integrative complexity in their public rhetoric than did those politicians who wanted to find a compromise on the issue of slavery. When it comes to slavery, there really aren't two sides, you might say, so taking multiple perspectives in that case may be downright wrong. (Notably, pro-slavery advocates showed equally low levels of integrative complexity. Psychologically speaking, those who were the most avidly opposed to slavery were surprisingly similar to those who most avidly defended it.)[51]

From the standpoint of the actor's traits, then, the two broad personality dispositions that most strongly shaped George W. Bush's life and his presidency were sky-high extraversion and low openness to experience. Put the two together under the best of circumstances and what do you have? You have tremendous social energy and a surging optimism that are sharply focused on a clear goal. You have a confident protagonist who will act boldly and decisively, with no second thoughts. You have a dynamic and personable leader who sleeps well at night because he knows in his heart that he has done the right thing.

On the social stage of the American presidency, the most monumental performances that the actor-in-chief displays are the *decisions* he makes. The actor's dispositional traits may not tell you exactly *what* decisions he will make – whether or not he will invade Iraq eighteen months after the 9/11 terrorist attacks, for example. But they may enable you to predict and understand *how* he makes decisions. What decision making process does he follow? What is his overall *style* of making decisions? On a visit to an elementary school in Crawford, Texas, President Bush talked about the process of making big decisions:

> Is it hard to make decisions as president? Not really. If you know what you believe, decisions come pretty easy. If you're one of these types of people that are always trying to figure out which way the wind is blowing, decision making can be difficult. But I find that I know who I am. I know what I believe in, and I know where I want to lead the country. And most of the decisions come pretty easily for me, to be frank with you.[52]

This is a remarkable passage. Has any president ever told people that the job is this easy? All you have to do is know what you believe, and the right decisions will quickly follow. To be fair, the president may have been trying hard to relate to the schoolchildren. Being the president of the United States may seem like an awesome and scary prospect, but it is really not all that difficult, he may be saying. You can do it when you grow up. He may have been trying to instill hope and optimism in his audience, as highly extraverted actors tend to do. However, the message he conveyed to the Crawford kids is basically the same thing he said in a private moment to Stephen J. Hadley, Deputy Assistant to the President for National Security Affairs. About a week after American troops poured into Iraq, Hadley asked the president how he was holding up under the stress of war. "I made the decision," Bush said. "I sleep well at night."[53]

As president, George W. Bush called himself "The Decider." As a confident extravert, he made his decisions quickly, relying on gut instincts and non-negotiable beliefs. In the words of Scott McClellan, "President Bush has always been an instinctive leader more than an intellectual leader. He is not one to delve deeply into all the possible policy options—including sitting around engaging in extended debate about them—before making a choice. Rather, he chooses based on his gut and his most deeply held convictions. Such was the case with Iraq."[54]

Throughout his life, George W. Bush made many of his most important decisions quickly and instinctively, without much deliberation, confident that he was making the right choice. He decided to marry Laura Welch after knowing her for just a few weeks. He called that "the best decision I ever made."[55] He suddenly decided to quit drinking on the morning after his 40th birthday party, and he never looked back. After major decisions were made, he committed himself heart and soul to carrying them out, regardless of the consequences. Extraversion supplied the necessary optimism and the relentless cheerleading that helped to sustain commitment to the choices made; low openness to experience brooked no uncertainties in the decision's wake, no doubts. After 5 years of unparalleled access to the decision-making process in the Bush White House, the journalist Bob Woodward concluded this: "it was the same play over and over. His [the president's] strategy was to make repeated declarations of optimism and avoid adding to any doubts."[56]

The actor high in extraversion will take bold risks on the social stage. He will swing for the fences. He will infuse his decisions with dramatic positive emotions—the excitement we feel for the noble quest, the joy we will all feel when we save the world from weapons of mass destruction, when we assure happiness, freedom, and democracy for the Middle East, now and for all time. He will work tirelessly to keep our spirits up. The actor low in openness to experience will trust his instincts or his deep convictions, and he will discount alternative points of view. He will never doubt that he is on the right side of history. Once the big decision is made, he will stick with it, no matter what. He will not debate himself. He will never second-guess. His admirers in the audience will marvel at his steadfast commitment. His critics will accuse him of being stubborn, inflexible, and dangerously out of touch.

***

We find ourselves this morning, September 11, 2001, at another elementary school—this time in Sarasota, Florida. It is a few minutes after 9:00 a.m., and George W. Bush is reading a story to a second-grade class. Chief of Staff Andrew Card whispers into the president's right ear: A second airliner has crashed into the World Trade Center. A hint of startle and perhaps confusion briefly passes over the president's face. In his head and his gut, he is making a decision. We are going to war. The president returns to the book and finishes the story. He walks to the school's media center to make a brief, televised statement to the nation. He looks shaken, unsteady. With weirdly informal language, President Bush announces that the full resources of the federal government will be employed to investigate the terrorist attack, to "find those folks who committed this act." Minutes later another plane slams into the Pentagon. President Bush reaches Vice President Dick Cheney by phone. "We're at war," he tells Cheney. Bush hangs up and turns to members of his staff on Air Force One. "That's what we're paid for boys. We're going to take care of this. And when we find out who did this, they're not going to like me as president. Somebody is going to pay." An hour later he is back on the phone with Cheney: "We're going to find who did this," Bush says. "And we're going to kick their asses."[57]

In the days that follow, President Bush channels his anger into deadly resolve. His "blood is boiling," he tells a journalist.[58] He must strike back, but he must do so with focus and discretion. The initial target of the president's rage must be Osama bin Laden and the Al Qaeda network, for it is clear to everybody that they were behind the attacks. He must get Osama bin Laden, must bring him in, dead or alive.

"We're angry," Bush tells the king of Jordan. "There's a certain level of blood lust, but we won't let it drive our reaction"; "We're steady, clear-eyed, and patient, but pretty soon we'll have to start displaying scalps."[59]

"This is an enemy that tries to hide but it won't be able to hide forever," he tells reporters. "We will rally the world. We will be patient, we will be focused, and we will be steadfast in our determination."[60]

On September 20, the president speaks to a joint session of the Congress. More than 80 million Americans watch on television. "Tonight we are a country awakened to a danger and called to defend freedom," Bush says, as fighter jets circle over the Capitol.

"Our grief has turned to anger and anger to resolution. Whether we bring our enemies to justice or bring justice to our enemies, justice will be done."

"I will not forget this wound to our country and those who inflicted it," he says. "I will not yield; I will not rest; I will not relent in waging this struggle for freedom and security for the American people."[61]

After the address, the president calls Michael Gerson, his head speechwriter. He tells him, "I have never felt more comfortable in my life."[62]

He is comfortable because his personality traits (and his life experience) have prepared him beautifully for this moment. This highly extraverted president is energetic and restless, loves to take the big risk that aims for the game-changing impact. He can turn negative emotions into positive emotions, sadness and anxiety into the joy of final victory. His anger activates a Behavioral Approach System that has rallied so many times before. Going back as far as anybody can remember, his greatest strength has been to take bold action on the social stage, now the global stage, to confront daunting challenges head-on with the power, fury, and exuberance of his extraverted will.

We have a clear enemy—an evil foe about whom no equivocation need be expressed. George W. Bush has never been comfortable with ambiguity and nuance. He is at his best when the emotional stakes are high and the instrumental task is crystal clear. The stakes could not be higher—the nation faces a threatening menace. And the task could not be clearer—remove the threat, hit it hard, kill it off. And here is the best thing: *We know exactly who the threat is*. We don't need to intellectualize it. We don't need to explore the niceties, the contingencies, the legalistic exceptions and qualifications, the maybe-this and maybe-that. We don't need to do nuance today. Instead, we can focus our grief and our rage on the simple, noble, and urgent cause of defending our country and our freedom.

In the months that follow, President Bush summons forth all of his psychological resources to take on the challenge of his lifetime, which he instantly sees as *the* challenge of *our* lifetime. To defeat terror. To make our country safe. To defend freedom. The president meets regularly with his national security team. Their first big decision is to focus on Afghanistan, whose Taliban government has provided safe haven for bin Laden and Al Qaeda.

When the president meets with his war advisors, Condoleeza Rice—his assistant for national security affairs—is careful to develop a tight script. The president does not like to waste time. He abhors digressions and petty disagreements; he wants clarity, decisive action. President Bush throws himself into the war planning effort. He participates forcefully in the discussions of strategy and tactics. He shapes the debates about the big issues: How do we get a foothold in Afghanistan? What is the role of covert operations? Where are our good targets for bombing? Who are the tribal chieftains we can trust? How do we win the allegiance of the people? What about humanitarian aid? The president is at the top of his game in the months immediately following 9/11. He is energized, focused, and informed.[63]

As American fighter planes bomb Taliban targets, a few hundred CIA officers and Special Forces personnel cross into Afghanistan to help organize Northern Alliance forces and their Pashtun allies. Although the forces never manage to find bin Laden, they are successful in overthrowing the Taliban government. On December 7, the Taliban's southern stronghold in Kandahar falls, effectively leaving pro-American forces in charge of the country. The Northern Alliance and the Pashtuns choose

Hamid Karzai as their new leader. He takes the oath of office in Kabul on December 22.

Although Osama bin Laden is still on the loose, the United States seems to have won the opening battle of the war on terror. In overthrowing the Taliban sympathizers and installing a friendly government in Afghanistan, President Bush and his national security team have set Al Qaeda back on its heels. America enjoys high standing in the world now. Shocked by the brutality of the 9/11 attacks, most of the world's leaders and their people sympathize with America's effort to defend itself, and defend the world, against militant Islamic terrorism.

The president is riding high when he delivers his State of the Union address on January 29, 2002. He is a study in focused energy, supremely confident, eager to move forward on America's mission to defend itself and to defend freedom. The success in Afghanistan is just the first chapter, he believes, in what will surely be a triumphant narrative of national redemption. From the ashes of the World Trade Center and the lives of 3,000 Americans lost on 9/11, America will rise again, and with it freedom and goodness. Our war on terror is a war on evil. All those who aid and abet the terrorists are as culpable as the terrorists themselves. They are enemies of freedom, too, along with Osama bin Laden and Al Qaeda. They threaten us today. They constitute an *axis of evil*: North Korea, Iran, and *Iraq*.

"The Iraqi regime has plotted to develop anthrax, and nerve gas, and nuclear weapons for over a decade," the president states. "This is a regime that has already used poison gas to murder thousands of its own citizens—leaving the bodies of mothers huddled over their dead children. This is a regime that agreed to international inspections—then kicked out the inspectors. This is a regime that has something to hide from the civilized world.

"States like these, and their terrorist allies, constitute an axis of evil, arming to threaten the peace of the world. By seeking weapons of mass destruction, these regimes pose a grave and gathering danger. They could provide these arms to terrorists, giving them the means to match their hatred. They could attack our allies or attempt to blackmail the United States. In any of these cases, the price of indifference would be catastrophic . . . .

"We'll be deliberate, yet time is not on our side. I will not wait on events, while dangers gather. I will not stand by, as peril draws closer and closer. The United States of America will not permit the world's most dangerous regimes to threaten us with the world's most destructive weapons."

The speech ends, and there is a final standing ovation. The actor strides off the stage. The applause goes on and on, thunderous.

TWO

Fathers and Sons

In the climactic scene of *W*, Oliver Stone's (2008) film about the life and presidency of George W. Bush, the father challenges the son to a fight in the Oval Office. George W. Bush is president now, and his father is an old man who returns to that most storied room in the White House, the hallowed space he himself occupied once upon a time, to go "mano a mano" against his first-born son.[1]

"Come on! Let's go! Bet you I can still whip your ass."

George Senior puts up his fists and takes a couple of swings at the president. He taunts the president, knowing that his son will never hit back. Then, he backs off. He lights a cigar. The former president tells his son that he has deeply disappointed him. He has ruined the Bush family name.

The son looks hurt, exasperated. It is the same old story coming out of the old man's mouth—about how he could never live up to the expectations of the family, how he would never be as good as his father or his younger brother, Jeb—the family favorite, the one who was *supposed to be* president.

Once again, as the son has done over and over in his life, he defends himself against his father's charge. Even now as president, he must prove that he is good enough.

"I dug myself out of the depths of hell to stand on my own two feet. To make something of myself. And I did it on my own!"

"Yeah, well you also wrecked it!" the father shoots back.

In the year 2008, the audience knows what this film maker, no fan of George W. Bush, intends the father's message to be: George W. Bush has failed; he has squandered the worldwide good will the nation enjoyed immediately after 9/11; he has plunged the United States into an endless, futile war in Iraq; he has presided over an administration that (implicitly, if not explicitly) condoned the torture of foreign combatants; he has shown ineptitude and callousness in responding to the devastation of Hurricane Katrina; he is largely responsible for the Republican Congressional losses in 2006; the deficit is at record levels, and the economy is on the brink of a disaster. The nation is a wreck. The Bush dynasty is disgraced.

"Get out of my office!" George W. Bush orders the old man to leave. "Get out of my life!"

"That's what it is. A God-damned fiasco."

"Get out!"

And then George W. wakes up, sweaty and panicked. It was all a dream. The president is safe in his bed in the White House, lying beside Laura. It will be okay in the morning, she counsels. It will be okay.

Like much of the film, Oliver Stone's Oval Office scene is fiction. There is no evidence that George W. Bush ever had a dream like this, and if he did it is hard to believe that he would have ever told anybody about it (except perhaps Laura).

The scene does, however, reprise and reverse, with a good deal of creative license, a well-documented event in the life of the film's protagonist. Here is the real event:

Sometime around Christmas in 1972, the 26-year-old George W. took his brother Marvin (aged 15 years) out for a spin in one of Dad's cars. They visited a friend's house and had a few drinks. Driving back, George W. ran over a neighbor's metal garbage can, and with the can wedged between the left front wheel and the car's body, he pulled noisily into his parents' driveway. Big George (Dad) was furious—not so much about the car but about George W.'s having gotten young Marvin drunk. He summoned his firstborn into his home office.

George W. charged in, his face red with anger. "I hear you're looking for me," he shouted, shaking his fist at his father. "You want to go mano a mano right here?"

Barbara rushed into the office and tried to break up the fight. Jeb rushed in, too. The second son saved the day by revealing a secret. George was out drinking because he was celebrating, Jeb told everyone. He was celebrating being accepted to Harvard Business School. Jeb's timely revelation was a total surprise. The parents hadn't even known that George W. had applied to Harvard. Proud that their difficult son had now achieved something impressive on his own, their tempers cooled.

But George W. was still hot. "Oh, I'm not going," he said dismissively. "I just wanted to let you know I could get into it."[2]

Only once before in American history have father and son both occupied the presidency. John Adams (the second president), was followed by his son John Quincy Adams (the sixth president). George H. W. Bush served as the 41st president of the United States, 1989 to 1993. His son was the 43rd president. Among the many Bush family nicknames, Dad was known as "41." The first-born son was "43."

Rivalries between fathers and sons are as old as ancient myths. We might imagine, then, that when both father and son ascend to the highest office in the land, the potential for rivalry and conflict would be enhanced to a fever pitch. With that in mind, it should come as no surprise that Oliver Stone sets up the father–son dynamic as the central dramatic theme in his story. Other biographers have done the same.[3] How could they *not*? At first blush, it would seem that the father–son rivalry has to be *the key* to any psychological analysis of the life and presidency of George W. Bush. Mano a mano. Father against Son. Son disappoints Father. Son loves and hates Father, deep affection and resentment all mixed up. Son wants to be like Father, and also does *not* want to be like him. Son wants to win Father's admiration, and wants to kill him off too, or at least surpass him. The whole thing screams Oedipus!

In the ancient Greek myth, Oedipus succeeds in killing off his father and sleeping with his mother. Of course, he does not consciously know he is doing these things while he is doing them. He does not know until years later that the man he kills at the crossing of three roads is his father, and does not know that the woman he is sleeping with as his reward for solving a famous riddle (the widow turned wife Jocasta) is indeed his mother. For a short while, Oedipus reigns as king, with Jocasta his queen. But it all turns out badly, once the truth of incest and patricide is revealed. Jocasta hangs herself when she learns the horrible truth. Oedipus rips the broaches off her death gown and plunges them into his eyes. Now that he sees the truth, he becomes blind. But in blinding himself, Oedipus identifies with the one wise man in the drama—the blind prophet Tiresias, who has *seen* the truth all along. In a symbolic sense, Oedipus has attained a kind of wisdom or maturity through his travails. Although he is banished to a distant land at the end of *Oedipus Rex*, Oedipus returns in subsequent dramas in the role of the wise sage.

In Sigmund Freud's classic take on the Oedipus myth, father and son compete for both power and love. At the beginning the father has it all. In the unconscious mind of the 4-year-old son, Freud argued, the father is typically omnipotent; he is aggressive and threatening; and he owns the one thing the son wants most of all—the soft, warm, caring, and alluring mother. The little son fears his father and hates him, for if his father were dead, his unconscious and primitive mind figures, he the son would have the mother all for himself. Like Oedipus the king, however, the son is fated to lose out in his unconscious bid for power and love. Freud argued that little boys eventually renounce their unconscious rivalry with their fathers and instead come to identify with the authoritative structure—the norms, rules, and constraints of society—that their fathers (and to some extent their mothers) represent. This is the key development in socialization, Freud argued. By unconsciously giving up the selfish desire to have it all, the son establishes what Freud called a *superego*, which is the beginning of a moral sensibility. Freud seemed to think that if little boys never had (and unconsciously resolved) Oedipus complexes, they would grow up to be ruthless tyrants or criminals.[4]

Read literally, Freud's concept of the Oedipus complex enjoys very little scientific credibility. Research psychologists have never been able to garner empirical support for the idea that very young boys struggle with unconscious desires to kill their fathers and make love to their mothers and that they eventually, by around age 6 years, resolve the complex through identifying with fathers and establishing a moral sensibility in the process. And don't even ask about how all this is supposed to apply to little girls and women.[5]

Still, as a more allegorical treatment of how fathers and sons sometimes relate to each other, and as a source for metaphors regarding how human beings relate to authority writ large, the Oedipus myth has sometimes provided insight. In the case of George W. Bush, the Oedipus story raises a host of questions about his relationship with his father: What were George W.'s basic feelings toward his father? What did he want from his father? Did he see his father as a rival? Did he wish to overcome his father, to (symbolically speaking) kill him off? Did he identify with his father and seek to be like him? Beyond his biological father, did George W. see other men in his life as father figures? If yes, what did he want from them, and what did they want from him?

Psychologically speaking, these are questions about *motivation*. Motivation is about what we want in life, what we desire, what we intend to accomplish. It is about how we go about trying to get what we want in life and trying to avoid what we do not want. It is about our goals, fears, dreams, hopes, and plans for the future. Even infants want things and act accordingly. Newborns want food and comfort, and their little minds and bodies are set up for them to respond in ways that meet these needs and achieve these implicit goals. But it is not until middle childhood—our grade-school years—that our recurrent wants, desires, and goals become important features of our developing personalities. A big step in this direction occurs around age 4 years, when we develop what psychologists call *theory of mind*.[6] A year or so before we enter kindergarten, our brains formulate a very simple theory about why people do what they do. The theory goes like this: *Because they want to.* People do things because they *want to do them.* People have wants, desires, and goals in their heads, and they act upon them. Around age 4 years, then, we figure out: *(1)* that people have minds, *(2)* in their minds they have wants and desires, and *(3)* those wants and desires motivate people to do what they do.

Once we consciously know that people (ourselves included) have particular wants and desires floating around in their minds and that human actions are motivated by those wants and desires, it is another short step to begin sorting through our own wants and desires, to begin evaluating how well we are doing in accomplishing them, and to make decisions regarding which wants and desires are most urgent, compelling, and realistic. Children begin to set up personal goals for themselves around age 7 or 8 years. Reflecting maturation of the brain and the effects of schooling, children's lives and their consciousness become somewhat more systematic, structured, and self-consciously goal-directed in the grade-school years.[7] Especially in middle-class settings, children's days become organized into tasks that must be achieved, goals that must be pursued, and projects that must be completed—in school, on the playground, with friends, at church, and in other social arenas wherein children are now expected to accomplish things that reflect their own personal goals. Partly as a result of the increasing importance of goals, children begin to show significant individual differences in early grade school with respect to *self-esteem*.[8] If the child feels satisfied with progress made in a given goal area (say, school or sports), then the child evaluates him- or herself in a positive way and experiences high self-esteem. Poor progress with respect to goals, by contrast, may produce negative self-evaluation and low self-esteem.[9]

Our recurrent desires, wants, and goals begin to form a new, second layer of personality in our grade-school years, layered over those underlying dispositional traits that have been developing since birth.[10] Personal goals—and the various values and strategies that form around them—are strongly influenced by the environments of our lives, especially the family environment. Whereas traits appear to be strongly driven by genetic predispositions, goals appear to be more contextual and contingent, more readily influenced by what is going on in a person's world. Over time and across situations, goals change more than traits, reflecting changing circumstances. Basic dispositional traits, like extraversion and agreeableness, establish a more-or-less consistent temperament core for personality. Our goals, by contrast move around more, wax and wane over time and across circumstances, sometimes showing rather sudden and dramatic transformations. A person can wake up one morning and set forth a brand new goal for life. A conversation with a friend can launch a new motivational agenda. By contrast, traits are more intractable, more stable, more impervious to changing relationships, situations, and social contexts.

George W. Bush was an extravert from very early on in life. But, like most of us, regardless of what our dispositional traits might be, he did not begin to own and act in accord with personal, self-defining goals until his grade-school years. Georgie began life as an actor, performing his traits on a social stage, as we all do. His high extraversion and low openness to experience continued to shape the way he performed his roles in Midland, New Haven, Cambridge, Austin, and finally the White House. But George W. Bush is, and from around second grade on was, more than an actor. He is and was also a motivated *agent. To be an agent is to act in a goal-directed and self-initiated manner, to act with purpose and intent.* Our traits shape how we act; our goals determine what we try to accomplish in our actions, and why. A motivational layer began to form in Georgie's personality, as it does for most all of us, around age 7 years, as he began to translate his wants and desires into goals, plans, and projects for the future. What, then, did he want? What were his biggest goals? And what did his goals say about his relationship with his father?

***

Georgie was *7 years old* when his sister Robin died.

It was 1953, and the family was living in Midland, Texas. Five years into the oil business, George Senior was about to make his fortune. By the end of the year, his new company, Zapata Oil, would drill 71 wells, and all 71 would strike oil. On February 11, John Ellis (Jeb) Bush was born. George Senior and Barbara (known in the family as "Bar") now had three children—Georgie, Robin, and Jeb. "Life," Bar later said, "seemed almost too good to be true."[11]

Georgie was fond of his 3-year-old sister. He sometimes helped his mother tend to the little girl. Before Jeb was born, the three of them went on walks around the neighborhood. Robin had blonde hair and blue eyes. She was nearly as energetic as her big brother, but she had a sweeter disposition. One morning, just a few weeks after Jeb was born, Robin woke up looking pale and lethargic. "I don't know what to do this morning," she sighed. "I may go out and lie on the grass and watch the cars go by, or I might just stay in bed."[12]

Bar figured her daughter had an advanced case of "spring fever." But she was still alarmed enough to take her to the family pediatrician, Dr. Dorothy Wyvell. Dr. Wyvell noticed bruising on Robin's legs. She drew a sample of blood and told Bar that she should come back the next day to discuss the test results. She told her to bring her husband. George Senior was in the next county over, going over land records for the upcoming oil deal. He rushed home to be at Bar's side and to learn the diagnosis.

Robin had leukemia. Dr. Wyvell had never seen a white blood count so high. The couple sat stunned as they were told to take their dying girl home and make her final days as comfortable and happy as possible. Instead, they checked Robin into Memorial Sloan-Kettering Hospital in New York City, a leading cancer treatment center. Bar moved into her grandparents' Sutton Place apartment, just nine blocks from the hospital, while George returned to Texas to work on the Zapata deal and to tend to family matters. Dorothy Bush, George Senior's mother, dispatched one of her own son's childhood nurses to take care of Georgie and Jeb back in Midland.

Bar stayed by her daughter's side as Robin underwent a series of painful bone marrow transplants and blood transfusions. George flew back frequently to be with Robin, too, and other family members from New England and New York made regular visits to the hospital. Robin was well enough to leave the hospital on a few occasions, spending some time in Kennebunkport, Maine (where the extended family gathered for summer vacations and other big events) and Midland. Georgie was told not to roughhouse with his little sister because she was sick. But he was never told she was dying.

Robin finally succumbed later that same year, on October 11, 1953. The family arranged a small, private memorial service, held in Greenwich, Connecticut. But there was no funeral. Instead, George and Bar donated Robin's body to the hospital for medical research. They returned to Midland. Georgie and one of his second-grade classmates at Sam Houston Elementary School were carrying a large phonograph back to the principal's office when Georgie spotted his parents' car pulling up in front of the school. For a quick second, Georgie thought he spotted his sister's little head bopping up in the back seat. He ran back to ask his teacher if he might go outside to see his parents and his sister. The teacher said okay.

"Hey, Mom! Dad!" he yelled. As he realized that Robin was not in the back seat, Georgie asked, "Where's Robin?" His parents told him she was dead. Georgie did not comprehend the news. How was this possible? "But why didn't you tell me she was so sick?" he asked repeatedly. "Why didn't you tell me she could die?"

"Well," his mother replied, "it wouldn't have made a difference. . ."[13]

In his campaign autobiography, George W. Bush would recall this moment as the "starkest memory of my childhood, a sharp pain in the midst of an otherwise happy blur."[14]

What were the effects? For the parents, Robin's death was an unspeakable tragedy. During the months at Sloan-Kettering, Bar steeled herself and refused to cry. After Robin's death, however, she was nearly inconsolable. George Senior was a basket case in the presence of his dying daughter. He frequently needed to leave the hospital room so that others would not see him break down in tears. Afterwards, he tried mightily to comfort his wife, even as he immersed himself in the biggest business deals of his lifetime. The couple did not talk about Robin's death very much, and family members and friends found the topic awkward as well. In Midland, Texas, in the 1950s, grief counseling for parents was not a common practice.

As far as the 7-year-old Georgie was concerned, at least three effects may be seen. First and foremost was sadness. "I remember being sad," George W. later wrote. "My [childhood] friends Susie Evans and Joe O'Neill remember the same thing, a great sadness."[15] Second was fear. George W. always insisted that Robin's death was not a traumatic event in his life. "Robin's death did not traumatize me," he later wrote.[16] But it should not be surprising to learn that he suffered from nightmares for years after. "He would wake up screaming in the night, and his mother would come running to comfort him," a childhood friend said.[17] Randall Roden was sleeping over one night when he was awakened by Georgie's shrieking.

Third, Georgie channeled his exuberant, extraverted tendencies into the *goal* of helping his grieving mother. Georgie took it upon himself to boost his mother's sagging morale. He told her funny stories and tried to divert her from her sadness by goofing around and playing the role that came so natural to him—the extraverted clown. He also showed a remarkable tendency to say weird things about his dead sister, producing curious smiles and making people feel a little better. At a Midland Bulldogs football game, Georgie announced that he wished he were Robin right now. When asked why he said that, Georgie replied that Robin had a much better view of the playing field than they did, from her perch up in the sky. Georgie tried to cover other people's tears with laughter. The prime target was his mother's tears. *Cheering his mother up became Georgie's first life project*—a personal goal into which he invested a great deal of his boundless energy. The goal became a top priority in his young life. When a friend stopped by one day and asked him to play, Georgie told him he could not come outside. His mother needed him.[18]

Georgie was right. With her husband on the road most of the time, his mother really *did* need her first-born. After Robin's death, Georgie became his mother's prime source of support and sustenance. "I wonder how I ever would have made it without my oldest son," Barbara later acknowledged. "I probably put more responsibility on him than I should have, especially for a boy of his age. But who else could I turn to with his father gone so much in those days? He was my Rock of Gibraltar, plain and simple, and because of that we have a very special relationship."[19]

That special relationship was built on deep love, common experiences, and shared personality traits. Like her first-born, Bar was an outgoing and extraverted performer on the social stage, outspoken and opinionated, with a sharp and biting wit. "My mother and I are the quippers of the family, sharp-tongued and irreverent," George W. wrote in his campaign autobiography. "I love her dearly, and she and I delight in provoking each other, a clash of wits and ready comebacks."[20] With a comeback not exactly ready for prime time, Bar once called Geraldine Ferraro a bitch. Well, almost. After the 1984 Democratic vice-presidential candidate accused the Bushes of being out of touch with real people, Bar told reporters that Ferraro was "a four million dollar—I can't say it, but it rhymes with rich."[21]

Bar fiercely defended the Bush family clan against criticism from the outside. At the same time, she could be highly critical of her own. Described as "The Enforcer" in the family, Bar played the role of daily disciplinarian when the children were little. When they grew up, she still reserved the right to slap down idiocy or impertinence with an icy stare or tart rebuke. After George W. announced that he planned to run for governor of Texas against Ann Richards, Bar told her son it was a dumb idea, and she predicted he would lose.

The mother–son relationship established a pattern that George W. followed with a small set of special women in his life— smart and authoritative women who had the guts to tell him what to do and redirect him when they thought he was headed the wrong way. Karen Hughes may have been the best example of this maternal dynamic. His most trusted aide during the years as governor and early on in his presidency, Hughes helped George W. Bush craft his message and public persona for the widest possible appeal. She was the ghostwriter behind his campaign autobiography,

A Charge to Keep. During times of crisis, Bush depended on Hughes for frank advice and critique. Bush speechwriter David Frum wrote that Hughes was the only person in the White House who was allowed to criticize the president. But she also offered the president unconditional admiration and love. Hughes loves Bush "the way a mother bear loves her cub," Frum wrote.[22] Another woman who played a close advisory role throughout the Bush presidency was Condoleeza Rice, first as assistant for national security affairs and later as secretary of state. Whereas Hughes kept Bush in touch with the soccer moms, NASCAR dads, and suburban white voters who made up the bulk of his political constituency, Rice schooled him on international diplomacy and briefed him on world events. In the run-up to the Iraq war, Rice worked tirelessly to organize information and distill arguments for the president and to keep national security meetings tightly focused on strategic goals. Like Hughes, she was fiercely protective of her boss.

The Bush family followed the strict gender roles so prevalent in the middle-class White mainstream of the 1950s. Bar stayed home and raised the kids—five in all, by the time Dorothy arrived, in 1959. Bar attended to all of the details regarding school, church, little league, neighborhood events, and the like. Although he tried to stay involved with the children, George Senior was gone much of the time. His expanding business deals made travel a frequent necessity.

The esteemed psychoanalytic theorist Nancy Chodorow asserts that in families like the Bushes—in which children are raised exclusively by mothers and other women, while fathers are gone much of the time—children develop a deep and visceral sense of what being a woman is fundamentally about, but mature maleness remains a mystery in their little minds.[23] For much of the normal day, little girls and boys interact with mothers and other female caregivers. They see mothers do what mothers characteristically do, from cooking to shopping to adjudicating disputes in the backyard. They develop a sense of what a day in the life of a mother is all about. As a result, little girls typically identify strongly with their mothers. Even if they consciously reject traditional gender roles when they grow up, they keep close to their psychological hearts a well-developed sense of what it means to be a mother. And they may even feel, perhaps at an unconscious level, that being a mother is the most authentically female experience a mature woman can have.

What about fathers and little boys? In traditional families like the Bush family of the 1950s, children spend much less time with men on a daily basis, and they have very little sense of what men actually do when they are "working." Of course, they see men in the community—teachers, policemen, merchants, and so on. But they do not usually follow their fathers around all day, the way they may follow their mothers or other female caregivers. They don't develop a broad and intimate sense of the masculine role. According to Chodorow, little boys often develop a *positional* identification with their fathers. They identify with a disembodied position in the world. They imagine what that position—being a man—might be, and they try to make themselves into that model. Eventually, of course, they will get on-the-job training, as it were, for masculinity. In their teenage years and beyond, they will obtain more direct experience regarding how to be a man. But the knowledge comes late. Until that time, little boys are left with guesswork in the face of an enigma.

Early on, Georgie identified with cowboys and baseball players. Very few little boys, after all, dream of owning an oil company when they grow up. Even if they were allowed to follow their fathers around from oil rig to office to board meeting, they would probably choose Willie Mays as their masculine idol, as Georgie did, over the man in the dark business suit. Nonetheless, the evidence suggests that Georgie also identified with his father's *position*, as Chodorow suggested, even if he had little understanding of what his father actually did on a daily basis; and he admired his father greatly, though from a distance. From an early age, he idealized his father. As he grew up and learned more about his father's daily routines and aspirations, he sought to connect his own goals to those his father pursued. As one biographer has asserted, "George W.'s father was the North Star of his ambition and idealization."[24]

Georgie also admired other men in the Bush family. Of particular importance in this regard was his paternal grandfather, Prescott Bush, who served in the United States Senate during those years when Georgie was first formulating his personal goals. A moderate Republican who represented the state of Connecticut from 1952 to 1963, Senator Prescott Bush was a dignified and imposing presence in the Bush family. Absurdly formal, even by the stiff standards of the 1950s, Prescott insisted that his grandchildren address him as "Senator." He was "scary," George W. admitted.[25] But during the years the Bush boys were growing up, Prescott personified all that a Bush man was supposed to be. He modeled a *motivational agenda* that has been passed down from father to son in the Bush family ever since. As Prescott saw and lived it, a Bush man sets for himself two large and noble goals in life. First, he must *make money*, lots and lots of it, and on his own. Inherited money is no good—the Bushes are not like the Kennedys, they are quick to point out. Each young man must first prove himself in the world of money; politics is not a birthright, no matter how wealthy a man's family of origin may be. Second, a man should commit himself to *public service*. He must pursue these two goals in the order specified—make money (tons of it) first, to take care of the family, and then, second (and only if the first goal is resoundingly achieved) aim to serve the public good, to take care of the broader community. Money and service, in that order.

***

Prescott Sheldon Bush (1895–1972) was born in Columbus, Ohio, to Samuel Prescott Bush and Flora (Sheldon) Bush. Samuel Bush was first a railroad executive and then a steel company president. During World War I, he worked for the U.S. government to coordinate major weapons contracts. His firstborn son, Prescott, enrolled at Yale University in 1913, as his grandfather and uncle had, where he played varsity golf, football, and baseball, was president of the Yale Glee Club, and was inducted into the legendary secret society Skull and Bones. At Yale, Prescott revealed a prodigious ability to memorize his classmates' names, as would his most famous grandson half a century later. After serving in the military in the last years of World War I, Prescott began a long career in business that took him from Simmons Hardware Store in St. Louis to jobs in Ohio and Massachusetts, before becoming an executive banker on Wall Street.

Prescott amassed a fortune between the mid-1920s and the early 1950s, eventually maintaining homes in New York, Long Island, and Greenwich, Connecticut, as well as the family compound at Kennebunkport, Maine, a 10,000-acre plantation in South Carolina, and a secluded island off the Connecticut coast. Along the way, he married Dorothy ("Dottie") Walker (1901–1992), a fiercely competitive and athletic woman, who was the daughter of George Herbert ("Bert") Walker (1874–1953). Bert Walker was a colorful and hard-drinking businessman who had once been a boxer. He founded Brown Brothers Harriman, a venerable Wall Street investment house, and he also served as a political advisor. Bert Walker was one of 12 men who gathered at a private meeting in the early 1930s to urge New York Governor Franklin Delano Roosevelt to run for the presidency. Prescott impressed both Bert and his demanding daughter with his athletic prowess (he was an accomplished golfer and was later named the head of the United States Golf Association), his classy Yale education, and his driving ambition. Prescott and Dottie eventually settled in Greenwich, where they raised five children in an eight-bedroom, three-story house with maids, cooks, and an expansive porch on tree-lined Grove Lane. They named their second child—George Herbert Walker Bush, born in 1924—after Prescott's flamboyant father-in-law. Because they called their own father "Pop," Dottie's brothers began to refer to her new son as "Poppy." The nickname stuck for the rest of his life.

Tall and athletic like his father, Poppy Bush excelled at almost everything he took on. He was a top-notch student, a slick-fielding first baseman, and an all-around nice guy. For high school, he attended Phillips Academy in Andover, Massachusetts, as would his oldest son two decades later. A few weeks after Japanese bombers attacked Pearl Harbor, George H. W. Bush met Barbara Pierce at a Christmas dance at the Round Hill Country Club in Greenwich. The daughter of the president of McCall Publishing Company, Barbara was a descendant of the 14th president of the United States, Franklin Pierce. Although she attended a private finishing school in South Carolina, Barbara resided in nearby Rye, a small town of stately homes and old money. Imagine it as chemistry, or perfect timing, or the way that impending war or crisis can stir the libido and bring two young people together, or even an inchoate sense that because they looked so good on the dance floor that it just might serve destiny to merge their two blue-blood families. Whatever the reasons, George and Barbara hit it off immediately. When he returned to Andover to finish out his senior year, Poppy was smitten. Barbara's classmates in South Carolina reported that she talked of little else but the handsome young man from Greenwich. George and Barbara got together again during spring break. They went on a double date to see *Citizen Kane*. After the movie, George walked Barbara home and kissed her goodnight. Barbara was 16 years old, and he was the first boy she had ever kissed.

Stirred to patriotism like so many young men graduating from high school in the spring of 1942, George H. W. Bush enlisted in the Navy. He became the war's youngest naval pilot, completing 58 missions over the Pacific. His plane was shot down during a raid in the Bonin Islands southeast of Japan. His crew was killed, but George managed to parachute out and was eventually plucked out of the water by a submarine. He received the Distinguished Flying Cross for heroism. During this time, Barbara was attending Smith College, in Northampton, Massachusetts. Home for a short furlough in the summer of 1943, George declared his love to Barbara, and the two were secretly engaged. They were married in January 1945, at the First Presbyterian Church in Rye.

After the war, George returned to Connecticut and, like his father before him (and like his older brother, Prescott, Jr.), enrolled at Yale. George and Barbara moved to a small house at 281 Edwards Street in New Haven. Their firstborn arrived on a hot and humid night at 12:30 a.m. on July 6, 1946. *The New Haven Register* for that day featured these front-page headlines: "First Phase of Atom Plan Nearly Ready"; "Truman Healthy after 14 Months, Strength Likened to Roosevelt's"; and "Baby is Born in Japan with 2 Faces and Bodies."[26]

Poppy did well in his courses at Yale and played first base for the varsity team. He joined the DKE fraternity. Like his father, George was inducted into the elite Skull and Bones Society. Even as they fanned out across the country upon graduation, "Bonesmen" pledged a remarkable lifelong allegiance to their brotherhood. Many have risen to the highest echelons of business and government, assisting each other along the way with advice, money, and an endless supply of social capital. Throughout his business and political career, George H. W. Bush would draw upon the Bonesmen network for support and social connections. Never one to dawdle, Poppy was a young man in a hurry during his Yale days. No beer bashes and fraternity high jinks for this college undergraduate, married with a baby at home. George was eager to get out into the world and make the kind of big money that Bush men are supposed to make. He completed his studies in 2.5 years and then drove his little family west to Texas, to make his fortune on his own.

Well, not *completely* on his own. Poppy left for Texas with a job awaiting him when he arrived. Neil Mallon—a longtime family friend, fellow Bonesman, and head of Dresser Industries— recognized George's drive and discipline and offered him a position as a sales clerk in the Odessa, Texas office of the International Derrick and Equipment Company, a subsidiary of Dresser. Mallon told George that if he worked hard he should have little trouble climbing the ladder of success in the oil business. Of course, Mallon was right. By the early 1960s, Poppy had realized the first goal of the Bush family's motivational agenda for men—to make large sums of money outside the direct family orbit. But his was no Horatio Alger story, no rags to riches tale about the ambitious young man who starts off with nothing and works his way to the top. Like Prescott before him and his sons after, George H. W. Bush began his ascent from an exalted position of privilege. Family ties landed him his first job at Dresser, and throughout his business career, and later in politics, he was able to cash in on the social and financial resources into which he was born. As critics of the Bush family are quick to point out, Bush men have, for generations, started down the path of life with huge inborn advantages—family wealth, the best schools, and social capital in spades.[27] How could they *not* succeed? At the same time, it would be unfair to ignore the pressure of high expectations that these advantages confer. Whereas some Bush men, like Prescott and Poppy, thrive in the family hothouse of competitive masculinity, others have wilted under the stress.

In the 1950s and early 1960s, Prescott fulfilled the second stage of the family's motivational agenda for Bush men (public service), as he served two terms in the United States Senate. An Eisenhower Republican, he took stands on many issues that were considered moderately liberal, if not progressive, at the time. He was an early champion of the United Negro College Fund. He supported civil rights legislation and the establishment of the Peace Corps. Eisenhower included Prescott Bush's name on an undated handwritten list of prospective candidates he favored for the 1960 GOP presidential nomination.

During the same period, Poppy became a millionaire, fulfilling for himself the first stage of the Bush motivational agenda and laying the groundwork for the second. After serving as chairman of the Republican Party for Harris County, Texas, George H. W. Bush set out to be elected senator from Texas. He won the Republican primary but lost in the general election to Democrat Ralph Yarborough. Two years later, however, he won a seat in the U.S. House of Representatives, defeating Democrat Frank Briscoe in the 7th Congressional District of Texas, which included Houston.

He was reelected in 1968. His voting record was rather more conservative than his father's. In 1970, President Richard Nixon convinced Bush to relinquish his position in the House and run again against Yarborough for the Senate seat. The national Republican establishment sensed that the outspokenly liberal Yarborough was particularly vulnerable. To their surprise, however, Yarborough lost the Democratic primary to the more conservative Lloyd Bentsen, who then defeated Bush in the general election, 54% to 43%. As a consolation prize, Nixon appointed Bush ambassador to the United Nations. During the Watergate years, Bush served as chairman of the Republican Party, and under President Ford, he was first appointed to head up the American embassy in China and later served as director of the CIA.

Re-enter George W. Bush, now a young man with little to show for himself beyond his Yale degree, son of George H. W. Bush, a millionaire businessman with an extraordinary political resume, and grandson of former Senator Prescott Bush. Even as he drank himself silly and chased the cutest girls all over Houston in the early 1970s, and even when he challenged his father, at age 26 years, to go mano a mano, George W. Bush never lost sight of, nor did he ever seriously question, the family's motivational structure for Bush men. Susan Munson, one of the women he dated in the early 1970s, reported that even then George W. "knew he wanted to own a baseball team, and he wanted to go into politics. [But] he wasn't sure how he was going to get to those goals."[28] He would later become part owner of the Texas Rangers. His initial investment of $800,000 would bring George W. more than $15 million when he sold his shares in the 1990s, providing him with the independent wealth that eluded him in the oil business. Prescott had achieved the first goal of the family's motivational program through banking; George Senior made his fortune in oil;

George W. achieved the same goal when he cashed out his ownership of a baseball team.

As a young man, George W. identified strongly with his father; indeed, he seemed to adore his father and tried to be like his father, in countless ways. Like his father, George W. Bush went to Andover, attended Yale, was a member of the DKE fraternity at Yale, and was inducted into Skull and Bones. Like his father, he was a fighter pilot, although he never saw combat. Like his father, he taught Sunday school at the First Presbyterian Church in Midland. Like his father, he tried to make it rich in the Texas oil business. Like his father, he even proposed marriage—at age 20 years, just as his father did—to a young woman from Smith College. Yes, the very same college Bar attended! Her name was Cathy Wolfman. In an eerie parallel to the Greenwich Christmas dance where Poppy met Bar, George W. and Cathy were engaged over Christmas break during his junior year at Yale. The couple planned to live in married student housing on the Yale campus, just as his parents had done. But the relationship with Wolfman faded away the following year.

George W., Jeb, Neal, and Marvin all idolized their father as the "beacon" of the family.[29] To one extent or another, all four brothers set out to make large sums of money in the business world, with the hope of then launching careers in public service. From an early age, Jeb focused most clearly on the motivational agenda for Bush men. Even as a child, he imagined himself as the president of the United States. Other family members saw Jeb as the one brother with the most promise for politics. He was smart, dynamic, hard-working, focused, and showed a strong interest in public policy. During George W.'s nomadic period, Jeb married, started a family, and began to make good money in the Florida real estate business. Seven years younger than his older brother, Jeb got a head start on fulfilling the family goals for Bush men. Had he not suffered defeat in his first run for governor in 1994, he might have achieved the ultimate public service goal, and thereby short-circuited forever his older brother's motivational agenda.

There is little doubt that Jeb and George W. experienced more than their fair share of sibling rivalry, and both competed for their father's attention and approval. George W. was more than a little bit annoyed, therefore, when his father seemed sadder about Jeb's loss in Florida than he was happy about George W.'s victory in Texas on election night in 1994. "The joy is in Texas, but our hearts are in Florida," Poppy told the media after the election results were in. Still, George W. was deeply moved when his father wrote him a loving letter of congratulations and gave him his prized cufflinks after the Texas gubernatorial victory, signifying a passing of the political baton from father to first-born son.

At a campaign stop in 2000, eighth-graders asked George W. about his father. "I didn't like it when people criticized my dad [as president]," he responded. "That's because I love him; I love him more than anything."[30] In his campaign autobiography, George W. insisted that the feeling was mutual. He described the love that both Bush parents provided their children as "unconditional love"; "Always. Forever. Unwaveringly. Without question. They said it and they showed it."[31] "Unconditional love is the greatest gift a parent can give a child," he wrote. "Once you know your family will always love you, you are free to try anything. You are free to fail. And you are free to succeed."[32]

George W. Bush may have been overestimating his freedom here. Was he free to scotch the entire goal program for Bush men and dedicate his life to a radically divergent motivational agenda? What if he had wanted to teach school instead of pursuing business?

Or write poetry instead of seeking public office? It all seems hard to imagine, both because George W. Bush never seemed to be cut out for these alternative sorts of goals and, just as importantly, because the idea that Bush men would pursue goals like these fits nowhere in the Bush family program for mature masculinity. Nonetheless, within the program, it seems clear that Father and Son loved each other very much and sought to promote each other's goals. George W. worked tirelessly on his father's presidential campaigns in 1988 and 1992, and Poppy mobilized his extensive network of friends and supporters to work on behalf of his firstborn's own presidential run in the late 1990s. Both men took great pride in each other's achievements. Asked early in his presidency whether his father had been helpful to him, George W. replied: "He's been helpful to me by telling me he loves me, and that he's proud of me."[33]

***

A son who loves and idolizes his father will hate his father's enemies.

George W. Bush was a freshman at Yale in the fall of 1964 when his father lost the Senate race in Texas to Democrat Ralph Yarborough. The summer before he worked on the Senate campaign. He posted "Bush for Senator" signs along Texas highways and handed out campaign literature door-to-door. Ever the extravert, George W. traveled across the state to organize rallies and whip up enthusiasm at his father's speeches and other campaign events. Confident of victory, he flew back to Houston for the election night celebration. But news of the defeat had already been broadcast when the Bush family pulled up to the Houston Shamrock Hotel to join supporters in the ballroom. Poppy gave a gracious concession speech. His 18-year-old son, however, was distraught. As startled campaign workers looked on, George W. broke down and wept bitterly.

Back at Yale, he was still feeling shaky. He sought out Yale Chaplain William Sloan Coffin, Jr. for some words of consolation. George W. knew that Coffin had attended Yale at the same time that his father had, and that both had been members of Skull and Bones. What he may not have known was that Reverend Coffin was now one of the nation's most outspoken advocates of nuclear disarmament and a critic of U.S. foreign policy. As the Vietnam war heated up, Coffin would emerge as a leading star in the anti-war movement. George W. spotted Coffin on campus and went up to introduce himself. "Oh yes," Coffin replied. "I know your father. Frankly, he was beaten by a better man." Coffin's remark cut deeply, and it reinforced a growing antipathy in George W.'s heart for arrogant, East-Coast intellectuals, counter-cultural activists, and other members of what he came to see as the liberal elite. For the next 30 years, men like Reverend Coffin would be among his father's strongest political enemies. George W. hated them. Once he became president himself, the sentiment was largely reciprocated.

Bigger enemies lay in wait. After 8 years as loyal understudy to Ronald Reagan, Poppy won the presidency for himself in the election of 1988. Less charismatic than Reagan and more willing to compromise with his political opponents, George H. W. Bush had some difficulty winning the trust of Christian evangelicals and other socially conservative groups that had become part of the broad Republican base. Nonetheless, world events (and his own measured responses to them) conspired to bring him considerable popularity in the early years of his presidency. The Berlin Wall fell, the Soviet Union crumbled, and American democracy finally emerged as the decisive winner of the Cold War—all under the watch of Bush I. When Iraq's Saddam Hussein invaded neighboring, oil-rich Kuwait, George H. W. Bush assembled a large coalition of nations to resist the aggression. Bush insisted on a complete withdrawal of Iraqi forces. When Saddam refused, allied forces launched air and ground attacks and drove the Iraqis out of Kuwait. His first-born son would later say that the coalition's triumph in Kuwait marked his father's finest moment as president.[34] He stood tall against a ruthless enemy.

The president halted the invasion once Kuwait was secure. Some critics asserted, however, that he should have continued the assault until Hussein's army was completely destroyed and Saddam himself removed from power. Bush explained that he had never intended to overthrow the Iraqi government, merely to force the Iraqis out of Kuwait, and that an extended invasion would have led to: *(1)* heavy American casualties, *(2)* the loss of international support for the operation, and *(3)* the long-term occupation of a hostile foreign country. The public seemed to agree. The president's approval ratings soared to the highest levels ever recorded.

Public approval, however, was short-lived. An economic downturn in the early 1990s helped to consolidate support for Democrat Bill Clinton, who defeated Poppy in the presidential election of 1992. A year later, the former President George H. W. Bush flew with family members to Kuwait to commemorate the coalition's victory over Iraq. The Kuwaiti authorities arrested 17 people who were allegedly involved in a plot to assassinate the former president with a car bomb. Through interviews with suspects and examination of the bomb's circuitry and wiring, the FBI concluded that the plot had been directed by the Iraqi Intelligence Service.[35] Later Saddam installed a mosaic of Poppy's face—complete with the slogan "Bush is Criminal"—on the floor of Baghdad's Al Rashid Hotel, where patrons could step on it all day.[36] "This is a guy that tried to kill my dad at one time," George W. Bush would later say.[37] His hatred for the Iraqi despot was boundless. Saddam "is a brutal, ugly, repugnant man who needs to go," George W. declared years later, as president.[38] "He is an evil man. I have seen a video of Saddam Hussein himself pulling the trigger on a man who didn't like his policies. He killed his two son-in-laws."[39]

It is difficult to overestimate the visceral hatred George W. Bush felt for the man who may have been his father's greatest enemy. Journalists Michael Isikoff and David Corn recount a scene involving Press Secretary Ari Fleischer and President George W. Bush from the spring of 2002, just under a year before Bush II would launch the fateful invasion of Iraq. Fleischer told the president about that morning's White House press briefing, wherein long-time correspondent Helen Thomas peppered Fleischer with questions about Iraq. Although no plans regarding a war in Iraq had yet been made public, Thomas wanted to know how the president could even consider a pre-emptive attack against Saddam. Fleischer reminded Thomas that regime change in Iraq had been a policy of the Clinton administration, too. The president "believes the people of Iraq, as well as the region, will be more peaceful, more better off without Saddam Hussein," he told Thomas. She shot back: "That's not a reason to go to war." As Fleischer later recounted this exchange for the president, George W. Bush turned grim and steely. And then this:

> "Did you tell her I don't like mother-fuckers who gas their own people?" the president snapped.
>
> "Did you tell her I don't like assholes who lie to the world?"

"Did you tell her I am going to kick his sorry mother-fucking ass all over the Mideast?"

Fleischer paused. "I told her half of that," he replied. Bush laughed, as did his aides. Still, Bush's reaction was telling. This wasn't bluster; this was real. The president meant what he said—every word of it.[40]

Armchair analysts and film makers have suggested that President George W. Bush pursued a war in Iraq to win an Oedipal battle with his own father. Mano a mano, Bush II needed to defeat Bush I in an ultimate test of masculinity. According to this common view, a wayward son who long resented his father's disapproval found his great Freudian opportunity to outdo the old man—to kill him off, in a psychoanalytic sense—by finishing the job that the old man started a decade before. By defeating Saddam, he might also defeat his father, or at least prove that he is the bigger and better man. A bold victory at war would finally convince all those doubters out there—including family members who worshipped Poppy and who thought Jeb was most deserving of the dynastic birthright—that he, George W. Bush, the first-born and bearer of his father's very name, deserved to be the king. Oedipus triumphant.[41]

The argument sounds good, but the evidence for it is slim. In Freud's classic formulation of the Oedipus complex, the son sees the father as an aggressor, for the father initially has all the power. The son's feelings towards the father are highly ambivalent. He hates the father because the father stands in the way of his most cherished unconscious goals—the goals of having power over others and having the mother all to himself. Yet he also may love and admire the father. Freud was a genius when it came to appreciating the deep ambivalence that lies beneath the surface of many human relationships.

But the standard Oedipal reading seems wrong in the case of George W. Bush. Sure, he felt ambivalence toward his father; most sons (and perhaps many daughters) do. When both father and son ascend to the presidency, some degree of rivalry is surely expected, and Oedipal comparisons are impossible to avoid. And growing up, George W. surely felt tremendous pressure to live up to his father's high standards, as did all the sons. *But the balance of this particular son's feelings toward his father seemed always to be shifted toward the positive end.* In the biographical accounts of the Bush family and in George W. Bush's own expressions, feelings of affection and admiration overwhelm resentment and hostility in the father–son relationship. I "would run through a brick wall for my dad," he once said. "I'm a fierce warrior when it comes to my father. I'm in it for love, not for power."[42] On this particular issue, perhaps we should just take George W. Bush at his word!

Rather than win out over his father, it seems more psychologically plausible to suggest that George W. Bush sought to win out over his father's *enemies*. For this psychologically crucial life goal, the son had little trouble summoning up hatred for political opponents of his father, especially East-Coast liberals and intellectuals. Helping Poppy defeat Massachusetts Governor Michael Dukakis in 1988 had to be almost as sweet (in George W. Bush's mind) as kicking Massachusetts Senator John Kerry's liberal ass in 2004. And sweeter yet to depose the biggest enemy of them all! "This is a guy that tried to kill my dad at one time." Here hatred rises to the boiling point. The animus that George W. Bush felt toward liberal elites, counter-culture protestors, and other Americans who opposed his father and his father's policy agendas for decades mobilized the son for political warfare, but politics is not literally war. Whereas political opponents can be defeated in elections, an evil man who tries to kill the good father must be defeated in real war, killed outright. There can be little doubt that President George W. Bush's decision to invade Iraq was partly motivated by the desire to avenge his beloved father.

When he was sworn into office on January 20, 2001, President Bush did not have an explicit plan to invade Iraq. But he was preoccupied with Iraq and with Saddam from the first month forward. On January 30, 2001, the president met with the principals of his National Security Council for the first time. According to Bush's first treasury secretary, Paul O'Neill, the meeting began with a discussion of the Israeli–Palestinian conundrum.[43] In the wake of Bill Clinton's recent failure to forge a peace plan between the Israeli government and Palestinian leader Yassar Arafat, President Bush announced that the new administration would tilt more strongly to the Israeli side. After some discussion of this policy shift, the president turned to Condoleeza Rice and began an exchange that the two had carefully scripted ahead of time.

"So, Condi, what are we going to talk about today? What's on the agenda?"

"How Iraq is destabilizing the region, Mr. President," Rice said. On cue, CIA Director George Tenet pulled out a large scroll, the size of an architectural blueprint, and flattened it out on a table. It was a aerial photograph of an Iraqi factory. Tenet suggested that the factory might be a "plant that produces either chemical or biological materials for weapons manufacture."

All the principals gathered around to peer at the grainy photograph. Tenet used his pointer to identify the railroad tracks that brought raw materials into the factory and the trucks lined up on the other end, into which finished weapons were assumedly loaded for transport to secret sites. Vice President Dick Cheney, typically dour and expressionless, was very excited. He waved his arms at the deputies, the backbenchers who sat against the wall, and urged them to step forward to see the photo. "You have to take a look at this!"

O'Neill was skeptical. He said that the factory looked like a thousand other factories he had seen in his long career as a businessman. There was no clear evidence in the photo that weapons were being made. Tenet did not dispute O'Neill's point, but it did not stop him from rolling out other scrolls that provided circumstantial evidence of Iraq's looming threat. The principals moved on to review the extant American policy regarding the enforcement of no-fly zones in Iraq, a Clinton-era program to keep Saddam in check. The president suggested that the policy was not tough enough. The president then gave everybody assignments for the next meeting. Secretary of State Colin Powell was to draw up tougher sanctions for Iraq. Secretary of Defense Rumsfeld was to "examine our military options." Might it be possible to employ ground forces in the north and south of Iraq to support an armed insurgency within, which might then lead to Saddam's ouster? Secretary O'Neill was to develop new financial strategies to squeeze the Iraqi regime.

Leaving the meeting, O'Neill concluded this: "Getting Hussein was now the administration's focus, that much was already clear." Ten days into the Bush presidency, and Iraq was already center stage.

Fastforward 8 months. Returning to the White House on the night of September 11, 2001, President Bush conferred with members of his national security team. As counterterrorism czar Richard A. Clarke recalls it, the president said this:

> "I want you all to understand that we are at war
> and we will stay at war until this is done. Nothing else

matters. Everything is available for the pursuit of this war. Any barriers in your way, they're gone. Any money you need, you have it. This is our only agenda."

The president then asked Clarke to focus on identifying what the next attack on the United States might be.[44] Later in the discussion, Secretary of Defense Rumsfeld noted that international law allowed nations to use armed force only to prevent future attacks, and not for retribution. "No!" the president shouted. "I don't care what the international lawyers say, we are going to kick some ass."

Clarke returned home for a few hours, and then returned to the White House in the early morning of September 12. Clarke knew that Osama bin Laden and Al Qaeda were behind the 9/11 attacks. All the evidence pointed to Al Qaeda. He was flabbergasted, therefore, to see that within 24 hours of the terrorist attacks the discussion in the White House had already begun to move toward Iraq: "By the afternoon on Wednesday [September 12], Secretary Rumsfeld was talking about broadening the objectives of our response and 'getting Iraq.' Secretary [of State, Colin] Powell pushed back, urging a focus on Al Qaeda. Relieved to have some support, I thanked Colin Powell and his deputy, Rich Armitage. 'I thought I was missing something here,' I vented. 'Having been attacked by Al Qaeda, for us now to go bombing Iraq in response would be like our invading Mexico after the Japanese attacked us at Pearl Harbor.'"[45]

Of course, Secretary Rumsfeld, Vice President Cheney, and President Bush did manage to focus attention on Al Qaeda in the fall of 2001. But the obsession with Iraq never went away.

Clarke describes a telling exchange he had with President Bush on September 12.[46] That evening, Clarke found the president alone, wandering around the Situation Room. President Bush "grabbed a few of us," closed the door, and then said, "Look, I know you have a lot to do and all . . . but I want you, as soon as you can, to go back over everything, everything. See if Saddam did this. See if he's linked in any way." Taken aback, Clarke reminded the president that over the past years he and intelligence officials repeatedly searched for a link between Saddam and Al Qaeda, and they repeatedly found nothing.

"I know, I know," the president replied, impatient and testy. "Just look [again]. I want to know any shred . . ."

Clarke promised to do his best.

"Look into Iraq, Saddam!" the president repeated, and then he rushed out of the room. Clarke's associates stared after the president as he disappeared from view, mouths agape.

***

President Bush was not the only man in his administration who wanted Saddam dead. Of special strategic and psychological significance were Dick Cheney and Donald Rumsfeld. Both served with Poppy in the Ford administration, and both functioned as in-house father figures for the new president. When it came to attitudes toward national security and Iraq, however, Cheney and Rumsfeld were very different from George W.'s real father. Whereas Bush Senior preferred careful diplomacy and building international alliances, Cheney and Rumsfeld favored a more muscular and unilateral American approach. Both believed that Bush Senior made a mistake by not finishing Saddam off in the 1991 Gulf War. They viewed Saddam as a menace in the Middle East and a threat to the security of the United States. As they saw it, the 9/11 attacks provided the perfect opportunity to depose the tyrant. Saddam was probably involved in the attacks in some manner anyway, they initially figured. And even if he wasn't, Saddam still threatened his neighbors, and ultimately would surely threaten the United States, with weapons of mass destruction. Because the Taliban government in Afghanistan provided refuge for Osama bin Laden and Al Qaeda, Afghanistan would have to be the first target of American retribution. But Iraq should be next.

From Day One of Bush II's presidency, Vice President Cheney was obsessed with the security of the United States. Heavy-set and balding, with an enigmatic crooked smile, Cheney was a survivor of multiple heart attacks. He harbored no political ambitions beyond the vice presidency, which helped to solidify his reputation as a deeply loyal and effective advocate for the president's policies. Cheney saw the world through a glass darkly. Threats to the security of the United States came from every corner of the globe, he knew. America should never let down her guard. Cheney was convinced that Saddam Hussein posed a serious and direct danger to the United States. He was convinced that the Iraqi dictator had produced and was stockpiling biological and chemical weapons and was working to build nuclear arms as well. But Cheney was realistic enough to know also that Al Qaeda demanded the first response. He agreed with the president when, 5 days after the 9/11 attacks, the president told his closest aides, "We don't do Iraq now; we're putting Iraq off. But eventually we'll have to return to that question."[47] At that precise point in history, much of the world saw the situation in starkly moral terms. The United States had been attacked. We were the victims, the good guys. The attackers must be punished. Cheney knew that the United States was duty-bound to punish the known attackers first. "If we go after Saddam Hussein, we lose our rightful place as the good guy," he acknowledged.[48]

Journalist Bob Woodward's first-hand accounts of the Bush administration's war planning for both Afghanistan and Iraq make it clear that Vice President Cheney was the most powerful and effective advisor to the president. Cheney was a master at seeming to defer to the younger president while never losing his position as a trusted father figure. Even though his hawkish attitudes about national defense contrasted sharply with Bush I, Cheney was careful to present his positions to Bush II in ways that did not denigrate the father. Cheney understood that George W. Bush loved and admired his father but that, at the same time, his political instincts and ideology differed substantially from his father's famously cautious approach. A bold and extraverted actor who (in accord with low levels of openness to experience) harbored few doubts regarding the righteousness of his actions, George-the-son displayed the kinds of personality traits that would make him amenable to the aggressive national security agenda that Cheney promoted. In going after Saddam as part of a broad war on terror, furthermore, George-the-son could achieve the cherished psychological goal of defeating his father's greatest enemy while, at the same time, fulfilling Cheney's ardent desire to defend America against a menacing threat.

Like Cheney, Secretary of Defense Donald Rumsfeld was eager to take Saddam out. With dust and smoke filling the operations center of the Pentagon on the afternoon of 9/11, Rumsfeld raised with his staff the possibility of going after Saddam in response to the terrorist attacks.[49] At a meeting of the national security team two days later, Rumsfeld was the first to suggest that the United States go to war against both Al Qaeda and Iraq.[50] When the president sampled opinions from his team on September 15, four key players—Cheney, Secretary of State Colin Powell, CIA Director George Tenet, and Chief of Staff Andrew Card— all voted to put Iraq on the back burner and concentrate first on Al Qaeda. Rumsfeld abstained.[51]

A former wrestler, Donald Rumsfeld was a fierce bureaucratic in-fighter who, like Cheney, pushed hard for an aggressive national defense. But Donald Rumsfeld's agenda was also filled with other things. One of Rumsfeld's most important goals was to streamline and modernize the military. Advanced technology and superior air power, he believed, would make obsolete the need for massive ground forces in future wars. A modernized military would make Americans more secure and enable America to exert more power on the world stage. A quick strike, Rumsfeld reasoned, would effectively depose Saddam, with minimal expense for the military and little cost of American lives.

The biggest goal on Donald Rumsfeld's motivational agenda, however, may have been simply to exert power—his own power, power for himself. He micromanaged the military's bureaucracy, bullied subordinates, and fought incessantly with his rivals on the Bush team. He was infamous for dashing off scathing and intimidating memos, called "snowflakes" (because they seemed to float down from the sky). Rumsfeld relentlessly fought to outmaneuver other advisors to the president. Even Condi Rice, a master of orchestration, had difficulty reining him in. Going back to the Nixon years, Rumsfeld had a testy relationship with George Senior. He advised President Ford to pick Nelson Rockefeller over George H. W. Bush as his vice-presidential choice for 1976. Nonetheless, George-the-son seemed to value Rumsfeld's counsel as an experienced father figure. Many White House aides were amazed that President George W. Bush cut Rumsfeld so much slack. Laura Bush despised the man. Whereas Bush was quick to lash out at aides like Andrew Card and Karl Rove when he was angry, he never rebuked Rumsfeld and often simply deferred to him.

If Cheney and Rumsfeld functioned as authoritative father figures for President George W. Bush, Colin Powell was—in temperament and worldview—much more like *the real father*. A military hero who commanded extraordinary respect with both Republicans and Democrats in the 1990s, Powell might have been the first black president of the United States, had he ever thrown his hat into the political ring. Powell believed that American troops should be sent to war only under conditions that posed the gravest threat to the interests of the country, and then only when the mission was clear and victory assured. To assure victory, the United States must act with overwhelming force in any military situation. Whereas Rumsfeld dreamed of military triumph through surgical strikes and streamlined deployments, Powell saw war as a long and brutal slog. Like the father but unlike the son, Powell knew the horrors of war up close. While Powell fought in the Vietnam War, Dick Cheney applied for and received five draft deferments, Donald Rumsfeld served in Congress and the Nixon administration (he was a Navy fighter pilot in the 1950s, but not during wartime), and George W. Bush flew airplanes for the Texas Air National Guard.

As a consistent voice of moderation in the Bush cabinet, Powell stood in stark contrast to Cheney and Rumsfeld. From the beginning, Powell cautioned against a bellicose response in Iraq. Like the first President Bush in 1991, Powell argued that invading Iraq would result in heavy casualties for American troops and might potentially leave the United States with no clear exit strategy. "If you break it, you own it," Powell famously warned, invoking what some have called the Pottery Barn doctrine of international relations. The better strategy, he suggested, was to build a diplomatic response. America should trust United Nations weapons inspectors to determine just how menacing the Iraqi threat was before launching any bold initiative. Working with other nations to exert economic and political pressure on Iraq, the

United States should support an international coalition to contain Saddam rather than overthrow him.

As president, George W. Bush did not seek direct counsel on Iraq from his own father. Nonetheless, he was aware of what kind of advice he might have gotten, had he tried to get it. His father always represented a relatively moderate, prudent, and internationalist expression of the Republican Party, even if he was more conservative than *his* own father, Prescott. To the extent that the father's political and strategic views were represented in the White House, they seemed to channel through Secretary of State Colin Powell. Yet Powell was never able to win the son over to his side, perhaps in the same sense that George I, so loved and admired by all his sons, was never really able to shape George II into the kind of force for moderation and compromise that he himself represented within the Republican party. But what father ever succeeds in making a son into his own image? In the battle among father figures for prime influence on the First Son, Powell lost out again and again to Cheney and Rumsfeld. The president admired Colin Powell, as he had always admired his real father. He listened respectfully to Powell's arguments. But he often rejected them.

Colin Powell shared one other attribute with George W. Bush's father—loyalty. George I labored in the Nixon, Ford, and Reagan administrations as a loyal subordinate who repeatedly sublimated his own ambitions for the good of the Republican Party. With ascension to the throne in 1989, his loyalty finally paid off. Likewise, Colin Powell exhibited fierce loyalty to superiors as he moved up the military ladder. Talent, ambition, and loyalty worked together to push him onward and upward, landing him at the top as a four-star general and, from 1989 to 1993, chairman of the Joint Chiefs of Staff. Like many military men, Powell believed deeply in the chain of command. Therefore, while he argued forcefully against the positions advocated by Cheney and Rumsfeld, Powell ultimately stayed loyal to the administration, even (and especially) when the final decision to invade Iraq was made. In the ironic end, he became as influential a public spokesperson *for* the invasion as Cheney and Rumsfeld had been in private.

War planning for Iraq began just 2 months after 9/11. It was the Wednesday before Thanksgiving in 2001, just as a National Security Council meeting was ending, that President George W. Bush pulled Donald Rumsfeld aside and asked him what he knew about the Pentagon's contingency plans for war in Iraq. Rumsfeld said that he had been reviewing all 68 of the department's secret war and contingency plans worldwide over the past few months, but recalled little that was new or significant regarding Iraq. As far as Rumsfeld knew, the combat commander for the region, General Tommy Franks, had not focused attention on Iraq.

"Let's get started on this," Bush said. "And get Tommy Franks looking at what it would take to protect America by removing Saddam Hussein if we have to."[52] Bush told Rumsfeld to keep the planning secret. If the press were to learn that the United States was planning a war with Iraq just as the Afghan operation was gathering steam, all hell would break loose. The president did not want it to appear that he was eager to pick a fight with Saddam.

As Rumsfeld and top military personnel worked furiously behind the scenes to develop a plan of attack, President Bush and Vice President Cheney began to prepare the American people for a new war. In his State of the Union address on January 29, 2002, Bush identified Iraq as one of three nations comprising an "axis of evil," posing a grave and growing danger to the world. With strong support from Cheney, Bush articulated a new doctrine of preemptive war. Rather than wait defenseless as enemies attack, the nation should strike down its enemies before they attack, Bush and

Cheney asserted. Saddam Hussein was the perfect target for a preemptive strike. In the latter half of 2002, CIA reports suggested, although never showed categorically, that Saddam was developing biological and chemical weapons and was intent on reconstituting the nuclear weapons program that Iraq had been forced to halt in the 1990s. And whereas no evidence ever surfaced to link Saddam back to the 9/11 terrorist attacks, many Americans believed that there must be some sort of connection. The Bush administration did nothing to dissuade them of their mistaken belief.

On August 26, 2002, Vice President Cheney delivered a pivotal speech at the Veterans of Foreign Wars convention in Nashville, Tennessee. "Simply stated, there is no doubt that Saddam Hussein now has weapons of mass destruction [and] there is no doubt that he is amassing them to use against our friends, against our allies and against us." The weapons are in the hands of a "murderous dictator," Cheney said. Saddam and his weapons are "as great a threat as can be imagined." The next day the headlines of *The New York Times* proclaimed: "Cheney Says Peril of a Nuclear Iraq Justifies Attack."

On October 10, 2002, the U. S. House of Representatives voted 296 to 133 to authorize the president to use armed forces in Iraq "as he deems to be necessary and appropriate." The Senate vote was 77 to 23, in favor. In November, the United Nations Security Council voted 15 to 0 that Saddam should face serious consequences if he violated disarmament obligations. United Nations inspectors were admitted into Iraq to search for evidence of chemical and biological weapons. Although no evidence was found, war drums continued to beat in the United States. Within the administration's inner circle, only Colin Powell and his aides continued to argue that the nation should take a cautious approach. On January 13, 2003, Bush finally told Powell that his mind was made up: The United States was going to war against Iraq. Are you with us or against us? Bush wanted to know. Powell might have walked away, resigned his post in protest against a war that he did not fully support. But instead, loyalty won out.

"I'll do the best I can," Powell answered. "Yes sir, I will support you. I'm with you, Mr. President."

"Time to put your war uniform on," the president said.[53]

The ex-soldier possessed more international credibility and cachet than any member of the Bush administration. He brought it all with him on February 5, 2003, when he addressed the United Nations Security Council to argue in favor of military action. It was the most important speech Colin Powell ever gave. Citing anonymous Iraqi defectors, Powell asserted: "There can be no doubt that Saddam Hussein has biological weapons and the capability to rapidly produce more, many more." In his heart, however, Powell likely did have doubts, serious doubts. Furthermore, some evidence he cited was widely held in intelligence circles to be highly suspect, such as the bogus claim that Iraq had once tried to obtain yellowcake uranium from the country of Niger. Years later in a television interview with Barbara Walters, Powell regretted having made the U.N. speech. He saw it as a "blot" on his legacy.[54] Nonetheless, Powell's address drew broad accolades at the time and was widely seen as making a strong case for an American invasion of Iraq. Six weeks later, America invaded.

***

George W. Bush burst on the social stage of human life as the extraverted actor with the uncanny ability to draw laughter, applause, and wide-eyed attention. From early childhood onward, he displayed boundless social energy, enthusiasm, and an aggressive tendency to inject excitement and emotional vitality into social situations of all kinds. Whereas his native extraversion sometimes brought him trouble as a young man, more often than not it brought him friends and bought him influence, as did his family ties and his family name. As Bush grew to maturity, extraversion joined forces with another strong trait in his personality make-up—low openness to experience. Together, these two cardinal personality dispositions produced a leadership style repeatedly characterized by the thousands who knew him socially and the millions who watched him on the world stage as bold, confident, restless, aggressive, steadfast, and unyielding. Guided by a few simple truths to which he swore all his allegiance, George W. Bush refused to focus his high-energy attention for more than a moment or two upon points of view at variance with his own. The confident swagger, the emotional intensity, the aggressive enthusiasm, the 100% commitment to a handful of unquestioned beliefs—the actor refined and elaborated these characteristics over a lifetime of blockbuster performances, from Midland, to Austin, to Washington, DC. As president, his traits helped to shape his response to the 9/11 terrorist attacks: bold action was required, focused aggression on an evil foe, no doubts, no looking back.

As Georgie moved through his elementary-school years, the *actor* became a motivated *agent*, too. It happens to most all of us. As personality develops through late childhood, goals and motives begin to layer over our basic dispositional traits. We begin to understand that life is about pursuing goals, and we begin to choose the goals we will pursue. To be an agent is to foresee goals, to develop plans to achieve goals, to learn strategies for responding to success and failure in goal pursuit. To be an agent is to know what you want in life and to set up your life so that you can get it. As actors, we continue to perform on the social stage, from our earliest years to our dying day. Actors are known by their traits—how they characteristically act on the social stage, as extraverts, for example, as performers with high energy or low energy, high conscientiousness or low conscientiousness, with a tendency toward depressiveness or no such tendency, friendly or not so friendly, anxious or calm, and on and on. The first layer of personality—our basic traits—is about the *how*, how we *act*. The second layer of personality is about the *what*—what we *want*, what personal goals we pursue in life. Beginning in late childhood, personality develops as a tandem, encompassing the social actor's developing traits and the motivated agent's developing goals.

What did George want? Over the course of his life, George W. Bush wanted many things. But four personal goals stand out in bold psychological relief.

PERSONAL GOAL #1

To raise his mother's spirits in the wake of Robin's death, to make her happy, to make her laugh. *Goal Accomplished*: 1953 to 1955, in elementary school.

PERSONAL GOAL #2

To make (large sums of) money on his own, to be a successful businessman, in accord with the Bush family's motivational agenda for men, passed down from Prescott to Poppy to Poppy's sons (George W., Jeb, Neil, and Marvin). *Goal Accomplished*: early 1990s, with the sale of George W. Bush's ownership share in the Texas Rangers.

PERSONAL GOAL #3

To perform public service, to hold political office or engage in non-profit public endeavors aimed at promoting a community, group, or nation—this also in accord with the Bush family's motivational agenda for men, passed down from Prescott to Poppy to Poppy's sons. *Goal Accomplished*: 1994 to 2009, as governor of Texas and as 43rd president of the United States.

PERSONAL GOAL #4

To defeat his father's enemies, to avenge the man he loves more than life itself by destroying his biggest enemy. *Mission Accomplished*: May 1, 2003.

Mission Accomplished. The invasion of Iraq commenced on March 19, 2003, and the Iraqi military was quickly defeated. American tanks rolled into Baghdad. On April 9, a small group of Iraqi men attempted to pull down the huge statue of Saddam standing in Baghdad's Paradise Square, opposite the Palestine Hotel where the world's press had gathered. U.S. troops finally joined in and used an armored vehicle to topple the statue— an iconic event in the war, seen around the world on television. U.S. troops continued to advance north, taking key towns such as Saddam's hometown of Tikrit.

By the end of the year, Saddam himself was captured, found hiding in a cellar in the town of Adwar, 10 miles from Tikrit. "He was caught like a rat," said Major General Ray Odierno. American troops confiscated two Kalashnikov rifles and Saddam's pistol. Four soldiers delivered the pistol—a 9-millimeter Glock 18C—to President Bush. For years after, Bush kept the mounted, glass-encased pistol in the Oval Office. With great pride, he often pulled the case out to show White House visitors, especially military veterans. Saddam's gun remains one of his most treasured possessions.[55]

In the story running through the mind of George W. Bush, Saddam's capture and his subsequent trial and execution are all anticlimax. They all follow naturally from the drama's high point, which happens as American forces stream into Baghdad and effectively depose the evil tyrant. With Saddam ousted, the son has avenged the father, and in the process he has liberated the Iraqi people. On May 1, the president declares victory in Iraq. The war is effectively over. Let us mark the triumph with a dramatic flourish. The president rides shotgun as a fighter jet lands on the aircraft carrier *USS Abraham Lincoln*, 30 miles off the coast of San Diego. He poses for photographs with pilots and members of the ship's crew while wearing his flight suit. A few hours later, he delivers a televised address to the American people.

"In the Battle of Iraq, the United States and our allies have prevailed," the president proclaims. Above the president's head and in the background, clear for all the world to see, a huge banner reads "Mission Accomplished."

Displaying the banner is not the president's idea. But the symbolism of the whole event is deeply simpatico with President Bush's driving motivational agenda. The war in Iraq turns out *not* to be over, not by a long shot. But the president has accomplished his own motivational mission by May 1, 2003. The mission is *not* about going mano a mano against his father but rather against his beloved father's greatest enemies. The dramatic landing in a fighter jet to mark the triumph of the war in Iraq consolidates an identification with Poppy, who flew his own fighter jet in his own war. With respect to George W. Bush's motivational agenda for life, all missions are now accomplished. With respect to his most cherished personal goals, it does not matter what happens from here on out.

Years later and after all that has happened and will happen in the aftermath of the American invasion of Iraq, let us not forget this fundamental truth: "This is a guy that tried to kill my dad at one time."

We defeated him, and now he is dead. And I've got his fucking gun.

THREE

On Being a Conservative

Let us travel back in our imaginations 50,000 years to the African savannah. We are the ancestors of modern human beings, living together in social tribes as foragers and hunters, migrating across grasslands and forests in search of food, shelter, and safety, forever on the move, on the outlook for opportunities and for dangers. Life is hard. Too often our babies live for but a season or two; our children sometimes starve. We are predators, for our young men hunt for wild game and bring back the meat to share with the clan. But we are also prey. The most vulnerable among us—our youngest, our oldest, and our weakest—are easy victims for hungry carnivores who are faster or stronger than us. We keep our most vulnerable close; we try to keep them safe in the group. Our biggest threats, however, come from other tribes of humans, hunters and foragers like us, who want what we want. There is just not enough to go around—not enough wild game, not enough food, not enough space in which to get our food, find our shelter, and live our lives the way we have tried to live them for generations. *We are under constant threat.* To survive, we must stick with our group. The group is everything.

Group life is human life. It is all we know. Our women care for our children in the group. We work together to raise our children, to feed them and keep them safe, and to teach them what they need to know so that they will grow up to raise children of their own. Our women tend to the home base, while our young men go off to hunt and to make war. A few of our older men are our leaders. They set forth our rules for living in the group. They preside over our ceremonies, such as when we bury our dead. We all cooperate in the group, for our very livelihood depends on *getting along*, sharing our resources, caring for and being cared for in the group. If truth be told, however, we also compete with each other in the group. We compete like crazy. We jockey for position. Each of us tries to get ahead in whatever way we can—by being more clever, more attractive, more dependable, more agreeable, more aggressive, more endearing, or more of whatever it takes and whatever we have in our arsenal of personality traits, cognitive skills, and physical wherewithal. Those who *get ahead* garner the most resources in the group. Getting along and getting ahead in the group—that is what human nature has always been all about.[1]

Everybody is different, although we are all part of the group. Some of us are more adventurous than others, willing to take risks, willing to explore what goes on outside the group or outside the group's rules. We tend to be a bit more adventurous when we are young, more willing to take risks, more eager to see things change, for change is exciting and, every once in a while, change brings with it good things. By contrast, some of us are more prudent than others, tending to rely on the tried-and-true, cautious and vigilant in our dangerous environment. We may become more vigilant and more sober as we get older, as we come to appreciate the group's traditions, the needs for stability and security, the wisdom of the way things have always been. The more cautious and restrained among us, whatever their age may be, tend to be suspicious of radical change. After all, we have built up our tribe, and we have survived and flourished over time. We have established strong traditions regarding how to live together, how to govern ourselves, who should be in charge, what authority to respect, how to relate to foreign tribes, what is right and what is wrong, and what to believe regarding the sacred. Our traditions have gotten us this far. Those among us who hew most closely to the group's timeless traditions aim first and foremost to keep us safe and secure. They typically urge us to keep things more-or-less the way they have always been, or to restore a golden time we may have lost. More than the rest of us, these especially restrained and cautious members of our group—deferential as they are to established authority—affirm the wisdom of ages past. *They are our conservatives.*

The starting point for understanding what it means to be a conservative, even as we move forward to the modern age, is to realize that conservatism is deeply ingrained in human nature. Human beings evolved to live in complex and highly ritualized social groups, competing and cooperating with each other to survive and reproduce. For Homo sapiens and their immediate predecessors, natural selection favored a strong identification with the group, for without it the individual human was destined for an early death. Even today, human beings feel an instant emotional preference for their own groups (in-group favoritism) and distrust rival groups (out-group antagonism).[2] Group loyalty is deeply valued, and blatant violations may be condemned as betrayal or treason.

Groups are typically organized in a hierarchical fashion; therefore, deference to authority is also highly valued. Groups develop over time, and they become defined by their history, and by the traditions they establish along the way. The natural human tendency is to *conserve* these established patterns of loyalty, authority, and tradition. At its heart, then, conservatism is about conserving patterns of group life that enjoy the imprimatur of tradition. It is about holding on to the past because the past is (perceived to be) good, safe, secure, trustworthy, comfortable, or simply the way things have always been, or were once upon a time, and *should* be. The tendency to conserve is enhanced under conditions of threat. Psychological research consistently shows that when people face threats to their security or their esteem, they embrace even more strongly the values and traditions of their self-defining groups. Under attack, we become even more conservative than we might otherwise be.[3]

In *The Conservative Soul*, Andrew Sullivan writes that conservatism looks with longing upon the past and wariness to the future. Time passes, and life invariably changes. But with each passing scene and chapter in our lives, something or someone is lost. We want to hold on to the good things we have known, to keep the best of life from slipping away. We want to conserve. As Sullivan sees it, all conservatism begins with loss:

> If we never knew loss, we would never feel the need to conserve, which is the essence of any conservatism. Our lives, a series of unconnected moments of experience, would simply move effortlessly on, leaving the past behind with barely a look back. But being human, being self-conscious, having memory, forces us to confront what has gone and what might have been. And in those moments of confrontation with time, we are all conservatives. . . . we get saddened when the familiar character disappears from a soap opera; or an

acquaintance moves; or an institution becomes
unrecognizable from what it once was. These little griefs
are what build a conservative temperament. They
interrupt our story; and our story is what makes sense of
our lives. So we resist the interruption; and when we
resist it, we are conservatives.

There is a little conservatism in everyone's soul—
even those who proudly call themselves liberals. No one
is untouched by loss.[4]

The past is known. It has become part of our story. But the
future is uncertain, and uncertainty can breed fear. What will
happen next in our lives? From the conservative point of view,
there is no reason to believe that the future will necessarily be
better than the past. It may be, or it may not. Progress is not
assured. What is for sure, however, is that threats are lurking
somewhere around time's corner. From the conservative point
of view, the seventeenth century philosopher Thomas Hobbes
got it right when he described the state of nature as forever
dangerous and human lives as potentially nasty, brutish, and short.
We are vulnerable creatures who confront new dangers every day.
The next person I meet will probably be harmless and maybe
even friendly, but I can never know for sure. I might meet 99 wonderful people in a row, but if the 100th is a murderer, my life will
be cut short. Better to be safe than sorry. For the individual, the
conservative approach is, as Sullivan puts it, to be "vigilant and
well-armed."[5] For the group, the first business of a conservative
approach is to assure safety. Sullivan writes:

So the first goal of conservative politics is not virtue, or
education, or liberty, or the integration of a divine or

eternal truth into every rule and regulation. It is much more basic than that. It is security. Without such security, it is impossible to have the peace necessary to cultivate virtue, apart from the virtue of courage.[6]

One of the great political texts in the history of conservatism is Edmund Burke's (1790) *Reflections on the Revolution in France*. Whereas many people in Burke's time saw the French Revolution as an inspiring triumph of the common people over tyranny, Burke lamented the wanton destruction of an old order. The French revolutionaries stormed the Bastille and overthrew the monarchy and the church. They executed dissidents by the thousands and ushered in a new era of terror and radical uncertainty. The French Revolution may have planted the seeds of liberty and fraternity, but Burke mainly saw chaos, anarchy, and loss. Reflecting a profoundly conservative attitude about time and human life, Burke rejected the idealism of revolutionaries and social visionaries, those dreamers who see history as the inevitable march toward enlightenment and the perfection of humankind. Transformative social agendas that break boldly from the past, that sever the precious and protective link with tradition and the wisdom of the ages, cannot be trusted, Burke asserted. Radical change is likely to cause more harm than good. Echoing Burke's warnings, Andrew Sullivan writes that as a political philosophy, conservatism has always been "based on doubt, skepticism, disdain for all attempts to remake the world and suspicion of most ambitious bids to make it better."[7] It is not that conservatives, like Burke, reject the idea of a better world in the future. Change is inevitable, and some change can be good. But they are suspicious of grand attempts to transform society and make human beings better people. They don't really trust the idea that human beings can be made dramatically better than they naturally are, at least not by social forces and idealistic agendas. Conservatives remain skeptical, cautious, vigilant, and well-armed.

For Sullivan and for Burke, being a conservative is fundamentally about feeling a particular sentiment regarding the nature of humankind and society. In describing a conservative *soul*, Sullivan suggests that conservatism is something deep and basic in a person's makeup, a dispositional tendency that is tied up with our emotions and desires. But conservatism also gives rise to particular values, ideals, and beliefs—thoughts and frameworks we have for making sense of self and society. In other words, conservatives not only *feel* a certain way about life, but they also *believe in* certain things.

Throughout American history, conservative intellectuals and policy makers have advocated a wide range of beliefs and ideals.[8] At the dawn of the American republic, conservative Federalists like John Adams and Alexander Hamilton argued for a strong federal government run by aristocrats and the landed gentry. They were highly suspicious of democracy. Before the Civil War, southern conservatives emphasized states' rights and small government. Many slave owners felt confident that their peculiar institution was a civilizing force grounded in tradition. In counterpoint to Jacksonian Democrats, the American political party known in the 1830s and 1840s as the Whigs favored economic growth in the context of moral restraint, the rule of law, and respect for tradition. In the early twentieth century, business leaders and their intellectual allies wanted to conserve an economic and political system that kept government out of the marketplace. Unfettered capitalism blessed some of these men with extraordinary riches; their conservatism was an effort to conserve their wealth and their standing. The richest of them had surely "gotten ahead" in their groups, and they wanted to keep it that way.

Different flavors of conservatism have proliferated in different regions and demographic niches in American society. Many conservatives shared a deep antipathy for communism, socialism, and other grandiose plans to create egalitarian utopias. After World War II, conservatism began to become a self-consciously organized ideological movement in American society. Leading intellectuals like William F. Buckley, Jr. and Irving Kristol brought together under one political banner a variety of interests and enthusiasms, such as militant anticommunism, free-market libertarianism, social and religious traditionalism, and opposition to state-sponsored liberalism. Republican Barry Goldwater carried the conservative banner to a crushing defeat in the 1964 U.S. presidential election. But 16 years later, Ronald Reagan achieved redemption and ushered in a conservative age in American politics.

Like President Reagan, George W. Bush rallied American conservatives of many different stripes when he won the presidency in the elections of 2000 and 2004. During the Bush years, being a conservative could mean many different things. Economic conservatives believed in the free market. They argued for low taxes and decried government interference in the good business of doing business. Defense conservatives believed in a strong military to keep America safe. In the wake of 9/11, the United States should hunt down its enemies and redouble its efforts to assure the security of all its citizens. Social conservatives cherished traditional family values, usually reinforced by strong religious beliefs. They believed that abortion should be illegal. They argued against gay marriage and other innovations in intimacy or social relations that threatened (as they saw it) the traditional American family. Like economic conservatives, social conservatives valued personal responsibility and individual liberty. For the most part, they distrusted government intervention in the everyday lives of people, even as they sometimes argued for more government support of religious schools and various faith-based initiatives.

Two months after the American invasion of Iraq, longtime conservative journalist Robert Novak described George W. Bush as "a president who may be more basically conservative than Ronald Reagan."[9] Novak was right. If ever there was a "conservative soul," it resided somewhere deep in the being of George W. Bush. Conservatism was a key to both his policies and his personality. Importantly, conservatism worked to motivate and to provide an ideological justification for the invasion of Iraq. But the story of being a conservative is complicated in the case of George W. Bush. After all, it is easy to imagine a different conservative president in office in 2003—pick any one from a long list of conservatives you can think of—who might have decided simply to leave Saddam alone. Many, if not most, conservatives would not have done what President George W. Bush did when it came to Iraq. The specific brand of conservatism that George W. Bush espoused as president, therefore, and the development of that brand from childhood through midlife conspired with a set of other personality and situational factors in his life to shape his presidency and influence his decision to invade Iraq.

One cannot understand Bush's decision to invade Iraq without considering the development of his conservative political belief system, a belief system that was as much a part of his personality as were his dispositional traits (Chapter 1 in this book) and his characteristic goals (Chapter 2). In the case of George W. Bush, a deeply conservative sentiment combined with important childhood experiences to produce an ideal image of how people should live together in security and freedom—a kind of Garden of Eden that he longed to conserve and restore. Bringing that mythic paradise back became part of his redemptive dream, a distinctively conservative dream to restore a world that he knew and loved as a child. The political philosophy George W. Bush developed as an adult provided him with a moral justification for the dream. Eventually, the dream came to encompass his vision for Iraq. The personality traits of high extraversion and low openness to experience set George W. Bush up for a transformative performance on the world's stage. His life goal to defeat his father's most hated enemies helped direct his energy toward Iraq. And the particular brand of political conservatism he developed over five decades of life provided a moral framework and idealistic rationale for the Iraq invasion. Bush's conservatism is key here. So, let us go back to the beginning. How did little Georgie become a conservative?

***

HYPOTHESIS #1: HE INHERITED IT

Maybe George W. Bush was simply born a conservative. Is it possible that being a conservative (or liberal) is (partly) a matter of what genes a person is born with? The answer is a qualified *yes*.

Political attitudes tend to run in families. Parents who espouse relatively conservative political values tend to have children who grow up to be fairly conservative, too. The same holds true for liberals. The cross-generational continuity of political attitudes is partly because of environmental influences. To a certain extent, children learn political values from their parents. There is also evidence, however, that heredity plays a role. For example, studies show that identical (monozygotic or MZ) twins tend to be more similar to each other on political values than fraternal (dizygotic or DZ) twins.[10] MZ twins are genetically identical whereas DZ twins have, on average, about half their genes in common. The simple logic of twin studies suggests that the more similar a person's genetic makeup is to another, the more similar will be their political attitudes. The similarities show up for broad self-ratings on questions like "How politically liberal or conservative are you?" and on more specific political beliefs such as "To what extent do you support the death penalty?" and "Should the government raise taxes to support more social programs?" Interestingly, even when MZ twins grow up in different families (as would be the rare case when identical twins are adopted into different families at birth), identical twins end up showing surprisingly similar scores on a dimension called *traditionalism*, which is the extent to which a person holds to traditional religious and generally conservative political values.[11] This is a remarkable scientific finding: it says that there is a strong probability that when two different people who happen to share the same genes are raised in different families and *never even know each other growing up*, they will develop fairly similar political attitudes. If one turns out to be a conservative, the chances are pretty good that the other will, too.

Behavioral scientists, therefore, are pretty sure that genes play *some* role in the formation of political attitudes. Still, nobody has ever identified a specific segment of DNA that encodes a tendency to be conservative or liberal. And scientists likely never will. It begs credulity to imagine that there is a particular gene determining whether a person believes that the federal government should provide universal health care or whether private citizens should be allowed to carry guns in the glove compartments of their cars. Genes regulate the production of proteins and other basic physiological processes, which interact in maddeningly complex ways with environments at many different levels and over time to produce structure, function, behavior, thought, and feeling. Even if scientists were able to decode George W. Bush's genome, they would be unable to identify a genetic pattern that made him into a conservative. Although it sounds wishy-washy, the most we can legitimately say is that genes have *something* to do with the development of a person's political values and beliefs. As science advances in the next few decades, we may learn more about what that something is. At most, certain genetic patterns may predispose a person to react to stimuli in a particular way, which may set up certain kinds of subtle preferences that are shaped by environments and experience over time. It is likely that genes get the story going. But there has to be much more to the story.

HYPOTHESIS #2: IT CAME FROM HIS PERSONALITY TRAITS

Perhaps George W. Bush became a conservative because the personality traits he began to show very early in life predisposed him to develop in a politically conservative direction. In a sense, this hypothesis is a variation on the first one, for evidence suggests that basic personality traits—such as the Big Five traits of extraversion, neuroticism, agreeableness, conscientiousness, and openness to experience (Chapter 1 in this book)—are partly determined by heredity. It may be the case, then, that a person develops his or her traits first, and then the traits give rise to corresponding political values. This hypothesis is plausible, and it adds a small but important piece to the story for George W. Bush.

How might a child's traits link up with the development of political attitudes? A study conducted at the University of California at Berkeley provides one clue. Personality psychologists Jack Block and Jeanne H. Block collected detailed personality ratings of nursery-school children made by their teachers when the kids were 3 years old and again, the next year, when the kids were age 4 years. Two decades later, the researchers recontacted the study's participants, who were now age 23 years, and asked them to complete a series of questions regarding their political beliefs and values. Block and Block found that those nursery-school children who were rated by their teachers as relatively inhibited, fearful, easily offended, inde-cisive, and easily victimized tended to show more conservative political beliefs at age 23 years. By contrast, self-reliant, energetic, dominant, and relatively undercontrolled children tended to grow up to be more politically liberal. Block and Block suggested that political conservatism in adulthood may spring from a more basic dispositional tendency, observable even in young children, to be especially cautious, inhibited, overcontrolled, vulnerable, and wary. The finding seems to resonate with the general view that conserva-tism involves a certain caution and wariness in the world.[12]

The findings from the Berkeley study are statistical tenden-cies in one particular group of American schoolchildren studied at a particular period in history. Even within the study itself, there were many exceptions to the general rule, which is almost always the case in behavioral science research. With little doubt, George W. Bush would have been a *big exception* to the rule. All of the biographical data available suggest that if 4-year-old Georgie had been in this study, he would have been rated by his teachers as dominant, relatively undercontrolled, and energetic. There was never anything timid, inhibited, indecisive, or overcontrolled about this kid. According to the study's statistical findings, then, he should have grown up to be a liberal. That didn't happen.

Assuming, furthermore, that the children in the Berkeley study carried with them into their early 20s some of the same personality tendencies that their nursery-school teachers saw, the study's findings seem to suggest that conservatives should show higher levels of *neuroticism* in adulthood, which is a basic personality tendency to experience fear, vulnerability, and other negative emotional states. Again, Bush doesn't fit. Psychologists have tended to rate him as low to moderate on the trait of neuroticism.[13] Although he could be hostile and tense, George W. Bush was rarely subject to sad moods, bouts of anxiety, or emotional instability. Moreover, the broad swath of scientific research on the topic shows that neuroticism is, in general, *unrelated* to political attitudes. In other words, conservatives are typically no more or less neurotic than liberals. Trait research does suggest a small correlation between being dutiful and controlled (aspects of the broad trait of *conscientiousness*) and tendencies toward conservatism, which fits the Berkeley study.[14] However, in the case of Bush, psychologists have tended to rate him in the moderate range on this variable, not especially high or low on conscientiousness, compared to other presidents.[15]

The primary sense, however, in which George W. Bush's basic personality traits line up with his political orientation targets a dispositional tendency that was not evaluated in the Berkeley study. That trait is openness to experience, which, as we saw in Chapter 1, was an especially strong tendency in his trait profile. It is clear that George W. Bush was extremely *low* on the trait of openness, indicating low tolerance for ambiguity and complexity, resistance to novelty and change, and a strong preference for simple, straightforward, black-and-white formulations for understanding the world. Comparing him to all the U.S. presidents, psychologists and historians rate Bush dead last on openness, as noted in Chapter 1.[16]

Openness to experience is the one personality trait that consistently predicts political orientation: on average, liberals tend to score higher on openness, conservatives lower. Conservatives often prefer strict moral rules and clear legal formulations that are consistent with society's conventional norms. They are highly suspicious of efforts to upset established conventions and to blur distinctions that have stood the test of time. As George W. Bush once said, "good and evil are present in this world, and between the two there can be no compromise."[17] It seems reasonable to suggest, therefore, that generally low openness to experience helped to pave the way for the development of conservative political beliefs and values in the life of George W. Bush. Similarly, the development of conservative values over time may have further reinforced Bush's inherent tendency toward low openness to experience.[18] Still, low openness to experience is a very general tendency, and it does not specify precisely what kinds of conservative values a person will hold and how those values may play out in his or her life. There must be more to the story.

HYPOTHESIS #3: IT'S BECAUSE HE WAS A FIRSTBORN

When I get to the topic of birth order in my personality psychology class, the students invariably perk up. Nearly every one of them seems to believe that your ordinal position in the family constellation—whether you are firstborn, second-born, last-born, only child, etc.—is a key to personality development. They will point to their own experiences and their observations of their siblings for proof. The students get very annoyed with me when I tell them that empirical research typically fails to support their folk notions about birth order. Because birth order is so easy to measure (you simply ask people), psychologists have routinely incorporated it into their studies over the decades. In general, their statistical findings show that birth order predicts almost nothing about personality.[19]

But there may be one exception. In his book *Born to Rebel*, Frank Sulloway makes a strong case for a link between birth order and a general tendency to rebel against the status quo.[20] According to Sulloway, children compete for the attention and love of their parents by adopting particular roles or niches in the family environment. Blessed with the natural advantage of being first on the scene, firstborns are likely to identify strongly with the parents and to adopt the traditional viewpoints of authority that the parents represent. By contrast, later-borns must define themselves over and against the dominant firstborns so that they can carve out a niche that will bring them what Sulloway calls "parental investment." Consequently, later-borns are more likely to adopt a rebellious and contrarian attitude toward authority. One interesting result of this development is that later-borns should be more open to innovation and change whereas firstborns should resist change and favor the status quo.

Sulloway finds rather extraordinary support for his hypothesis by examining historical records. In one of his studies, he surveyed the published responses of nineteenth century scientists to the introduction of Darwin's theory of evolution. Darwin (himself a later-born) launched a scientific revolution that defied the authority of the church as well as many accepted scientific canons of the day. Following the publication of his landmark *Origin of the Species* in 1859, the historical record shows that later-born scientists were 4.4 times more likely to support Darwin's revolutionary views than were firstborn scientists. Sulloway finds similar results for initial reactions of scientists to the discoveries of Copernicus and Newton and to the revolutionary writings of Sigmund Freud. Later-born scientists, therefore, appear to welcome dramatic changes; firstborn scientists, by contrast, tend to express skepticism. In other words, the firstborns tend to be more conservative, at least when it comes to scientific practice. Sulloway emphasizes that firstborn scientists are skeptical about *any* kind of new idea – good ones (like evolution) and dumb ones (like phrenology, which was the nineteenth century theory that bumps on the head correspond to personality traits – later-borns loved that one, too). Eventually, of course, firstborn scientists will catch on to a new idea, if it turns out to be a very good idea. Today the scientific community (firstborns, later-borns, everybody) overwhelmingly accepts the theory of evolution—even if, as surveys show, most American adults (and the 43rd president) don't.

Because they are the first children to enter the family system and to encounter family and societal traditions, Sulloway argues, firstborns are likely to be more *traditional* than later-borns. When it comes to evaluating Sulloway's thesis with objective survey data from living people, however, the scientific jury is still out.[21] But let us give Sulloway's hypothesis the benefit of the doubt and assume that it has some validity. In the case of George W. Bush, we see a firstborn who consistently expressed a very strong preference for tradition. More so than his younger brothers (all of whom would be characterized as politically conservative), George W. Bush seemed to embrace tradition and identify with the conventions of his parents' generation. We have already seen (Chapter 2) how strongly he identified with his father, to the point of attending the same schools his father attended, forming an engagement to a Smith College woman in the same way his father did, aiming to be a fighter pilot like his father, and following his father into the oil business. Although all of the brothers admired their father, none of them felt more pressure to follow so closely in his footsteps. To reinforce how much it fell upon the firstborn to embody what

Sulloway depicts as the traditionalism niche in the family, let us not forget that George W. was the one son in the family who carried his father's name.

The conservative tendency toward traditionalism expressed itself repeatedly in George W. Bush's life, from Andover to the White House. Although he loved to tweak authority with humor and mild forms of rebellion, George W. identified strongly in high school with the traditional values espoused by Andover Academy. In his senior year, he was appointed as a proctor for underclassmen, charged with assuring that the younger boys followed the rules and adhered to the school's traditions. At Yale, he joined the DKE fraternity and was inducted into the legendary Skull and Bones Society. Both accomplishments bespeak popularity and prestige, for sure, but they also underscore a strong identification with the most veritable and traditional organizations on campus. When George W. did violate rules, he did so in the tried-and-true ways of conventional college life—by staging college pranks or getting deliriously drunk and making a fool of himself, and not through campus sit-ins and protest marches.

Throughout his adult years, George W. Bush felt a strong attraction to tradition. One of the most telling examples comes from his days as part-owner of the Texas Rangers. In the 1980s and 1990s, Major League Baseball (MLB) developed a playoff system, whereby the best second-place team from each league (the wild card team) would qualify for post-season play. MLB also introduced interleague competition, such that, for example, the New York Yankees (American League) could play the New York Mets (National League) and the Chicago White Sox could play the Chicago Cubs during the regular season. These innovations have proven to be wildly popular. A baseball fan myself, I know almost nobody who now believes that these changes were a *bad* idea.

But this was not the case for George W., whose contrary views reflect his strong tendency toward tradition. In his campaign autobiography, Bush "admit[s] to almost mystical feelings about America's pastime." He writes that in speeches to college students he typically emphasizes the "essential truths," or "fixed stars," of faith, family, and personal responsibility, and then, "partly joking," he often adds a fourth fixed star: "Baseball should always be played outdoors on grass, with wooden bats." On the traditions of baseball, Bush writes:

> I'm a traditionalist when it comes to our national sport. I voted against wild-card play, because I don't believe baseball should reward a second-place finish. I didn't like interleague play because I worried it would diminish the World Series. I thought the best future for baseball would be found in reverence and respect for its history and traditions.[22]

HYPOTHESIS #4: ROBIN'S DEATH PLAYED A ROLE

Andrew Sullivan suggests that experiences of loss build a conservative sensibility in life. When we lose something or someone dear to us, we hold on ever more tightly to what is left behind. We seek to conserve those things, ideas, feelings, experiences, communities, and institutions that link us to the past, and to what we have lost. No doubt the biggest loss in the early years of George W. Bush's life was the death of his little sister from leukemia. When Poppy and Bar told their 7-year-old son that Robin was dead, Georgie was stunned. He had known that Robin was sick, but his parents had never let on that her illness could be fatal. A deep sadness set in, punctuated by the flashes of fear that produced the young boy's nightmares. In response to Robin's death, Georgie channeled his extraversion into the social role of family clown. His antics helped him achieve the first important personal goal in his life—the goal of lifting the spirits of his grieving mother. Is it possible that Robin's death also activated or reinforced a tendency toward conservatism? Might George W. Bush's lifelong embrace of tradition—what he called the "fixed stars" and "essential truths" of "faith and family"—stem, in part, from Robin's death?

It is hard to say. As far as I know, behavioral scientists have never documented a relationship between experiences of early loss on the one hand and the development of conservative sentiments and values on the other. Are children who lose siblings or parents to death more likely to grow up to be more conservative than those children who do not experience loss? It seems doubtful. Nonetheless, studies have shown that conservatives tend to express a stronger fear of death, or sensitivity to the negative prospects of death, than do liberals.[23] Does this fear or sensitivity stem from actual losses in life? Or is there something about being a conservative in the first place that makes death a more salient psychological concern? When people are exposed to stimuli that remind them of death, they typically embrace more tightly the traditions and conventions that they have grown up with, a move toward conservatism in most cases. All in all then, there does seem to be some sort of psychological connection between death (the ultimate loss) and conservatism, as Sullivan suspected. But research does not support a simple causal story in which early experiences with death give rise, later on, to a conservative sentiment in life.

The psychological effects of Robin's death for George W. Bush depend, in part, on what meaning or lesson Bush derived from this early tragedy. Beyond expressing how sad Robin's death was and how it motivated him to raise his mother's flagging spirits, George W. Bush was never especially expansive in discussing the death of his sister and the effects of her death on his life. In *A Charge to Keep*, he offers three sentences:

> I was young enough, and my parents loved me enough, that Robin's death did not traumatize me. I guess I learned in a harsh way, at a very early age, never to take life for granted. But rather than making me fearful, the close reach of death made me determined, determined to enjoy whatever life might bring, to live each day to its fullest.[24]

Written with Karen Hughes as a campaign autobiography and filled with such clichés as "live each day to its fullest," this passage must be read with some skepticism. Given the reports from his parents and childhood friends regarding nightmares, it seems unlikely that Robin's death did not stimulate some fear in little Georgie's heart. And the emphasis on being "determined" seems as much an effort to convince voters of his steady convictions as it is a statement of psychological reality. Nonetheless, Bush's words express a natural, but also naturally *conservative*, response to loss. He did *not* write that Robin's death inspired high ideals in him, or motivated him to change the world, or taught him that a person must make himself into something good or better or transcendent—the kinds of responses that might inspire a more liberal sensibility. He writes instead that Robin's death taught him at an early age "never to take life for granted." Hold on to what you've got, for it may be gone tomorrow. The "close reach of death" teaches us to "enjoy whatever life may bring." As Hobbes, Burke, and Sullivan would have it, there are no guarantees of growth or progress in life. One grabs what one can grab, and holds on desperately to what one has—a simple truth that resonates deeply with the conservative soul.

HYPOTHESIS #5: IF YOU GREW UP IN MIDLAND, TEXAS, YOU WOULD BE CONSERVATIVE TOO

When it comes to the effects of social environments on the development of personal beliefs and values, psychological research confirms common sense. People *do* learn basic lessons about God, goodness, society, truth, fairness, virtue, and so on from parents, teachers, pastors, rabbis, and many other authority figures in their environment, as well as from siblings, peers, television celebrities, rock stars, and even authors of books. We are not born with beliefs and values etched into our brains, even if we come into the world with certain predispositions and preferences. We learn what to believe, and we learn it from the environment. How could it be otherwise? With this in mind, it is important to mention, even if it is patently obvious, that the Bush family was a bastion of conservative values for most of the twentieth century. Tracking the political mood of the country as it evolved from World War II through 9/11, Prescott proved to be moderately conservative as a senator from Connecticut (in the 1950s and 1960s), George H. W. Bush tacked further to the right as vice president and president (1980s and early 1990s), and George W. Bush outflanked them both as governor and president. It is also important to mention, though perhaps even more patently obvious, that Midland, Texas in the 1950s was a pretty conservative place—like Midland, Texas today. Of course, political liberals can spring up anywhere. But it is hard to find them in the Bush family, and hard to find *lots of them* (outside Austin and a few other liberal enclaves) in the great red state of Texas.

One could argue, therefore, that George W. Bush turned out to be a conservative because he grew up in a very conservative family and lived in a very conservative community in a very conservative state within the United States. So much exposure to conservative environments virtually assured that his values and beliefs would ultimately reflect the lessons he learned from these environments. There is surely some truth in this broad generalization, as George W. Bush himself repeatedly acknowledged. In tracing the development of his own conservative beliefs, he was always quick to identify his parents, his family environment, and various other people and institutions that espoused traditional values, as well as his experiences in the National Guard and the business world.

Amidst all these environmental factors, however, the town of Midland, Texas loomed especially large. In *A Charge to Keep*, Bush asserted that his most basic values in life all trace back to Midland. To reinforce the point, he gave Chapter 2 the title, "Midland Values." Like Robin's death, moreover, the town's importance may lie less in the actual psychological effects it produced and more in its symbolic *meaning* in the life story of George W. Bush. This is because a deeply conservative traditionalist like George W. Bush needs an *Eden*—an idealized setting from the distant past, lost but never forgotten, whose simple goodness must be *conserved* or restored. For George W. Bush, Midland, Texas was Eden.

In the beginning, there was Midland. And it was good:

> Midland was a small town, with small-town values. We learned to respect our elders, to do what they said, and to be good neighbors. We went to church. Families spent time together, outside, the grown-ups talking with neighbors while the kids played ball or with marbles and

yo-yos. Our homework and schoolwork were important. The town's leading citizens worked hard to attract the best teachers to our schools. No one locked their doors, because you could trust your friends and neighbors. It was a happy childhood. I was surrounded by love and friends and sports.[25]

Midland was a place where children enjoyed the freedom to play in a safe environment. Security was assured because adults looked out for children and taught them the rules:

Everyone played together. Everyone's parents watched out for everyone else's kids. Midland was a place where other people's mothers felt it was not only their right, but also their duty, to lecture you when you did something wrong, just as your own mother did. I'll never forget the time Mike Proctor's mom came running out of her house to yell at me for running out into the street without looking. She got my attention, and I never did it again.[26]

Remarking on these idyllic passages from *A Charge to Keep*, one biographer asserts that "the Midland of memory is the core image" of George W. Bush's life, "his West Texas version of a New Jerusalem."[27] This is a keen psychological insight. His nostalgic memory of Midland captures perfectly George W. Bush's image of how people, all people everywhere, should live together. Like most utopian visions, there is peace, harmony, happiness, and love. But notice what else—notice how deeply *conservative* this image is. The first business of conservatism is to assure *security*. No one locks their doors in Midland. The only hint of danger is the traffic in the street—symbolizing, perhaps, out-groups, that is, those outsiders who happen to drive through town. Remember never to run into the street without looking. Stay vigilant, even in Eden. There is legitimate *authority* in Eden. Children learn to respect their elders, the parents who "watched out for everyone else's kids" and the "town's leading citizens." There is *discipline* and a clear sense of *right* and *wrong*. Moms have a duty, as authorities within the community, to lecture children when they break the rules. Mike Proctor's mom lectured the future president when he acted in a heedless way, and he "never did it again."

The emergence of Midland as the idealized community for social life—the good group wherein people live together in security and freedom as they strive to get along and get ahead in the world—marks the end of the first stage of George W. Bush's development as a conservative. By the time he headed off to high school, Georgie had established the rudiments of a profoundly conservative and traditionalist sensibility towards life. A firstborn son from a politically conservative family who identified strongly with authority, he probably inherited dispositional tendencies that favored the development of traditional values and beliefs. Among these tendencies was a predisposition toward low openness to experience, and with it a strong preference for those simple, tried-and-true frameworks for right and wrong that promise stability, continuity, and security. The death of his sister may have (as a young boy) sensitized him to, or (as an adult) symbolized for him, the fragility of human life, and fueled his desire to hold on to, or conserve, that which is familiar, cherished, and tied to the past. Midland values reinforced the lessons he learned in the family— respect authority, stay vigilant and disciplined, work hard and show personal responsibility. Life as a child in Midland, reconstructed in memory during his adult years, set up for George W. Bush a conservative paradise, to which his longing and his striving were forever oriented.

At the end of childhood, then, George W. Bush was well on his way to becoming a conservative. He had a taste for it, a visceral feel for being a conservative. But his beliefs were still vague and general. Beyond his penchant for traditionalism and his tendency to identify with the authoritative status quo, he did not have a political ideology. It would take decades before he developed a specific brand of conservatism to shape his moral and political agendas. By the time he left Texas for Andover, George W. Bush seemed to be heading down a conservative path. But what kind of a conservative would he turn out to be?

***

There are many different kinds of conservatives in the United States.

Economic conservatives favor small government, low taxes, and pro-business policies. They have strong faith in the free market. Government should limit its involvement in the daily enterprise of Americans so that workers can be maximally productive and businesses can make maximum profits. High taxes and excessive government regulations are almost always bad because they stifle innovation in business and obstruct open competition among economic entities. Economic conservatives tend toward laissez-faire, libertarian viewpoints when it comes to the role of government in the lives of its citizens, or else they favor government interventions designed to strengthen business and build wealth. For economic conservatives, making money is close to a moral virtue, and free enterprise has a strong moral cachet. The family business, the family farm, the self-made entrepreneur, the profitable company that brings increasing wealth to its shareholders—these are all highly valued images for American economic conservatives.

Building wealth is almost always good. At the end of the day, some people will end up vastly wealthier than others. But this is okay, for open competition makes for winners and losers. And as the economy grows, there should be more winners. A rising economy lifts all (well, many) boats.

In the twentieth century, economic conservatives in the United States tended to gravitate to the Republican Party. Like Calvin Coolidge in the 1920s, they have tended to believe that what is good for business is good for America. Economic conservatives fought Roosevelt's New Deal with tremendous passion and vitriol. They abhorred government intrusion into the marketplace and insisted that unfettered capitalism and free enterprise would eventually bring America out of its Great Depression. After World War II, they continued to advocate for pro-business policies like low taxes and free trade, and they rallied against communism, which they saw as the ultimate threat to capitalism and the American way of life. A self-made banker who earned his millions on Wall Street, Prescott Bush personified the kind of economic conservatives who made up the Republican establishment at mid-century. His son, George H. W. Bush followed right along, making millions in oil in the 1950s before he helped to build up the Texas Republican Party in the 1960s. Although far less successful in business than his grandfather and father, George W. Bush internalized the standard ideological playbook for economic conservatives in the Bush family environment, at Harvard Business School, in the oil business, and as part-owner of the Texas Rangers. When he made his failed run for Congress in 1978, he called himself an economic conservative who hoped to deregulate the energy industry and do battle with the "bureaucratic spread of federal government that is encroaching more and more on our lives."[28]

Research shows that Americans who identify themselves as politically conservative tend to adopt what the political psychologist John T. Jost calls *system-justifying* beliefs.[29] Resistant to broad societal changes and accepting of the economic status quo, conservatives tend to adopt beliefs that reinforce and justify existing structures, hierarchies, and institutions in society. Things are pretty much fine as they are—no need to meddle in the natural or established state of social reality. Economic conservatives tend to believe that people generally get what they deserve anyway, so idealistic efforts to level the economic playing field or redistribute resources from rich to poor are misguided. They believe that if you work hard enough you will succeed. They believe that individual merit will typically win out. Therefore, if people take personal responsibility for their lives, work hard, and do the right things, they will usually get ahead (and get along). System-justifying beliefs help to shield economic conservatives from the anxiety or guilt they might otherwise feel in the face of rampant disparities in American society. Whereas liberals may experience deep angst when they encounter broad economic inequalities in the United States and in the world, economic conservatives may be more likely to accept these disparities as the way things simply are or have to be. This may be one reason, Jost argues, that conservatives tend to report higher levels of happiness than liberals report.[30]

Although they share many similarities with economic conservatives, *social* conservatives have a very different ideological agenda. Their main concern is the regulation of social behavior. They favor policies that aim to assure order, stability, and traditional values in the family and the community. In the 1960s and 1970s, social conservatives rallied around politicians who promised to get tough on crime and drugs and to make America's communities safe again. They tend to favor stiff sentences for criminal offenses. They tend to favor the death penalty. With the political rise of the Moral Majority, the Christian Coalition, and other manifestations of the religious right over the past three decades, social conservatives have become increasingly identified with the regulation of sexuality and reproduction. They ardently oppose abortion. Roe v. Wade, the 1973 Supreme Court ruling that struck down certain restrictions on abortion, galvanized the social conservative movement like no other event of the twentieth century. Conservative Christians who oppose abortion usually invoke strong religious justifications for their stance. Social conservatives today also tend to oppose expanded rights for gays and lesbians. They view themselves as the vanguard against all threats to the sanctity of traditional family life, from pornography to divorce to euthanasia.

Beginning in the 1960s, white social conservatives migrated en masse to the Republican Party. Many working-class and middle-class whites in the South, who had voted Democratic ever since the days of FDR, began to switch party affiliation once Lyndon Johnson signed civil rights legislation. Johnson once remarked that having now gone on record as supporting the rights of African-Americans, the Democratic Party would lose the deep South for a generation. His prognosis turned out to be optimistic—it is two generations now, and counting. Richard Nixon's "southern strategy" brought many white, working-class former Democrats, who feared crime and racial integration, into the Republican Party. After Roe v. Wade, many conservative Christians, who had previously been apolitical or leaning (for economic reasons) Democratic, began to join ranks with the Republicans, to the benefit of Ronald Reagan and George H. W. Bush in the 1980s.

In the 1988 presidential campaign, his firstborn son proved to be an invaluable asset for George H. W. Bush in his quest to win the votes of social conservatives. Episcopalian and tending toward moderation, George H. W. Bush was never comfortable with the religious, born-again fervor of many social conservatives, especially those of fundamentalist and evangelical persuasions. But his son George W. Bush learned to talk the evangelical talk, and walk the walk. He became the real thing in the 1980s, a bona fide social conservative, a champion of faith and family values. He would later win the hearts and most of the votes of evangelical Christians across America.

George W. Bush's evolution as a social conservative was gradual. The traditionalist sensibility laid down during his childhood in Midland did not translate into a coherent body of beliefs and values until his middle-adult years. During adolescence and young adulthood, when many people explore and crystallize their ideological beliefs, George W. Bush did neither. It is true that in high school, he read, or at least carried around, Barry Goldwater's *Conscience of a Conservative*, at the suggestion of his father. George W. seemed mildly interested in the book's ideas, but he rarely talked about them.[31] He felt uncomfortable with campus protestors and others opposed to the Vietnam War, but he never really expressed clear positions on the burning issues of the day—the war, civil rights, the rising women's movement. At Yale and during his 20s and early 30s, he continued to show little by way of an ideological inclination.

After he married Laura and after the birth of their twin daughters, however, George W. began to settle down and focus his life on socially conservative principles. In his late 30s and early 40s, he attended Bible readings and discussion groups. His religious faith, which had heretofore been a peripheral feature of his psychological makeup, began to intensify and to move in an evangelically Christian direction. He began to stake out positions on social issues that were to the political right of his more moderate father but simpatico with the rising evangelical movement in America—unequivocal opposition to abortion, affirmation of traditional family values, advocacy for faith-based philanthropy, and so on. By the time he ran for president in 2000, George W. Bush was carrying his Bible with him everywhere. According to an evangelical friend who often joined him on the campaign trail, "The nights I was with him [in the same hotel], when I looked by the bedside, it [the Bible] was there. And he just disciplined himself into the Word [reading the Bible] every day."[32]

Behavioral scientists (many of whom do *not* read their Bibles every day) tend to be socially liberal, for the most part. Yet, they have traditionally held an almost morbid fascination with social conservatives. Psychologically speaking, what makes social conservatives tick? One strong line of behavioral-science research suggests that the psychological roots of social conservatism lie in the development of an *authoritarian personality*. The theory suggests that harsh and repressive parenting styles, especially under conditions of economic stress, tend to produce in children a set of traits and values that emphasize: *(1)* strong adherence to society's laws and conventions, *(2)* submission to established authority, and *(3)* aggression (e.g., hatred, scorn) toward those who violate the established norms of society.[33] Authoritarians are what one research team calls "in-group specialists"—they show strong allegiance to the norms of their own groups (e.g., family, church, nation) and strong distrust of outsiders, or "out-groups."[34] Among Americans, high scores on measures of authoritarianism are associated with a wide range of socially-conservative political positions, as well as involvement in fundamentalist religious traditions, prejudice against homosexuals and other members of out-groups, suspiciousness regarding the humanities and the arts, cognitive rigidity, militaristic sentiments, and self-righteousness.[35]

In his book *Conservatives without Conscience*, John Dean, the former White House legal counsel for Richard M. Nixon during the Watergate era, argues that authoritarians dominated the presidential administration of George W. Bush and the conservative politics of the era.[36] Prominent on his list of authoritarian personalities were some of Bush's closest political advisors (e.g., Dick Cheney, Karl Rove), Republican leaders in Congress (e.g., Congressman Tom Delay, Senator Bill Frist), and socially conservative religious figures such as Pat Robertson. Dean may be right about Cheney, Rove, and the others. But George W. Bush himself should probably *not* make Dean's list. Despite his strong social conservatism, Bush showed few of the classic features of the authoritarian personality. For example, there is little evidence to suggest that he was overly *submissive* to authority or that he was especially *prejudiced* against out-groups, such as ethnic and racial minorities, or gays and lesbians. Although he stood for law and order, he seemed to harbor little *hostility* or cynicism regarding those American citizens who violated the norms of society. In the general population, scores on measures of right-wing authoritarianism tend to correlate positively with self-ratings of social conservatism.[37] But George W. Bush may have been an exception to this rule, as well. At most, his score on authoritarianism would be in the moderate range.

Whereas George W. did not fit closely the profile of the authoritarian personality, he did, as do all social conservatives, deeply value *authority*. In his idealized image of growing up in Midland, Texas, Bush depicted an orderly society in which legitimate authorities, like parents and town elders, enforced rules and provided guidance for the town's citizens. According to the psychologist Jonathan Haidt, the broader social philosophy suggested in "Midland Values" invokes a moral universe that stirs socially conservative souls the world over. In a brilliant synthesis of religious, philosophical, and evolutionary ideas, Haidt argues that we are hard-wired to feel strong gut reactions in response to five moral domains: harm/care, reciprocity/fairness, authority/respect, in-group loyalty, and purity/sanctity.[38] People *in all societies* feel that: *(1)* it is wrong to hurt innocent people and good to relieve suffering (harm/care); *(2)* it is wrong to cheat and good to treat people fairly in social interactions (reciprocity/fairness); *(3)* people should respect legitimate social hierarchy in order to assure social order and peace (authority/respect); *(4)* people should be true to their group, and betrayal is bad (in-group loyalty); and *(5)* the body and certain aspects of life are sacred and pure, and violations of chastity and piety are bad (purity/sanctity). These five moral intuitions—deeply set in human nature—form the basis of the many different religious and ethical codes that human beings have developed since our hunting and foraging days. To one extent or another, all human beings feel these five moral intuitions. But conservatives tend to feel *three of them* especially strongly—authority/respect, in-group loyalty, and purity/sanctity. By contrast, liberals tend to have stronger feelings about harm/care and reciprocity/fairness.

Research support for Haidt's thesis regarding differences between conservatives and liberals with respect to basic moral intuitions comes from two different kinds of studies. In the first line of research, Haidt and his colleagues ask self-identified conservatives and liberals how they might react in response to moral violations of various kinds and what it would take to get them to violate each of the five moral intuitions. For example: "How outraged would you feel if you saw a mother slap her child ?" (harm/care); "How much money would I need to pay you to get you to curse your parents to their face?" (authority/respect); "If you were really hungry, would you ever cook and eat your dog?" (purity/sanctity). Findings from studies like these show that the more conservative a person is, the stronger priority he or she puts on the values of authority/respect, in-group loyalty, and purity/sanctity. You might have to pay a conservative $100,000 to get him to burn an American flag or to betray his family (in-group loyalty), or to urinate on the floor of the Vatican (purity/sanctity). You could get a liberal to do these things for, say, $20,000, though he might still feel bad about doing them. By contrast, the more liberal a person is, the greater the emphasis on harm/care and reciprocity/fairness. In the hypo- thetical scenarios that researchers pose, liberals report much stronger reluctance than conservatives to engage in any kind of behavior that involves physically hurting others or violating basic norms of fairness and equality.[39]

A second line of research examines how values play out in people's life stories. In a study that my students and I published in 2008, we asked highly religious members of various Christian congregations to describe the development of their own religious and ethical beliefs.[40] The participants also completed short ques- tionnaires regarding political ideology and voting patterns. Supporting Haidt's argument, those Christian adults who reported that they were politically conservative tended to underscore the power of authority, in-group loyalty, and sanctity in their religious and ethical belief systems. More so than liberals, they tended to describe God as a powerful authority figure ("Lord," "Sovereign," "Master") and to emphasize the importance of hierarchy in the church; they tended to describe their faith community as an exclusive "family" or in-group to which they felt strong loyalty, contrasting it to out-groups (e.g., other religions, the secular world); and they repeatedly emphasized the contrast between humankind's sinful nature and the purity or perfection of God. By contrast, those equally devout adults who reported that they were politically liberal tended to emphasize Christian teachings regarding healing the sick and feeding the poor (harm/care) and principles of fairness and equality as captured, for example, in the Golden Rule.

Throughout his adult life, George W. Bush placed prime importance on the values of authority, group loyalty, and purity/sanctity. A good society requires a strict chain of command, Bush believed. Good children answer to their good parents, who as good citizens answer to the legitimate authorities of their communities, such as elected officials and religious leaders. People should be fiercely loyal to their communities. Going back to Prescott's days as a Wall Street banker, the extended Bush clan was famous for its loyalty to the family, and its distrust of outsiders who sought to reveal family secrets. As president, George W. Bush insisted on the same kind of loyalty among staff members and his inner circle of advisors. Indeed, critics of the Bush administration often singled out the reluctance that advisors felt to disagree with the president, lest they be accused of disloyalty. In his book *The Price of Loyalty*, journalist Ron Suskind describes how Bush's first treasury secretary, Paul O'Neill, repeatedly refused to toe the line, believing instead that a president is best served when he hears a wide range of different opinions. O'Neill was soon labeled as disloyal, and was forced out.[41]

Like many presidents, furthermore, George W. Bush viewed his exalted office and his responsibility to serve the American people as a sacred trust. But his emphasis on purity/sanctity extended in interesting ways to other features of his presidency, too. As he saw it, the dignity of the presidency required that White House staff always dress in formal business attire and observe formal norms of decorum. Certain areas of the White House were deemed sacred spaces, as if they were altars in churches or holy religious sites. The Oval Office was the most sacred space. Therefore, Bush found especially disgusting the fact that President Clinton engaged in sexual shenanigans in the Oval Office. Even late at night and all by himself, George W. Bush would not permit himself to enter that sanctum sanctorum unless he was dressed appropriately. One night President Bush was watching a movie with friends in the White House theater. Wearing a sweater, the president left the room to fetch something from the Oval Office, which was just down the hall. After half an hour, the friends asked what was taking him so long. An aide to the president explained that he went upstairs to change into a suit and tie: "He doesn't believe anyone, including the President, should set foot in the Oval Office without correct attire. To him, it's hallowed ground."[42]

George W. Bush ran for president in 2000 as a *compassionate conservative*. Although derided by many as a repackaging of old ideas, the term "compassionate conservative" conveyed a developmental achievement for Bush. As a young man he displayed a deeply conservative and traditionalist sentiment about life, but it was not until midlife that he finally filled in the ideological details and spelled out exactly what his conservative values and beliefs were. The term came to represent an important piece of Bush's unique brand of conservatism. As described in the final chapter of *A Charge to Keep*, compassionate conservatism combined standard tenets of economic conservatism (lower taxes, support for free markets and free trade) with a set of principles (e.g., smaller government, tough penalties for crime, education reform, encouragement of faith-based volunteerism) aimed to encourage personal responsibility and affirm "the worth and dignity and power of each individual."[43] "I am a fiscal [economic] and a family [social] conservative," Bush wrote. "And I am a compassionate conservative, because I know my philosophy is optimistic and full of hope for every American."[44]

Compassionate conservatism gave an ideological frame for a redemptive dream in the life of George W. Bush. As a moral outlook on government and society, compassionate conservatism aimed to restore the lost Eden of his childhood—Midland, Texas in the 1950s, as romanticized and reconstructed in the adult mind of the little boy who grew up there and then. It is not that George W. Bush needed, as an adult, to reexperience his childhood paradise. Instead, he felt the need to share that paradise with others, to bring back its simplicity, beauty, and goodness for Americans living in the twenty-first century. In content and tone, compassionate conservatism expressed a paternalistic attitude about society and morality designed to bring authority, loyalty, and sacredness back to American communities. The paternalistic attitude was one of *tough love*, the kind of love that authorities (parents, churches, elected leaders) provided for children in the mystic chords of his Midland memories. It was also the kind of love that society writ large should feel for all its members who refuse to obey authority, fail to be loyal, or desecrate that which is sacred.

Bush began his final chapter of *A Charge to Keep* by describing a visit he made as governor to a juvenile detention center in Marlin, Texas. At the end of Bush's speech to the inmates, one young man (probably 15 years old, African-American) surprised the governor and his staff by raising his hand and asking a question: "What do you think of me?" Johnny Baulkmon asked. As Bush describes it in his campaign autobiography, he told the young man that he and all Texans cared about his well-being, and he encouraged him to work hard and get an education when he was released from jail. The journalist Robert Draper, however, provides a more vivid account of this incident. Draper notes how Governor Bush struggled at first for a response to the question posed by young Johnny Baulkmon. The governor looked as if he were going to cry. But he finally rallied and said this:

> You look like kids I see every day. And I'm impressed by the way you're handling yourselves here. I think you can succeed. The state of Texas loves you all. We haven't given up on you. But we love you enough to punish you when you break the law.[45]

The Johnny Baulkmon incident marked an important step forward in Bush's eventual run for the presidency. Karen Hughes and other advisors felt that the young man's question enabled Bush to find his authentic voice as a compassionate conservative. The incident also shows how George W. Bush managed to steal a page from the liberal playbook, to his consummate advantage in 2000. Compassionate conservatism could appeal to those political moderates, and even some liberals, for whom *harm/care* was their deepest moral intuition. The state of Texas loves Johnny Baulkmon, loves him enough to punish him when he is bad, like the good parents of Midland. And loves him enough to hope for his redemption. In the Midland Eden, people always look out for each other; they care about what happens to their neighbors; they punish rule-breakers, but they do so in love rather than vengefulness, like parents; tough love will eventually lessen suffering and pain, and it will provide hope. Tough love showed that conservatives could be compassionate—that along with their deep feelings regarding authority, in-group loyalty, and the sacredness of human life, conservatives could feel empathy for the suffering of others.

***

Compassionate conservatism got hijacked on 9/11. But the redemptive dream never died.

When the twin towers came crashing down, the national emergency that ensued overwhelmed President Bush's domestic plans for compassionate conservatism, as it overwhelmed everything else. In an instant, the nation's security became the paramount concern. In the manner of threatened in-groups throughout human evolution, the American people reembraced the time-tested traditions of their group, turned to their leaders for strength and assuredness, and readied themselves to fight back against the out-group responsible for the attack. Patriotism and church attendance surged, the government launched a slew of security initiatives, and Islamic terrorists were identified as the hated out-group. The moment was tailor-made for the classic conservative response— be vigilant, be well-armed, and prepare to defend yourself against the enemy. It was the kind of moment that seems perfectly designed for the elevation of a great conservative leader, ready-made for a Churchill or a Reagan who is perceived as standing tall against the enemy, the champion of all that the in-group holds to be dear and self-defining—its traditions, its heritage, its very way of life. Within 2 weeks of the attack, George W. Bush's approval ratings soared into the stratosphere.

After 9/11, defense conservatives replaced social and economic conservatives as the main players in the game. Vice President Cheney emerged as arguably the most powerful force in the Bush administration, and a leading spokesman for an aggressive military response. Secretary of Defense Rumsfeld saw the threat as an opportunity to strengthen and showcase the newly streamlined armed forces. Those conservative politicians and pundits who had always advocated for the strongest possible American military and the most vigorous defense of the homeland suddenly found that the broad majority of Americans were now firmly on their side. The conservative consensus—be vigilant, be well-armed, prepare to defend yourself against the hated out-group—was further reinforced when letters containing deadly anthrax spores began showing up in the mail. In the weeks after 9/11, letters filled with anthrax were mailed to several news media offices and two Democratic U.S. senators, killing five people and infecting 17 others. The administration immediately suspected that Osama bin Laden and Al Qaeda might be the source of the anthrax attacks, just as they were the enemy on 9/11. But suspicion quickly spread to Iraq. In an October 15, 2001 article, *The Wall Street Journal* asserted that the anthrax mailings could be readily connected to Osama bin Laden through "several circumstantial links" but that bin Laden "couldn't be doing all this in Afghan caves." Therefore, "the leading supplier suspect has to be Iraq."[46]

As fear spread, the targeted out-group expanded. The Bush administration cautioned Americans to beware of weapons of mass destruction. Biological weapons like anthrax spores, chemical weapons, and nuclear weapons—all of these might easily find their way onto American shores, killing people in their own homes, potentially destroying American cities. Protecting America against weapons of mass destruction, even by preemptively attacking a state harboring such weapons, became the new Bush Doctrine. To ignore the grave and gathering threat posed by these states—especially Iraq—was to be naïve and unpatriotic, tantamount to betrayal of the in-group. The political analyst Craig Unger describes the country's mood: "Somehow, in the wake of 9/11, there had been a radical shift to the right in the

American consciousness. Fear was everywhere and unabashed patriotism appeared to provide the answer."[47]

Fear of an out-group is almost always a friend to conservative leaders. In 2002 and early 2003, President Bush and his conservative allies convinced many Americans to target Iraq as a paramount out-group to fear. By the time Secretary of State Colin Powell appeared before the United Nations to make his monumental case against Iraq, most Americans had come to believe that Saddam Hussein had developed and was stockpiling weapons of mass destruction. Deposing Saddam and ridding the world of these weapons became the prime justification for the American invasion of Iraq. In the minds of millions of Americans, the war was justified as an effort in self-defense. Once we overthrew the enemy and defused the weapons, our fears would abate.

Fear of the out-group continued to be a strong political ally for President Bush in the early period of the Iraq War and throughout his first term in office. After the president marked "Mission Accomplished" on May 1, 2003, the Iraq War devolved into a protracted and brutal struggle between different political and religious factions, resulting in thousands of lost American lives and the deaths of countless Iraqis. Even as support for the war began to wane in the United States, the fear that helped to motivate the war in the first place continued to buoy President Bush. Psychological research has long shown that fear of out-groups motivates support for the conservative forces of the in-group. In 2004, a team of social scientists conducted a series of studies wherein college students rated their support for President George W. Bush and his policies after being exposed to different kinds of stimuli.[48] When the students were presented with stimuli that reminded them either of the 9/11 attacks or (relatedly) their own death, they tended to show high support for the president. When they were presented with more neutral stimuli, however, they tended to show relatively low support for President Bush and stronger support for his Democratic challenger, Senator John Kerry. Bush defeated Kerry in a close election in 2004. Had terrorists attacked the United States again, in the months just before the election, Bush probably would have won by a landslide.

For many defense conservatives, like Dick Cheney, hitting back against the feared out-group was more than enough justification to invade Iraq. But it was never enough for George W. Bush. On the eve of 9/11 and long before he invaded Iraq, George W. Bush had evolved into that special (and relatively rare) kind of conservative who needs a lofty principle, even a righteous cause, to justify his biggest decisions and his most daring acts. With its redemptive message of tough love and Midland values, compassionate conservatism provided George W. Bush with the right kind of political ideology to inspire good works in the domestic sphere. He needed an inspiring ideological counterpart for foreign affairs, a set of beliefs and values that affirmed America as a force for good *in the world*. The answer came to him in the late 1990s, when he began to consider a run for the presidency. His father introduced George W. to Condoleeza Rice, who was then a political science professor at Stanford and the school's provost. Over the next 1 ½ years, Rice teamed up with another academic, Paul Wolfowitz, to run regular tutorials with Governor Bush in order to school him on international relations and foreign policy. A professor of international relations at Johns Hopkins, Wolfowitz had served in a number of Republican administrations, and he would later serve as deputy secretary of defense under George W. Bush. Wolfowitz was a leading *neoconservative*.

Although the term is controversial, neoconservatism in America is typically described as a political philosophy that supports the use of economic and military power to bring democracy and human rights to other countries. Like conservatives of most stripes, neo-conservatives place prime importance on national security. But they believe that America's security is best assured through an activist foreign policy that takes on anti-American forces in other countries. Neoconservatives seek to spread those most valued American ideals—democracy and freedom—to the rest of the world. Their vision is both idealistic and pragmatic. They see democracy and freedom as ultimate human ideals, and they argue that because freely elected democracies rarely make war on each other, exporting democracy to the rest of the world ultimately enhances American security. Although many neoconservatives are Republicans, they trace part of their lineage back to the hawkish views espoused in the 1970s by Henry ("Scoop") Jackson, the Democratic senator from the state of Washington who advocated an aggressive militarism in foreign affairs. Many senior neoconser-vatives, like Irving Kristol and Richard Perle, were once liberals who became disenchanted with the 1960s counterculture and with what they perceived as America's going soft on communism. When the Soviet Union dissolved, some neoconservatives turned their attention to the Middle East. They typically express strong support for Israel and agitate for the spread of democracy in the Arab world.

Irving Kristol once said that a neoconservative is a liberal who has been mugged by reality. Like classic liberals, neoconservatives hold to a transformative vision for society. They believe that gov-ernment should intervene, especially on the world stage, to improve the prospects of people everywhere. Like classic conser-vatives, however, they see the world through a glass darkly. After all, they have been mugged by reality. From the neoconservative point of view, there is a tremendous amount of danger out there, evil forces that threaten America and her best ideals. It is not enough to be vigilant and well-armed, ready to defend the homeland when it is under attack. One must assume a more proactive stance, energized by the ideals of freedom and democracy to fight the *good* fight and to *take that fight* to the enemy. Going back to the presidency of Richard Nixon, neoconservatives have lambasted "realist" foreign policy efforts, such as those implemented by Henry Kissinger, wherein American leaders tolerated authoritarian dictators and sought peace through negotiation, diplomacy, and arms control. As vice president and president, George H. W. Bush was mainly a realist when it came to foreign policy, as were some of his closest aides, such as Brent Scowcroft and James Baker. Under the tutelage of Wolfowitz and other neoconservatives, however, his firstborn son adopted a more idealistic and interventionist philosophy.

When George W. Bush completed his tutorials with Wolfowitz and Rice, he had finally filled in the details for his full political ideology. By sentiment and sensibility, he was a conservative—that much was never in doubt. His penchant for traditionalism went all the way back to his childhood days in Midland. By the time he entered the oil business, he had internalized the standard tenets of economic conservatism. He never lost his belief in small government, low taxes, and free enterprise. Through his 30s and 40s, he developed his characteristic positions as a compassionate conservative. Building on conservative moral intuitions regarding authority, loyalty, and sacredness, Bush added a touch of tough love to the mix, just enough to activate in the minds of voters that generally more liberal moral intuition regarding harm/care. Laced with the language and sentiments of Christian evangelicals, compassionate conservatism inspired a redemptive attitude about social life. When people do bad things, they should be punished;

but, like the idealized parents and town leaders of Midland, authorities hope to redeem those under their control, to make people *good*, to *conserve* that which is good in society, and to *restore* goodness to society when society loses its way. What compassionate conservatism might achieve for the in-group (American society), neoconservatism could achieve for the ultimate out-group—the rest of the world. Let us go boldly, then, to export Midland Values to the entire Middle East.

Sigmund Freud wrote that human behavior is *overdetermined*. He meant that every piece of human conduct, every decision we make, is determined by a multitude of forces, both inside and outside the person. When it comes to George W. Bush's decision to invade Iraq, Freud could not have been more right. From inside the *actor*, the dispositional traits of very high extraversion and very low openness to experience helped to produce a president who was psychologically primed to make a dramatic and decisive performance on the world stage. He would act boldly, and he would never doubt that his action was right. As a motivated *agent*, he set forth the life goal of defeating his beloved father's most fearsome enemy. With the attacks of 9/11, he found an opportunity to accomplish the motivational mission of a lifetime, to put Saddam away for good. As fear and patriotism spread across America in the wake of the terrorist attacks, George W. Bush felt a level of energy and a depth of conviction that may have exceeded anything he ever felt before. Saddam was evil—he had no doubt. Saddam possessed weapons of mass destruction—little doubt there, as well. To protect the in-group, he must attack the group's greatest external threat, that same threat, as beautiful coincidence would have it, who "tried to kill my dad at one time." The invasion is justified as self-defense, to defeat a treacherous enemy and destroy his weapons of mass destruction. But George W. Bush can provide further justification too, a justification, and a motivation, that flows naturally from the particular brand of conservatism he developed and articulated in his midlife years. Conservatives every one of them, Richard Nixon, Henry Kissinger, George H. W. Bush, and even Dick Cheney would never have said this:

> Let me make sure you understand what I just said about the role of the United States. I believe the United States is the beacon for freedom in the world. And I believe we have a responsibility to promote freedom that is as solemn as the responsibility is to protecting the American people, because the two go hand-in-hand. . . . I say that freedom is not America's gift to the world. Freedom is God's gift to everybody in the world. I believe that. . . . And I believe that we have a duty to free people.[49]

Journalist Bob Woodward recorded George W. Bush's words in December 2003, almost nine months after Bush launched the invasion of Iraq. Even when the world learned that what Saddam Hussein was concealing in those Iraqi bunkers and other secret sites was exactly *zero* weapons of mass destruction, George W. Bush never wavered in his belief (an authentic and principled belief) that invading Iraq was the right thing to do. Part of his motivation and his justification for the invasion (what made him do it, and what gave him the moral justification for doing it) derived directly from his lessons in neoconservatism. Like compassionate conservatism, neoconservatism inspired idealism and hope in the mind of George W. Bush. It provided further validation and moral meaning for the overdetermined decision to declare war on Iraq. Like compassionate conservatism, furthermore, his neoconservative values resonated with a broad narrative of redemption that George W. Bush projected onto the in-group, the out-group, and his own life. The redemptive narrative he *authored* across the course of his life is a deeply conservative story about the restoration of all that was once good and natural about the world—Midland lost, and then found.

It is to that redemptive story that we now turn.

FOUR

Variations on a Redemptive Theme

Nobody recorded when George W. Bush took his first drink. But he claims to have taken his last sometime in the summer of 1986, while celebrating his upcoming 40th birthday with friends and family members at the Broadmoor Hotel in Colorado Springs. His career in alcohol abuse, therefore, spanned at least two decades, from the fraternity parties at Yale to the morning after the celebration of his 40th, when he woke up with a terrible hangover, went for his customary 3 mile run, and informed Laura upon his return that he would never drink again. And, as far as the public record can be trusted, he never did. He quit cold turkey. Around the same time in his life, George W. Bush experienced a religious transformation that helped consolidate his commitment to sobriety. In essence, he found Jesus, and he gave up drinking. The two developmental moves—from sin to salvation, from drinking to recovery—were inextricably linked in his mind to a grand narrative of personal redemption. President George W. Bush once said: "There is only one reason why I am in the Oval Office and not in a bar. I found faith. I found God. I am here because of the power of prayer."[1] As George W. Bush saw it, the redemptive arc of his life moved from the dissolute years as a prodigal son to sobriety, faith, and public service. He believed that his own redemptive story culminated in his ascension to the presidency. What he may not have believed or recognized, however, was how the same redemptive story brought him, and the United States, to the Iraq War.

The serious drinking began in college. When George W. pledged the Delta Kappa Epsilon fraternity in 1965, the DEKEs were known to have the biggest bar and the best parties on the Yale campus.[2] The parties got even better with the arrival of George W. Bush, the exuberant extravert who was the life of nearly every party he ever attended and a regular supplier of alcohol for the fraternity. The DKE house was like the movie *Animal House*, recalled one fraternity brother, and George W. Bush played John Belushi.[3] Before football games, young George would mix up batches of screwdrivers in garbage cans. He was a star participant in fraternity beer-chugging contests. Heading home one evening after downing innumerable drinks, George W. suddenly collapsed on the pavement and began rolling down the street. A classmate recalled that he "literally rolled all the way back to the dorm."[4] Back on his feet, George W. might hop on a chair or table to lead his fraternity brothers and their dates in rounds of drunken revelry. Although no photograph has ever surfaced to confirm the story, he was once rumored to have stripped off his clothes and danced naked on top of the bar. Asked about the purported incident years later, George W. conceded that his memory was hazy, but he doubted that it ever occurred: "I'm too modest to have danced on a bar naked."[5] His modesty may have kept him from taking his clothes off, but nothing seemed to hold back the drinking. As one fraternity brother remembers his times with George W., "we drank heavily at DKE. It was absolutely off the wall—appalling. I cannot for the life of me figure out how we all made it through."[6]

Beginning in his DKE years and running through age 30 years, George W. Bush was arrested three times for alcohol-related activities. The first time was in December 1966 when he and a few fraternity buddies, after consuming more than a few drinks, stole a Christmas wreath from a hotel. George W. told the police officer that he and his merry band of brothers were "liberating" the wreath and taking it to the DKE house, because the DKE house did not have a Christmas wreath and it needed one. Evidently unable to appreciate the humor, the police officer arrested George W. on the spot, hauled him down to the police station, and charged him with disorderly conduct. A Bush family friend arranged to have the charges dropped. On November 18, 1967, George W. was arrested at the end of the Yale vs. Princeton football game, when he and inebriated fraternity brothers stormed the Princeton field and tried to tear down the vintage wooden goalposts. He was escorted to the police station and then told to get out of town. "So I was once in Princeton, New Jersey," George W. later quipped, "and haven't been back since."[7]

The third incident was more serious. On September 4, 1976, George W., his 17-year-old sister Doro, and a few of George's regular drinking buddies met up with Australian tennis star John Newcombe and Newcombe's wife at a bar in Maine. After 3 hours of drinking, George W. headed back to the Kennebunkport family compound, drunk behind the wheel. Officer Calvin Bridges was just finishing his shift when he spotted the car swerving back and forth on Ocean Avenue. He pulled George W. over, gave him a sobriety test (George W. failed), arrested him, and drove him to the Kennebunkport police station. His blood alcohol level registered 0.12, over Maine's 0.10 legal limit. George W. pleaded guilty to the DUI charge. He was fined $150, and his license was suspended. (The story of the 1976 DUI incident remained under wraps for 24 years, only to surface in the week before the 2000 presidential election.)[8]

The time between his Yale graduation in 1968 and the DUI arrest in 1976 corresponds roughly to what George W. Bush characterized as his "nomadic period." Lacking a clear direction in his life, he moved from one job to another, served in the Texas Air National Guard, and eventually attended Harvard Business School. He drank heavily throughout this period. At the Chateaux Dijon apartment complex in Houston's Galleria District, George W. hung around the pool on Mondays through Thursdays, awaiting his regular weekend duties as a Texas Guard pilot, chain-smoking Winstons and downing one Budweiser after another. Or else he tooled around Houston in his blue Triumph, looking for a good party. Wherever George W. was living, the good parties and the best bars were never hard to find. The music might be blasting from the jukebox, the drinking contests might begin once he arrived, and the opportunities for chasing pretty women were endless, as was the endless enjoyment of what George W. once characterized as "the 4 B's" in his life: beer, bourbon, and B & B.[9] He returned nightly to a disheveled bachelor apartment, stumbling over dirty laundry, unread magazines, empty bottles, and beer cans strewn about the path to his bed. On one particular night of heavy partying, he needed badly to relieve himself on the way home. A woman reported that she observed him urinating on a car in an Alabama parking lot.[10]

Excess alcohol tended to shift George W.'s extraversion into overdrive. As he later admitted, drinking "magnified aspects of my personality that probably don't need to be larger than they already are—made me more funny, more charming (I thought), more irrepressible."[11] And more boorish, as even his friends would say. "He was not the classic mean drunk," one acquaintance remembered. "But there was a point at which he crossed the line over into nastiness, and the comments that he thought were hilarious were just asinine, and sometimes malicious. You just sort of held your breath when he walked up to a stranger in a restaurant—you never knew what he was going to do or say."[12] At an elegant cocktail party in Kennebunkport, George W. (bourbon in hand) wobbled up to an older, grey-haired woman, a good friend of his parents, and blurted out: "So—what's sex like after fifty anyway?"[13] He was even less funny, indeed menacing, a decade later when he spotted *The Wall Street Journal* Washington Bureau Chief Al Hunt, his wife Judy Woodruff (a prominent television correspondent), and their 4-year-old son in a Dallas restaurant. Hunt had recently written an article critical of Vice President George H. W. Bush. Colliding with tables and bumping into diners, the vice president's firstborn made his drunken way toward the family, pointed a finger at Hunt, and then, as the little boy and shocked patrons looked on, began to scream: "You no good fucking son of a bitch! I won't forget what you said and you're going to pay a fucking price for it!"[14]

By the mid-1970s, some family members and friends began to fear that George W. Bush's drinking problem was spinning out of control. After he married Laura Welch (in 1977) and even after the birth of their twins (1981), George W. continued to drink heavily. Laura herself enjoyed a good drink on social occasions, but she became increasingly critical of her husband's alcohol abuse during the early years of their marriage. She was not amused, for example, when he showed up for the annual Midland Country

Club Wildcatter party dressed as a diaper-clad Mahatma Gandhi. "He kept doing this pretty terrible Indian accent," said one party-goer, "but I got the impression he really didn't know who Gandhi was, and why his being drunk and practically naked might be seen as offensive to some people."[15]

As he moved through his 30s, George W. worked hard in the oil industry, continued his jogging routine, attended church regularly, coached Little League, and developed strong and meaningful relationships in the Midland community. But he would still come home drunk many evenings, often yelling or picking fights with Laura, and often passing out on the couch. "He was wild when he drank too much," Laura conceded. In late 1985, Laura finally delivered an ultimatum: "It's either me or Jim Beam." But her threats to pack up the girls and leave did not, at first, have the desired effect. One night in June 1986, George W. came home drunk again and inadvertently woke up his daughters. Laura was livid. "This has got to stop!" she said. George looked his wife up and down, adopted a thoughtful expression and then a smirk—and then he ambled over to the kitchen counter to pour himself another bourbon.[16]

A few weeks later, however, he finally did put an end to it—turned stone sober, for good.

Resolving to give up alcohol on that morning at the Broadmoor Hotel in Colorado Springs, sometime near his 40th birthday, was the most important turning point in George W. Bush's life. Why, after two decades of abuse, did he make the change? Laura's threats must certainly have had some effect. He loved his wife and cherished his daughters; he did not want to lose his family. Another factor was his father's run for the upcoming presidential election. By 1986, it was clear that Vice President

George H. W. Bush would be pursuing the 1988 GOP. candidacy for president. All family members worried that George W.'s antics could jeopardize Poppy's once-in-a-lifetime chance. George W. himself has suggested that he quit alcohol because it "began to compete with my energy."[17] With his 40th birthday looming ahead of him, George W. may have been feeling the physical toll of impending midlife. He was a step slower, a little more tired—and alcohol made it all worse. One biographer argues that as George W. began to see just how debilitating alcohol was for both himself and his family, he simply and dramatically *willed* himself to quit.[18] He just said no—no more booze, no more parties. It was an exercise in consummate self-discipline.

But self-discipline typically requires some sort of social or ideological support. George W. Bush found this support in religion. Invoking a classic New Testament image, George W. claimed that the idea of giving up alcohol was a "mustard seed" that was planted the year before his vow of sobriety. As George W. told the story in *A Charge to Keep*, the Reverend Billy Graham visited the extended Bush family in Kennebunkport sometime during the summer of 1985. Gathered around the fireplace on a Saturday night, Bush family members asked Graham to answer various questions they had about Christian faith. The discussion continued the next day when George W. and Billy Graham took a private walk together on the Maine shoreline. Bush was impressed with Graham's "gentle and loving demeanor" and by the power of his example as a man of faith. He was also impressed with Graham's message—that "God sent his Son to die for a sinner like me." George W. wrote that he had "always been a religious person," but that his faith "took on new meaning" after his meeting with Graham. According to Bush's autobiography, his encounter with

Graham helped to change what had heretofore been a casual Christian faith into a growing, evangelical commitment:

> Over the course of that weekend, Reverend Graham planted a mustard seed in my soul, a seed that grew over the next year. He led me to the path, and I began walking. And it was the beginning of a change in my life.[19]

George W. Bush believed that his reembrace of Christianity at midlife led directly to his resolution to give up drinking. In the "official version" provided in his campaign autobiography, an encounter with one of America's most respected religious leaders planted the mustard seed that eventually grew into full faith and sobriety. After all, what better catalyst for the conversion of a would-be American president could a story have than the Reverend Billy Graham? Graham was the most well-known and widely admired American religious figure of the late twentieth century, and a spiritual confidante for Presidents Johnson, Nixon, and Reagan. The Billy Graham story, however, does not provide the full account of George W. Bush's redemptive move from sinner to saved. When asked about the Kennebunkport weekend years later, Billy Graham did not recall having had an important role to play in Bush's religious development: "I was with him and I used to teach the Bible at Kennebunkport to the Bush family when he [George W.] was a younger man, but I never feel that I in any way turned his life around."[20]

Graham may not have felt he made much of a difference in Bush's life because the turnaround had already occurred by the time he met with the Bush family in 1985. According to respected sources, the mustard seed may have been planted a year before, when George W. met with a very different man of faith. That man was a self-proclaimed evangelical preacher named Arthur Blessitt. No heartwarming, all-American picture here of the wholesome family gathered together in the living room. A "Jesus Freak" from the 1960s who boasted of carrying a 12-foot, 45-pound wooden cross more than 37,000 miles (what *The Guinness Book of World Records* proclaimed to be the longest walk in human history), Blessitt took his traveling salvation show to Midland, Texas in April 1984. His visit corresponded with one of the worst economic periods for the Midland oil industry. Oil prices had plummeted from $40 per barrel to $8; unemployment lines, repo signs, and bankruptcies signaled desperate times. George W. Bush himself had known little but failure in the oil business.

For a week, Blessitt preached to thousands who filled the Chaparral Sports Center in Midland. Local radio stations broadcast his sermons. In classic evangelical fashion, Blessitt saved hundreds of souls in Midland, encouraging men, women, and children to give their lives over to Jesus. After preaching one night, he prayed together with several Midland oilmen who had become born-again Christians, including Jim Sale, a friend of George W. Bush. Because Sale had no olive oil in his kitchen, Blessitt anointed the men's heads with Mazola. The unorthodox religious ritual was vintage Blessitt. Back in the 1970s, he presided over "toilet baptisms" of drug addicts, who would flush their controlled substances down a toilet and announce that they were now "high on Jesus."[21]

Intrigued with Blessitt and his message, George W. asked to meet with him, so a rendezvous was arranged.[22] On April 3, 1984, Arthur Blessitt, Jim Sale, and George W. Bush met in a coffee shop at the Midland Holiday Inn. Blessitt recorded what happened in his diary (Sale later confirmed that Blessitt's record was accurate):

Bush started things off. "Arthur, I want to talk to you about how to know Jesus Christ and how to follow Him."

Blessitt asked, "What is your relationship with Jesus?"

"I'm not sure," Bush replied.

"If you died this moment, do you have the assurance you would go to heaven?"

Bush said, "No."

After some further explanation, Blessitt said, "The call of Jesus is for us to repent and believe. The choice is like this. Would you rather live with Jesus in your life, or live without Him?"

"With Him," Bush replied.

"Jesus changes us from the inside out," Blessitt continued. "The world tries to change us from the outside in. Jesus is not condemning you. He wants to save you and cleanse your heart and change your desires. He wants to write your name in the Book of Life and welcome you into His family now and forever."

Jim Sale then told his own story of salvation. Further discussion ensued. Then, Blessitt said, "I want to pray with you now."

"I'd like that," Bush replied.

Blessitt then prayed aloud, asking Bush to repeat each phrase after him:

Dear God, I believe in You, and I need You in my life. Have mercy on me a sinner. Lord Jesus, as best as I know how, I want to follow You. Cleanse me from my sins, and come into my life as my Savior and Lord. I believe You lived without sin, died on the cross for my sins, and rose again on the third day, and have now ascended unto the Father. I love You, Lord; take control of my life. I believe in Your way. I forgive everyone, and I ask You to fill me with Your Holy Spirit and give me love for all people. Lead me to care for the needs of others. Make my home in heaven, and write my name in Your book in heaven. I accept the Lord Jesus Christ as my Savior and desire to be a true believer in and follower of Jesus. Thank You, God, for hearing my prayer. In Jesus' name I pray.[23]

When the prayer was finished, Bush smiled broadly, and Blessitt began to rejoice in the power of the Lord. "There is joy in the presence of the angels of God over one sinner who repents," Blessitt proclaimed, quoting Luke 15:10. He gave Bush a pamphlet entitled "A New Life."[24] Later that evening, Blessitt wrote this in his diary: "A good and powerful day. Led Vice President Bush's son to Jesus today. George Bush, Jr.! This is great! Glory to God."[25]

***

As we move from our teenage years into our 20s, we begin to need and to seek a *story* for our lives. The prime psychological challenge of young adulthood is to develop an identity—a deep and coherent sense of who we are and what our lives mean as adults in society. The challenge of identity is particularly daunting in modern societies like ours, advanced post-industrial societies wherein young men and women typically grow up to live lives that may not resemble closely the lives lived by their parents. Who am I? What do I believe to be true and good? What should I be doing with my life? What does my life fundamentally mean? These are the identity questions that people living in modern societies must come to terms with in their early-adult years, when they need to start thinking seriously about finding a job, finding a mate, beginning a family, making a home, getting a life.

Modern societies do not provide ready-made answers for these questions. Instead, young people confront an ill-defined menu of identity options. They are encouraged to choose what works well for them—to pursue a career that will bring them success, given their own skills and opportunities; to find a partner and develop a personal life that will sustain love and commitment;

to build an adult life that is meaningful and good. The various choices people make in this regard, and the ways they think about those choices in the context of their entire lives, come together into a broad story of the self—an internalized and evolving narrative about who they are, who they were, who they will be, and what it all means. Each of us begins to work on a narrative for our lives by the time we reach our 20s, and we continue to work on that story for much of the rest of our lives. Let us call that story a person's *narrative identity*. For each of us, narrative identity is the story we work on, and live by.[26]

Throughout his 20s and 30s, George W. Bush struggled to find a story for his life. Amidst the drinking and the carousing of his nomadic period, young George was looking for a narrative that might help him to settle down into the adult world and make sense of his chaotic life. The original model for the story was his venerable father. Young George admired his father greatly and tried to be like him in many ways. As we have already seen, he followed his father's path to Andover, Yale, Skull and Bones, and the oil industry. Like his father, he flew military jets. At one time, he even planned to marry a young woman from Smith College, as his father did. But as he moved into young adulthood, George W. Bush must have realized that his father's story could never be his own. The discrepancies between their early life paths (and their respective temperaments) were simply too great. Whereas the father was a star student at Andover and Yale, young George pulled mediocre grades. Whereas Poppy played first base on the college varsity team, his firstborn son and namesake distinguished himself, instead, in the fraternity beer chugging competitions. George Senior was a bona fide war hero; George Junior sat out the Vietnam War. The father made millions in the oil industry; the son's oil career turned out to be a bust.

Having a distinguished father can be both a blessing and a curse when it comes to developing a narrative identity. The advantages, as we see in the case of George W. Bush, can be considerable. His father provided him with an explicit model for how to be an adult—a life of business success followed by public service, embodying the motivational agenda for Bush men laid out by Prescott Bush, Poppy's own father. His father and the broad swath of Bush family friends set young George up with numerous opportunities for achievement. It is probably safe to say that young George would not have gotten into Yale or the Texas Air National Guard if he had not been the son of his particularly distinguished father. His father's friends helped him get started in the oil industry.

In a less tangible sense, furthermore, the Bush family provided all of the sons with a rich storehouse of expectations and stories about how a young man should make his way in the world. George W. Bush enjoyed not only the best schools, the most extensive social networks, and the greatest material comforts that a young American man might enjoy in the middle decades of the twentieth century, but he also enjoyed the best stories from which to draw inspiration. These include heroic tales of his grandfather's rise on Wall Street, his grandmother's example as an extraordinary athlete and a woman of faith, and the many achievements of great uncles and aunts and sundry other luminaries on both sides of the family. A big identity problem for many young men and women of lesser means in American society is that they often have little direct exposure in their families to models and stories about how to live as a mature adult who contributes something important to society. George W. Bush did not have that problem.

The same advantages of wealth and prominence, however, can double as disadvantages for narrative identity. In American society, young men and women are expected to establish their independence from their families and to distinguish themselves over and against their origins. We like our men, and increasingly our women, to be *self-made*. In the case of George W. Bush, this cultural expectation led to double trouble. First, he had to realize in his 20s and 30s that he simply did not measure up to the standards set by his father. It was as if reality had a clear message for young George W. Bush during this time. The message was a twist on what the Democratic vice presidential candidate Lloyd Bentsen famously said to his Republican counterpart Dan Quayle in the 1988 debates, when Quayle, responding to charges that he was too inexperienced for the office, identified himself with a young and glamorous former president of the United States, John F. Kennedy.[27] Bentsen's retort suggested that Dan Quayle was no JFK. In a similar vein, social reality was sending a parallel message to the young George W. Paraphrasing Bentsen, the message went something like this: " I knew *George H. W. Bush*. George H. W. Bush was a friend of mine. Young man, you are no George H. W. Bush!"

Second, young George was surely also aware of the general expectation in American society that young men need to distinguish themselves from their fathers and make it on their own. Our families may provide us with the resources we need, but we are supposed to create our own singular identities, our own unique and self-defining stories. Young George: Give it up! You will never be a George H. W. Bush. And you shouldn't be trying to be him anyway! Hey dude: *You need your own story*.

But what kind of story might that be? Narrative identity is a story in two parts. The first part is the past. In developing a self-defining narrative for life, a young man or woman looks back on the past in search of an explanation for what has come to be. How did I get to where I am right now? The psychologists Tilman

Habermas and Susan Bluck argue that it is not until late adolescence and young adulthood that we are able to understand our past as a coherent story that explains who we are today.[28] We do this by finding what we believe to be *causal sequences* in our past. In a causal sequence, the narrator tells how an event, or a series of events, caused something to happen in the story. For example, an aspiring doctor may claim that her interest in medicine has its origins in her caring for her sick brother when she was in junior high school. Or a 40-year-old man may explain his recent decision to run for public office as the realization of a lifelong dream. He traces it back to a song his second-grade class used to sing: "Young Abe Lincoln was a poor man's son; never knew when his work was done . . ." He loved that song. And then in seventh grade, he watched a movie about U.S. President Woodrow Wilson, and he found that inspiring. In college, he took lots of courses in history and government, which furthered his interest in politics. And over the past 20 years as he advanced in his job and raised a family, he kept following political developments in his community, and now he thinks this is the right time to take the plunge and make a run for public office. And if this works out, then . . .

In the two contrived examples I have provided, the narrators identify a key *scene* in the story—the young girl's caring for her brother, the young boy's learning a song about Abraham Lincoln—that precipitates a cascade of events, resulting eventually in a particular life outcome. Both examples illustrate a fundamental feature of narrative identity: It is *only a story*—a person's own subjective, biased, explanatory account about how things came to be. As a causal explanation for how the past has given birth to the present, there is no way to confirm or disprove the story. How can we ever really know if learning a song in second grade really stimulated a lifelong interest in politics? Had our aspiring politician never heard that song, he might have still decided to run for office at age 40 years. When it comes to explaining how we came to be, the best we can typically ever do is to make up a story about it. But we all feel the need to do this, to make sense of who we are through stories. Narrative identity, then, involves a subjective, selective, and imaginative re-interpretation of the past. People are not like digital video recorders who faithfully remember and play back the past as it really was. Instead, people forget most of the past. (The brain is not big enough to remember it all, and there is no good reason to remember most of it anyway.) In the long run, we remember but a small subset of what happens in our lives. Picking through the bits and fragments of autobiographical memory, we select for special treatment certain key scenes and characters that stand out for being personally significant in some way. We unconsciously decide that certain pieces of our past are really important for explaining how we came to be. And we feature those pieces as the high points, low points, and turning points in our narrative identity.

If the first part of narrative identity is the reconstructed past, the second part is the *imagined future*. We construct stories for our lives that explain how the past, as we have created it in memory, sets the stage for *who we will be* in the future. Both the young doctor and the aspiring politician hold aspirations for what is to come next in their lives. These aspirations are as much a part of their respective narrative identities as are their stories about how the past has produced them. Importantly, should the aspirations for the future change, the narrator most surely will change the story of the past. If he loses the election, for example, our middle-aged narrator may decide that he is not cut out for politics after all. He may decide instead that he wants to go back to school and get an advanced degree in education, because, after all, he has long admired teachers, and this may be traced back to a class he took in fourth grade when . . . (and a new story begins to take form). The human mind is endlessly creative when it comes to narrative identity. Its storied creations function as personal myths that give our lives unity, purpose, and meaning.

In his 20s and 30s, George W. Bush faced a difficult task when it came to narrative identity. His past was undistinguished; his future, uncertain. Looking back on his autobiographical memories, what might he summon up to launch a story for the future? What had he done with all the resources he was given? Not much, if truth be told: President of his seventh-grade class. Organized a stickball league at Andover. Always popular but never excelled in anything of note. Flew some planes for the Texas Air National Guard. Drilled some oil wells, but came up dry. Lots of great parties. Lots of drinking. Drinking and partying. Partying and drinking. How do you make a good story out of this? What kind of good future can you create out of such a mediocre and chaotic past?

Here is the answer: *You make it all into a story of redemption.*

Stripped to its essence, a redemptive story is a tale wherein bad is transformed into good. The story begins with a socially, emotionally, or morally negative situation, which then gives way to a socially, emotionally, or morally positive situation. The hero of the story endures suffering of some kind at the beginning, but the suffering gives way to happiness in the end. In a redemptive story, the good ending depends on there being a bad beginning. No pain, no gain. No sin, no salvation. In the logic of a redemptive sequence, the negative sets up the conditions for the positive's eventual emergence. The protagonist of a redemptive story cannot know the joy, security, enlightenment, or nirvana that comes with the transformation if he or she has not first experienced the depths of despair, anxiety, ignorance, or some other extraordinarily negative state of mind or existence, from which he or she is ultimately delivered. Redemption is that deliverance from suffering to an enhanced or ennobled state.[29]

How do you make a life into a narrative of redemption? There are two steps. First, you need to do things that you can later look back upon as having turned your life around. Second (and later), you need to look back on those things as the scenes through which redemption was achieved. The first step is behavioral; the second step is interpretive.

Around the age of 30 years, George W. Bush took his first behavioral steps down the road to redemption. As happens in the redemptive stories of many men who squander their youth, an important early step was finding a woman who might save him. Enter Laura Welch. In the summer of 1977, George met Laura at a backyard barbecue in Midland. The hosts, Joe and Jan O'Neill, had been trying for some time to fix George and Laura up with each other, although they worried that their two friends might not mix well. The chemistry and the timing, however, were just right. Levelheaded and serious, Laura was attracted to the young man's energy, extraversion, and bombast. That night she told her mother, "The thing I like about him is that he made me laugh."[30] As for George W., he was smitten by the librarian's beauty and intelligence, and by the steady calm she projected. About meeting Laura that night, George W. later said: "By then, I'd lived a lot of life, and I was beginning to settle down. When we met, I was enthralled. I found her to be a very thoughtful, smart, interested person—one of the great listeners. And since I'm one of the big talkers, it was a great fit."[31] George W. proposed marriage weeks later, and the two were married on November 5, 1977. In *A Charge to Keep*, George W. Bush characterized his marrying Laura as "the best decision I ever made."[32]

Marrying Laura was a good decision for at least two reasons. First, Laura's steady and tranquil disposition helped to exert a soothing effect on George W.'s life. As he spent more and more time with her, George W. felt calmer and more secure in his daily interactions with others. Laura modeled a steely discipline that George, at age 31 years, seemed to lack. She quietly focused her energy on accomplishing the goals that were important to her; she was not easily distracted. Furthermore, Laura was able to provide George W. with both unconditional love and a check on his unruly impulses. She affirmed his best nature while quietly critiquing his foibles and occasional outbursts. Bush family members noticed that she was the first person to come along in years who seemed to be able to influence George W.'s behavior for the better.[33]

The second reason that marrying Laura was a very good decision pertains less to her admirable traits and more to the opportunity the marriage provided George to move into a new stage in the life course. The famous psychological theorist Erik Erikson wrote that the development of a long-term intimate relationship, as we see in a good marriage, serves the prime developmental function of moving an adult into the critical stage of *generativity*.[34] Generativity is the concern for and commitment to providing for the next generation, through parenting, teaching, mentoring, and/or engaging in a range of important behaviors that aim to leave a positive legacy for the future. According to Erikson, generativity is and should be the central psychological and social task for adults as they move into and through their 30s, 40s, and 50s. This is the time in the human life course when adults must step up to take responsibility for the next generation and to make a positive contribution to society and social institutions. Adults can be generative in many different ways. For many, generativity is largely about parenting—trying to provide care, love, and discipline for one's own children and working with other parents, with schools, and the community to create positive environments for children. But generativity often expands well beyond the realm of parenting and children, as generative adults assume leadership roles in their neighborhoods, churches, workplaces, and other settings wherein they feel that they can make a positive difference.[35]

George W. was not without generative inclinations before he met Laura. But Laura helped to put these inclinations into practice. George W. may have sensed that she would have this effect soon after he met her. In describing why he found Laura so appealing, he later wrote that she believed deeply "that each individual has a responsibility to be a good neighbor and a good citizen."[36] Through their marriage both George and Laura found new opportunities for assuming generative social roles. They became active in a range of civic organizations in Midland. After their children were born (1981), they joined the First United Methodist Church. George W. served on the church finance and administrative committees. He became involved in United Way and eventually chaired one of its campaigns. Laura volunteered with the Junior League. They both savored their roles as parents. George W. spoke often of how much he enjoyed being a father. Of course, any politician with children who claimed that he or she did not value and enjoy parenthood would be doomed in the next election. But George W.'s fondness for the role seemed genuine. He wrote that he "loved being a dad and playing with the girls." "A friend once told me he never realized how to enjoy his children until he watched me playing with mine."[37]

As George W. Bush became more deeply and meaningfully involved in the generative roles that came with marriage, parenthood, and civic engagement, the contrast between his serious commitment to making a positive difference in the world on the one hand and his abuse of alcohol on the other became more and more glaring. By day, he worked hard to make a go of it in the oil business; in the evenings, he often drank away the frustrations and disappointments he experienced in his business. Drinking was partly an escape from his failures; but it was also, as it had been back at Yale, an opportunity for socializing and having a damn good time. Heavy drinking seemed clearly at odds with his growing religious faith, however, which tied closely (as it does for many Americans) with his generative roles. Indeed, survey research shows that high levels of generativity among American adults are often positively associated with strong involvement in a faith tradition.[38] George W.'s generativity and his religious involvement were developing in tandem during his 30s, even as his heavy drinking continued to be a big problem for him and his family. On any given weekend, George W. might both get drunk and teach Sunday school.

Even after Arthur Blessitt brought Jesus into his heart in 1984, George W. continued to drink heavily. He continued to drink even after he joined the Community Bible Study in 1985, meeting regularly with other evangelical Christians to discuss the gospels and other biblical texts. He continued to drink even after his fabled walk on the beach with Billy Graham. But the midlife demands of generativity and Bush's growing understanding of himself as a generative man of faith finally won out. When he finally gave up alcohol, he gave the lion's share of the redemptive credit to God.

***

By the time he turned 40 years old, George W. Bush had taken the necessary behavioral steps to turn his life into a story of redemption. He had married a mature and serious-minded woman. He had begun to raise a family. He had taken on an array of generative roles in the church and the community. He had experienced a religious conversion and renewal of his personal faith. He had given up drinking. For the first time, he could begin to discern an overall pattern for his life that might provide a coherent and satisfying narrative identity. His story was not to be his father's. It was instead to be a self-defining and forward-looking story of redemption. Around age 40 years, George W. Bush finally became the *author* of his life. He began to reconstruct his past and imagine his future as a grand narrative in which a flawed protagonist endures years of waywardness and depravity only to emerge, at midlife, as a generative man on a mission.

In crafting his life narrative into a story of redemption, George W. Bush did what research suggests many highly generative American men and women tend to do at midlife. Over the past two decades, my students and I have studied the life stories told by American adults who score very high on well-validated measures of generativity—typically questionnaires that assess the extent to which a midlife person is involved in many different generative roles and committed to making a positive difference for future generations.[39] We have consistently found that highly generative American adults—caring and productive men and women who tend to be deeply involved in community, religious, and civic endeavors—tend to see their lives as stories in which personal loss, defeat, frustration, and suffering of various kinds consistently and repeatedly lead to positive outcomes. The redemptive stories that generative Americans tend to tell often follow a pattern comprised of five themes. All five themes are central to the story that George W. Bush began to construct for his own life around the age of 40 years.

THEME #1: EARLY ADVANTAGE

Compared to their less generative counterparts, American men and women who score high on measures of generativity are about three times more likely to identify childhood scenes or circumstances in their lives through which they received a special blessing, distinction, or advantage. In their narrative accounts of childhood, they may emphasize the positive impact of an early skill they developed or a teacher who took a special interest in them. They may point to favorable economic or psychological circumstances that they enjoyed. They may simply claim: "Mom liked me the best." Now, it is certainly true that most people, if they think about it hard enough, can come up with an early advantage that they enjoyed in life. But highly generative adults need no prompting or encouragement in this regard. They have a ready-made script that says they were fortunate early on, they were special, they were blessed, they were *chosen*—chosen by luck, by good genes, by propitious circumstances, even by God. They consistently begin their stories by illustrating how the protagonist was chosen early on for a special destiny.

Key point: I am *not* claiming that highly generative American adults *really did enjoy a special advantage* over others when they were children. I am saying instead that *they think they did*. It is a story they have constructed about the past, a narrative interpretation that comes from the standpoint of midlife. As generative adults, they now look back upon the past and they construe a special advantage that they enjoyed, once upon a time.

George W. Bush construed just such a special advantage in two very different ways. The first is obvious: He was the firstborn son of George H. W. Bush! It doesn't get much more advantageous than that. Even as a child, Georgie must have known that the Bush clan was no run-of-the-mill American family, struggling to eke out a reasonably respectable middle-class existence. It was a family that saw itself as specially chosen to have impact, and to lead. The realization of the family's special status and his own special place as the firstborn heir became clearer and clearer as George W.'s father climbed the political ladder all the way to the White House. Of course, the fact that he was the son of one of the planet's most prominent men doubled as a burden, too. But George W. was never so delusional to believe that this big advantage was not a big advantage, even when he may have occasionally wished he were not so advantaged in this way.

The second way in which George W. Bush authored his life to underscore an early advantage was his emerging conviction in midlife that *God had chosen him* for a special destiny. In a sense that seems paradoxical only if you don't understand how evangelical Christianity works, George W. Bush received this blessing, in his mind, *because he was a sinner*—and not just any old, garden-variety sinner, but a drunken, wayward sinner, the prodigal son who squandered his birthright for 20 years. Going back to the New Testament tale of St. Paul's conversion on the road to Damascus, born-again Christians have typically loved this kind of redemptive story the most. God chooses the worst sinner for a special blessing. In this kind of paradigmatic conversion story, the hero does not get the special advantage—does not get chosen—unless he has screwed things up really, really badly. Think: debauchery, a life of crime, drug addiction. For George W. Bush, therefore, alcohol abuse becomes the very mechanism through which he receives his special call from God. By squandering the original early advantage (his privileged status as a Bush), he gets a second (and better) chance. Like many recovering alcoholics in American society and many reformed criminals, George W. Bush framed his transformation from drunkenness to sobriety as a salvation sequence guided by a Force beyond his control.[40] From age 40 years onward, he believed that God had chosen him to make a big difference in the world. This became the starting assumption for his new narrative identity.

THEME #2: OTHERS SUFFER

Compared to their less generative counterparts, highly generative American adults are about four times more likely to identify an early scene in their lives in which they witnessed the effects of suffering or injustice on other people. They present vivid memories of, say, children being bullied, friends enduring family tragedies, people suffering racial or religious discrimination, and other scenes wherein bad things happened to other people. As with the first theme of early advantage, most anybody can surely recall an experience from childhood in which they saw something bad happen to somebody else. But again, highly generative adults seem to have a ready-made script for this sort of thing. Furthermore, they are likely to suggest that the suffering of others had a profound effect on them—opening their eyes to the injustices in society, for example, or sensitizing them to other people's difficulties. Highly generative people may even suggest that they had a precocious awareness in childhood of the cruel turns that life can take, and a special empathy for life's victims.

In the narrative identity that George W. Bush eventually constructed for his life at midlife, the death of his sister Robin stood out as the clarion childhood scene of suffering. When his parents finally told him that Robin was dead, 7-year-old Georgie sat "sad, and stunned. I knew Robin had been sick, but death was hard for me to imagine. Minutes before, I had had a little sister, and now, suddenly, I did not. Forty-six years later, those minutes remain the starkest memory of my childhood, a sharp pain in the midst of an otherwise happy blur."[41]

In the development of George W. Bush's personality, Robin's death turns out to have wide implications. As we saw in Chapter 1, Georgie the *actor* responded to the death by enacting his dominant trait of extraversion. He became the family clown, whose social performances brought laughter amidst the tears of grief. In Chapter 2, I argued that Robin's death led directly to the establishment of the first long-term personal goal in Georgie's young life. He made it his business—as a motivated *agent*—to raise his grieving mother's spirits, to make her laugh again. In Chapter 3, I suggested that George W. Bush later made sense of his sister's death in ways that resonated with and reinforced his deeply conservative political values and sentiments. As he reconstructed the event in adulthood, Robin's death taught him that life is fleeting and that one must *conserve* the best of life for as long as possible, to hold on to what one has and to thereby "live each day to its fullest."[42]

In terms of his emerging narrative identity at midlife, Robin's death becomes a key scene expressing how George W. Bush *authored* a redemptive story of the self. The story's first theme, early advantage, tells the protagonist that he has been given a special opportunity to make a positive difference in the world. The story's second theme, others suffer, reinforces just how much the world needs the protagonist to do his generative thing. As an author of his own narrative identity, George W. Bush was not especially original. Like many highly generative American adults, he put together a story that basically says this: "I am blessed" (Theme #1), "but others suffer" (Theme #2). Or: "I am the gifted protagonist who journeys forth into a dangerous world."

The world's dangers are ever present: Bad things will invariably happen to others, as I knew early on; my sister died of leukemia, when I was only 7 years old, and she was only 3 years old. But I am special; I am chosen; I can make a difference, and as a mature generative man at midlife, I need to make a difference, because the world—ever dangerous and threatening—needs me.

THEME #3: MORAL STEADFASTNESS

When highly generative American adults describe how they came to hold the religious, ethical, and political values that guide their lives, their stories tend to go like this: "I have held steadfast to my particular beliefs and values for almost as long as I can remember; I may have questioned them back in my teenage years, but I got things worked out pretty well back then; and I haven't suffered from much doubt since." More so than their less generative peers, midlife men and women who score high on self-report measures of generativity tend to hold strong beliefs about what is good and true in the world. They tend to make those beliefs central to their understanding of who they are. They tend to suggest, furthermore, that those most cherished beliefs have changed surprisingly little over the course of their lives. They exude a quiet confidence that what they believe is true and good, even when they realize that other people do not necessarily share the same beliefs and values. Although they may admit that long ago they struggled to figure out the answers to ultimate questions regarding morality, society, God, and so on, they report that they do not struggle anymore. Now in midlife, they are steadfast in their moral beliefs.

Research suggests that moral clarity and steadfastness are a prime feature of the life stories of highly generative American

adults in their midlife years, whether they are liberal or conservative, Christian or Jewish, black or white, male or female.[43] The case
of George W. Bush is among the most extreme examples of this
general tendency to be found anywhere. "I know what I believe,
and I believe that what I believe is right," George W. Bush once
said, at an international conference of world leaders in Italy.[44]
He was famous for his moral steadfastness, a quality that was both
a major source of admiration for his admirers and a major target
of scorn for those who saw Bush as dogmatic, stubborn, narrow-
minded, and self-righteous. Reinforcing the life-narrative theme of
moral steadfastness was Bush's low level of openness to experience, as we saw in Chapter 1. Whether they live generative lives or
not, people low in openness to experience tend to favor simple,
clear, and highly consistent moral ideologies. They dislike ambiguity; they want to be certain about things. In the case of George W.
Bush, the personality trait of low openness, readily traced back to
his childhood years, seemed to have a big influence on the kind of
narrative identity he developed later in life.

Another huge influence was religious faith. Check that:
His religious faith was more than a mere "influence" in the life
story of George W. Bush; it was instead the very essence of his
moral steadfastness. The very word "faith" suggests steadfastness
and certitude. After listening to an inspiring sermon in 1998, then
Governor George W. Bush phoned James Robison, a Southern
Baptist evangelist, and told him: "I've heard the call. I believe God
wants me to run for president."[45] In a 2000 presidential debate,
Governor Bush was asked to name his favorite political philosopher. He identified Jesus Christ. On his first day in office, President
Bush declared a day of prayer and cut federal funding for what
may be the one thing that most disgusts Christian evangelicals:
abortion. He hired or attracted many evangelicals for work in the

White House and government agencies. He usually began Cabinet meetings with a prayer. The journalist and former Bush aide David Frum writes that the very first words he heard when he walked into the Bush White House were these: "Missed you at Bible study," words from one earnest young Christian directed not at Frum himself (a Jew) but at Michael Gerson, a chief Bush speechwriter and evangelical Christian.[46] When a White House courier once entered the Oval Office unannounced, the only signs he detected of the president were his shoes protruding from behind the desk. President Bush was lying prostrate on the floor *in prayer*.[47] In a 2003 interview, George W. Bush said: "I pray daily, and I pray in all kinds of places. I mean, I pray in bed, I pray in the Oval Office. I pray a lot . . . as the Spirit moves me. And faith is an integral part of my life."[48]

THEME #4: REDEMPTION SEQUENCES

Psychological research shows clearly that highly generative adults in their midlife years tend to reconstruct and imagine their own lives as following a redemptive arc. They see early setbacks and failures in their lives as paving the way for later success and happiness. When they summon up vivid emotional scenes from the past, they tend to recall them as redemption sequences. In a redemption sequence, a particular scene in the story begins very badly but concludes in such a way as to bring something positive to the protagonist. The positive ending may be a favorable change in the protagonist's life, or it may be a long-term lesson or insight that the protagonist gained from the original bad event. Many studies have shown that construing negative life events as opportunities for gaining new lessons and insights is itself associated with greater levels of happiness, mental well-being, and physical health.[49]

Around the age of 40 years, George W. Bush began to see the redemptive arc that his own life might take. The frustration, the drinking, and the waywardness of his 20s and 30s became the necessary lead-in to a new chapter of faith, sobriety, and generativity. In his newly emerging narrative identity, he was the sinner who was now saved, the drunk who was now sober, the party animal who would now reign in his impulses and channel all of his prodigious energy into generative roles and commitments. Just how powerful the theme of redemption became for George W. Bush in his midlife years is nowhere more apparent than in his campaign autobiography, *A Charge to Keep*. In this public telling of his own story, the promise of redemption appears in the very first paragraph:

> Most lives have defining moments. Moments that forever change you. Moments that set you on a different course. Moments of recognition so vivid and so clear that everything later seems different. Renewing my faith, getting married, and having children top my list of those memorable moments.[50]

In the first sentences, the author informs the reader that the story about to be told will feature life-changing moments. The three examples given—renewing faith, getting married, having children—suggest that these moments will feature redemptive moves wherein the hero of the story consolidates his generative commitment. The author follows through on his promise. Each of the first four chapters in *A Charge to Keep* is structured as a redemption sequence. Chapter 1 (entitled "A Charge to Keep") begins with an account of political defeats—George W.'s own loss in the 1978 congressional race, his father's loss to Bill Clinton in the 1992 presidential race, and his brother Jeb's loss in the Florida governor's race in 1994. The chapter ends hopefully with George W.'s decision to run for president, motivated in part by an inspiring sermon he heard in 1998. Chapter 2 ("Midland Values") begins with Robin's death and ends with George W.'s evocative descriptions of the happiness, security, and freedom he felt growing up in Midland, Texas. Chapter 3 ("What Texans Can Dream Texans Can Do") begins with an account of the long odds he faced when he decided to run for governor against the popular Democrat incumbent, Ann Richards. The chapter is structured like a David defeats Goliath narrative; the underdog who faces an overwhelming challenge at the outset emerges the victor at the chapter's end. Chapter 4 ("Yale and the National Guard") begins with a vaguely negative description of campus unrest and the general chaos, as George W. has reconstructed it, of the late 1960s. It ends with his flying a jet plane high above the clouds. Sharply disciplined and in perfect control, he soars free and clear above the turmoil on the ground.

In Chapter 10 ("The Big 4-0"), George W. provides an account of the religious transformation he experienced in the run-up to his 40th birthday, and he tells the story of how he resolved to quit drinking. The chapter ends with a simple proclamation of the redemptive power of Christian faith: "Faith changes lives. I know because faith changed mine."[51] The redemptive power of faith runs throughout George W. Bush's campaign autobiography, and is captured in the book's very title. *A Charge to Keep* is named, in part, after a Methodist hymn written by Charles Wesley. The hymn's first two verses suggest that God redeems Christian lives so that men and women will follow their generative calling to serve Him:

> *A charge to keep I have,*
> *A God to glorify,*

A never dying soul to save,
And fit it for the sky.

To serve the present age,
My calling to fulfill;
O may it all my powers engage
To do my master's will!

THEME #5: FUTURE GROWTH

The stories we live by are about both the past as we have reconstructed it and the future as we imagine it. Highly generative American adults tend to imagine the future in upbeat, optimistic terms. Even if they believe, at some level, that the world is going to hell in a handbasket, they believe that they themselves are making a positive difference in their own family, neighborhood, and community. In the circumscribed worlds wherein they love and they work, they see and hope for the long-term positive outcomes of their generative efforts. The seeds they are planting will grow to become healthy plants, they believe. Their children will prosper. Their fledgling projects will mature and reap benefits for generations to come.

At midlife, George W. Bush began to see how his renewed faith, his newfound sobriety, and his commitment to a generative mission in life would eventually pay off. He had always dreamed of greatness. As a child, he wanted to be like Willie Mays when he grew up. Later, he modeled himself after his father. Neither of these aspirations was realized. At midlife, his newfound narrative identity suggested a different way to think about the future. As the prodigal son who drank his way through two decades of waywardness and failure, he had finally found his calling. As a disciplined man of faith, he would now fulfill the mission that God and destiny had set him up to fulfill. In the decade after his midlife redemption, George W. Bush worked hard to assure his father's election as president in 1988, successfully shepherded the Texas Rangers franchise through an important transitional period (which brought George W. substantial profits when he sold his shares as part-owner), and positioned himself to run for public office in Texas. His prospects for the future brightened significantly once he gave his life over to Jesus Christ and swore off alcohol. After his 40th birthday, he was finally able to see the future in hopeful and realistic terms. He would never be a centerfielder for the San Francisco Giants. He would never be his father. But he could be a man of faith who turns his life around at midlife to pursue a God-given vocation. His story told him this: The mustard seed is finally planted, and now we will see it grow.

***

Redemptive stories in American lives come in many different flavors and forms. There are a million varieties of misery out there, from unemployment to being spurned by a lover, and just as many different ways that misery can turn into something positive in the end. My father left my mother when I was 5 years old (bad); but that made me a stronger and more independent person later on (good). We were poor (bad), but it taught me that love is more important than money (good). I flunked out of college (bad), but then I took a low-level job with a company and today, after 30 years, I own that company, and I am rich (good); and, you know, I wasn't really mature enough for college back then anyway, and I might never have become mature if I hadn't had to swallow my pride and start at the bottom of that company and work my way up. He left me (bad), but then (thank God) I found a better man (good).

Despite the countless ways to author a story of redemption, certain grand forms of redemptive narrative enjoy a favored position in American culture. These are the stories that we often like best. Among these are stories of atonement (from sinner to saved), liberation (from captivity to freedom), recovery (from illness to health), and upward social mobility (from rags to riches—this one we often call, *the American Dream*).[52] In broad terms, George W. Bush adopted the forms of *atonement* and *recovery* in formulating a meaningful narrative identity for his own life. Finding personal faith and recovering sobriety after alcohol abuse were key elements of the redemptive story he authored at midlife. His story, furthermore, captured certain other ideas that reflected his psychological standing as a deeply conservative man with an evangelical Christian value system. To understand the nature of these ideas and how they worked for him as he moved through his midlife years, we need to consider recent psychological research on the life narratives of devout Christian adults—those Christians who identify themselves as politically conservative and their Christian counterparts, equally devout, who identify themselves as political liberals.

Whether or not you hold religious beliefs and sentiments, let us imagine for a moment that you are a devout Christian. You attend Protestant services or a Catholic mass on a regular basis— not just at Christmas and Easter, but weekly, sometimes more than once a week. You believe in God. You believe that Jesus Christ was/is, in some sense, the Son of God. You believe in the Christian message of redemption. You cherish your religious beliefs, and you have a hard time imagining what your life might be like if you were not a religious or spiritual person. Now I ask you this: What if there were no God in your life? What would your life be like if you had absolutely no religious faith?

In a psychological study published in 2008, each of nearly 150 highly religious Christian adults was asked this set of questions, as part of a long life-narrative interview.[52] Almost every participant in the sample found the prospect of life without faith to be very negative. Responses often sounded like this: "Oh my God! I can't imagine it. My life would be horrible. My life would be meaningless. It would be really, really awful." In the lingo of social psychologists, the participants in this study were asked to think through a *downward counterfactual.*[53] For these highly religious adults, their Christian faith was a fact of their life. Now, they had to imagine a world that would be counter to that fact, something that virtually every one of them saw as a huge step downward in what life would and should be like.

Each participant in this study described his or her own litany of bad things that might follow from a life without God. Many identified loss of meaning in life. Many suggested that they would feel bitter, angry, sad, fearful, or lonely if they had no religious faith. Among the many different responses, certain patterns tended to line up with how these Christian adults identified their *political orientation.* (As part of a series of questions administered at an earlier time, the participants rated their overall political viewpoint on a 1 to 5 scale, from "1" for highly liberal" to "5" for "highly conservative.") Those Christian adults who rated themselves as highly or moderately liberal tended to say that life without God would make them feel "empty" or "bereft." Life would be like the surface of the moon—a barren landscape, a desert, without energy or sustenance. By implication, faith fills them up, gives them sustenance and resources—the bread of life. By contrast, those Christian adults who rated themselves as highly or moderately conservative tended to say that life without God would be "chaos," "out of control." There would be nothing to stop people from acting on their selfish impulses. Drug addiction, rampant crime, infidelity, the breakdown of marriage, the dissolution of social institutions, dog-eat-dog, every man for himself—a world without God would be like a war zone. By implication, faith keeps us in check, as Christian conservatives see it. Faith tamps down the raging conflicts within, protects us from our darkest and most selfish impulses.

The initial findings from this study vividly confirm sentiments that have been identified with conservatism for centuries, as I described them in Chapter 3. Recall that political conservatives have traditionally turned a jaundiced eye toward human nature. Suspicious of liberal programs to perfect humankind, conservatives remain skeptical and vigilant. People cannot be fully trusted. The world is a dangerous place. The first order of business for good government is to protect its citizens from danger, from the potential chaos of unregulated human life. Substitute religious faith for government, and you have the basic sentiment described in the downward counterfactuals from the Christian conservatives asked to imagine their lives without God. Faith protects us from the chaos of unbridled human impulse. Faith regulates the self.

How do government and religious faith work to regulate the self? One way is to establish rules of proper conduct. Call them ordinances, laws, commandments, moral imperatives, and the like. Another way is to encourage people (citizens, believers) to *regulate themselves*. In the study I just described, the same sample of Christian adults described in vivid detail 12 important scenes in their narrative identities, including a life story high point (the best moment in your life), low point (the worst moment in your life), turning point, positive childhood scene, negative childhood scene, and an early scene regarding religious faith. Researchers carefully coded the content of the stories told about each of these scenes.

Compared to politically liberal Christian adults, the conservative Christians told significantly more stories about their lives wherein authority figures laid down *rules and reinforcements* for good conduct. They also told significantly more stories in which they or some other character in the scene learned lessons regarding *self-discipline*. In other words, Christian conservatives in this study were much more likely than Christian liberals to emphasize in their life stories the different ways in which authority figures (parents, teachers, schools, the church, the police, the government, God) worked to regulate the self. Authority figures established rules, laws, commandments, and the like, and encouraged people to obey these norms. Or they urged people to summon up or develop the discipline necessary to regulate and control themselves. Put simply, we can be regulated from outside (rules and reinforcements) or from within (self-discipline). Either way, we must be regulated. Otherwise, there is chaos.[54]

The central redemptive move in George W. Bush's narrative identity, as he authored it in midlife, was from chaos to regulation. The high-energy main character in this story was often out of control during the two decades leading up to the big turning points in his life. After marrying a fine woman, experiencing a religious conversion, and giving up alcohol for good, however, the protagonist emerges around age 40 years as a model of self-discipline. He has developed strategies for keeping his very strong impulses under tight control. He now reads his Bible every day. He never touches a drink. He keeps to a rigorous schedule. He focuses unswervingly on generative goals for the future. The bombastic, fun-loving, over-the-top extravert is still an extravert. His Behavioral Approach System—the BAS, as I described it in

Chapter 1—is still running on all 12 cylinders. But the high-performance Jaguar is now equipped with a new set of brakes, and a package of safety features worthy of a Volvo.

Even as a young man, George W. Bush had the capacity to exhibit remarkable self-discipline. Although he lost the 1978 Congressional race, his opponent later described George W. as a tireless campaigner: "The way he focused on what he had to do was extraordinary. He didn't relax. He worked all the time."[55] Even as drinking took a physical toll, George W. stuck with a rigorous regimen for physical fitness. He ran five or six times a week, pushing himself hard to improve his times. In an interview with *Runner's World*, he said: "Running does a lot of important things for me. It keeps me disciplined. . . . Running also enables me to set goals and push myself toward those goals."[56] For the young George W., the most impressive feats of discipline involved *the high-stakes mastery of power*. Like flying a jet. In *A Charge to Keep*, Bush described the exhilarating experience of tremendous speed combined with steely self-discipline. "I shifted the plane into afterburner, and with a loud bang the acceleration intensified, with the sudden increase from 10,000 to more than 16,000 pounds of thrust. The movement was amazing." As the speed increases, the pilot must "master" himself, "mentally, physically, and emotionally. You have to stay calm and think logically. One mistake and you could end up in a very expensive metal coffin."[57]

Laura Bush once said that she always believed that her husband had strong self-discipline but that he didn't know that he had it until he quit drinking at age 40 years.[58] Whether or not he really "had it" before midlife, it is clear that the redemptive story George W. Bush created for himself as a middle-aged man featured the deliverance from personal chaos through self-discipline. The story proved a valuable asset for both his own psychological development and his long-term political prospects. In the 1994 gubernatorial race, Ann Richards tried to paint her opponent as an impetuous and spoiled rich boy who could not possibly have the gravitas and the discipline to be the governor of Texas. George W. Bush kept his cool throughout the campaign and marketed himself as a steady, reasonable, and highly disciplined man of faith.

In the 2000 presidential election, he marketed himself as the anti-Clinton (even though, technically speaking, his opponent was Al Gore). "Leaders who cheat on their wives will cheat their country," he wrote in his campaign autobiography.[59] Unlike Clinton, Bush was able to control his strong impulses, the story suggested, and thereby bring back discipline, honor, and integrity to the White House. In Freudian psychology, the Latin word "id" is often used to refer to the unruly selfish, sexual, and aggressive urges that run rampant in human nature. As people grow up, they must learn to control the id. Early in Bush's first term as president, David Frum invoked Freud's famous concept in characterizing the new president, and the president he replaced: "George W. Bush's id seems to have been at least as powerful and destructive as the Clinton id. But sometime in Bush's middle years, his id was captured, shackled and manacled, and locked away. By the time he entered politics, he was the disciplined, guarded man I saw in the Oval Office."[60]

The conservative hero of George W. Bush's redemption story begins as the prodigal son who repeatedly falls prey to temptation. Although he shows flashes of discipline in his teenage and young adult years, he finds it very difficult in general to control his impulses and channel his kinetic power into a productive and self-defining life plan. Beginning with his marriage to Laura, however, and running through his religious conversion and his turn to sobriety, the conservative hero masters himself, atones for his sin, and resolves to move forward in life with energy, discipline, and generativity. It is a redemptive story of atonement through self-discipline, the kind of transformative narrative that evangelical Christians have always found appealing. It is also a redemptive story of *recovery*. Through religious faith and self-discipline, the conservative hero recovers from alcohol abuse. In the kind of conservative fashion I described in Chapter 3, furthermore, the hero seeks to *recover* something good that has been lost, seeks to *conserve* or *restore* something good that was either experienced or imagined from the past. As it is for many men and women who abuse alcohol or drugs, that something good that they seek to recover is the sobriety they enjoyed before they lost control. But it can be more than that, encompassing their remembered/imagined way of being before they fell prey to addiction—the innocence, the goodness, the freedom that was their life, or should have been their life, *once upon a time*.

For deeply conservative adults like George W. Bush, the redemptive dream may look forward and backward—to restore in the future something good from the past. As I suggested in Chapter 3, that something good was George W. Bush's idyllic childhood in Midland, Texas and all that Midland came to represent for him as he grew up. His family left Midland for Houston when Georgie was entering junior high school. Andover, Yale, the Texas Air National Guard, and Harvard Business School were to follow, punctuated by sojourns up north to the Kennebunkport family retreat. In 1975, at the age of 29 years, George W. moved back to Midland, where he hoped to make an adult life in the oil business. His inchoate plan may have also included becoming the kind of responsible adult—one of the movers and shakers and leaders of small-town, all-American Midland—that he so admired when he was a boy, or that he came to admire later as he reconstructed Midland into an imagined paradise of youth. For the children of Midland, there was an environment of security, parental love, gentle discipline, and freedom to run, ride bikes, play baseball, and have fun. For the adults of Midland, there was the satisfaction they experienced in raising their children in a safe, wholesome, and God-fearing community. And there was freedom, too—the endless opportunity to make a good life under the protective canopy of Midland values. George W. wrote:

> When you step outside in Midland, Texas, your horizons suddenly expand. The sky is huge. The land is flat, with not even the hint of a hill to limit the view. The air is clear and bright. The impression is one of the sky as a huge canopy that seems to stretch forever. Appropriately, "the sky is the limit" was the slogan in Midland when I arrived in the mid-1970s, and it captured the sense of unlimited possibilities that you could almost feel and taste in the air.[61]

***

It was on September 14, 2001 that George W. Bush's redemptive dream for America began to take public form. Only 72 hours after the attacks on the World Trade Center and the Pentagon, September 14 turned out to be the fateful day when his entire presidency was transformed.

The transformation began around noon at the National Cathedral in Washington, DC, where political dignitaries, military personnel, select members of the press, and others who managed to secure a ticket of admission were gathered for a National Prayer Service. President Bush addressed the congregation. Hinting at the redemptive message he would convey, he began his remarks with the theme of suffering:

> "We are here in the middle hour of our grief. So many have suffered so great a loss, and today we express our nation's sorrow. We come before God to pray for the missing and the dead, and for those who loved them."

After recalling the deaths of thousands, the heroism of fire-fighters and rescuers, and the nation's overwhelming grief, President Bush assured the congregation that America was ready to respond:

> "Just 3 days removed from these events, Americans do not yet have the distance of history, but our responsibility to history is already clear—to answer these attacks and rid the world of evil. War has been waged against us by stealth and deceit and murder. The nation is peaceful, but fierce when stirred to anger. This conflict was begun on the timing and the terms of others; it will end in a way and at an hour of our choosing."

America had been caught off guard. But she will summon forth her resolve and regain control, the president asserted. She will ultimately defeat the evil forces that were responsible for the attack. Chaos will give way, and goodness will be restored. This ultimate redemptive sequence for history *has to happen*, Bush insisted, because a just God governs all the world:

> "This world He created is of moral design. Grief and tragedy and hatred are only for a time. Goodness,

remembrance and love have no end, and the Lord of life holds all who die and all who mourn."

And then President Bush made a transition of historic proportions, a rhetorical move from the singular to the collective that represented a coming together of one man's life history and the historical moment. He made a claim that he knew to be true for his own life, and he projected that claim onto the nation as a whole:

"It is said that adversity introduces us to ourselves. This is true of a nation as well."

President Bush knew that adversity was at the center of the story he authored for his own life. His own narrative identity was a redemptive story of atonement and recovery through self-discipline. With God's help, he had overcome the chaos of his own life and restored a goodness he knew long ago and once upon a time. In the wake of 9/11, *this could be America's story, too.*

"America is a nation full of good fortune, with so much to be grateful for, but we are not spared from suffering. In every generation, the world has produced enemies of human freedom. They have attacked America because we are freedom's home and defender, and the commitment of our fathers is now the calling of our time."

Invoking the powerful religious idea of a *calling* from God, President Bush identified Americans as the blessed and chosen people, a nation that has always enjoyed good fortune but that has now come to know suffering as well. As freedom's home and defender, America must again take up the Providential mission to defend freedom against its enemies. Like their forefathers, the current generation must remain *morally steadfast* in the righteous battle against chaos and evil. America must summon forth all of her *self-discipline* to defeat the enemy and restore the goodness that she knew, once upon a time.

At the conclusion of the service, the congregation stood to sing "The Battle Hymn of the Republic." As the presidential party walked out of the cathedral, they saw that the morning's grey skies and rain had lifted. The sky was sunny and brilliantly blue.[62]

A few hours later, President Bush met New York Governor George Pataki and New York City Mayor Rudy Giuliani at McGuire Air Force Base, south of Princeton, New Jersey. The three men helicoptered to the Wall Street heliport on the East River and then drove in a motorcade around the bottom of Manhattan island to Ground Zero. The president stepped out of the limo and toured the ruins where just days ago the World Trade Center had stood. The crowd of workers pressed against him. They wanted him to say something, but unlike the cathedral scene, the president had not prepared any remarks. He had no notes. There was no sound system. With a gas mask dangling from his neck, a retired New York City firefighter named Bill Beckwith jumped up and down on a charred fire truck pulled from the rubble, to test if the truck was strong enough to serve as a platform for the president. Bush then climbed up beside him. At 4:40 p.m., somebody passed the president a bullhorn.

"Thank you all," Bush began. "I want to tell you how . . ." But the bullhorn was ineffective, and the president's voice did not carry.

"Can't hear you!" a rescue worker shouted.

"I can't go any louder," Bush said with a laugh. "America today is on bended knee in prayer for the people whose lives were lost here . . ." Another voice yelled out from the crowd: "I can't hear you."

The president paused for a moment. Then with his arm around Beckwith's shoulder, he shouted back: "I can hear you. The rest of the world hears you. And the people who knocked these buildings down will hear all of us soon!"

The crowd began to shout, and then roar: "USA! USA!"

A defining scene in his presidency. A moment for the ages. A high point in what George W. Bush was beginning to construe and portray as a grand narrative of American redemption. On September 14, he began to tell the story for the American people. He began to give a voice to the redemptive dream in two very different registers—the lofty and inspiring call to mission at the National Cathedral, and the gritty discourse of revenge at the prime site of the 9/11 attacks.

In the months that followed, the redemptive dream expanded to encompass the Middle East more generally, with a growing focus on Iraq. In his January 2002 State of the Union address, the president identified Iraq as part of an "axis of evil." Restoring America's security and assuring freedom became a matter of defeating both the terrorists responsible for 9/11 and those enemies of America who harbored or condoned terrorism. By the middle of 2002, the Bush administration had articulated a new American policy of preemptive war. To assure security and freedom, America must strike her enemies before they strike her. Along with Osama bin Laden, Saddam Hussein began to share the limelight as America's Public Enemy Number One. The exact date when President Bush made up his mind to invade Iraq to topple the Hussein government is open to debate. In his careful analysis of the administration's meetings and dealings in the run-up to the Iraq War, journalist Jacob Weisberg concludes that Bush made the final decision in late June or early July 2002.[63] Whether or not Weisberg is right, it became clear to the entire world in the fall of 2002 that the Bush administration was poised to strike back at Saddam, as if Saddam himself had colluded with Al Qaeda to attack the United States on 9/11.

It drove the critics crazy when the Bush administration blurred the distinction between those who, on 9/11, really did turn airplanes into bombs—Osama bin Laden and the Al Qaeda terrorist network—and the Iraqi dictator who had nothing to do with the original attacks. At first, President Bush hoped that a clear link between the two might be found. But when it became obvious that no evidence connecting Al Qaeda to Saddam was to be discovered, President Bush and his neoconservative allies did the next best thing: they connected the two *through narrative*. America must defend herself against her enemies. But her nobler goal is to defend her gift (which is God's gift) to the world. That gift is freedom. Here the neoconservative vision of a Middle East transformed by democracy and freedom dovetailed with President Bush's redemptive take on his own life and on the world. To the extent he harbored terrorists and developed weapons of mass destruction, Saddam Hussein was a mortal enemy for America. But even if he did none of the above, the ruthless Iraqi dictator was an enemy of freedom, just like the Al Qaeda operatives who took the towers down. America was now called to defend freedom for herself and for the world.

In George W. Bush's deeply conservative redemptive dream, the reborn protagonist makes it his mission to recover (restore, conserve) a state of affairs that has been lost. In his own life, the lost state is the sobriety he enjoyed before he went off to Yale to begin a chaotic period of drinking and waywardness. But the lost state is also the security, innocence, goodness, freedom, and opportunity that was Midland, Texas when Georgie was a little boy, as he reconstructed and romanticized it in midlife. With self-discipline, moral steadfastness, and God's blessing, the protagonist seeks to restore something of the paradise that once was Midland. Of course, Iraq was never Midland (even if some Christian literalists locate the original Garden of Eden near the Tigris and Euphrates Rivers, not too far from present-day Baghdad). George W. Bush knew that Iraq was not like America in many ways. But in his mind and his story, freedom is the good and natural state of humankind. By defeating Saddam and liberating the Iraqi people, America would restore something that God has given to all people. The 9/11 attacks and Iraq, therefore, were part of the same redemptive story. The generative protagonist would transform tears into joy, oppression into freedom—a gift for generations to come. As one neoconservative advisor to the president proclaimed when he learned that the United States was now ready to invade Iraq, "Our children will sing great songs about us years from now."[64]

The American president who launched a preemptive war on Iraq in March 2003 was convinced that God would help him restore the redemptive dream for America and for the Iraqi people, just as He had helped George W. Bush himself find personal redemption. On the eve of the war, David Gergen (longtime advisor to many presidents) told *The New York Times* that President Bush "has made it clear he feels that Providence intervened to save his life, and now he is somehow an instrument of Providence."[65] Baptist minister and Interfaith alliance leader Welton Gaddy came to the same conclusion at the same time, in an interview with the *Pittsburgh Post-Gazette*: "You see a growing feeling he [believes] he is, in fact, a divinely chosen leader in this moment in history. It's as if he discovered the power of religion late in life and thinks the nation needs to [do the same]."[66]

Like many who have noted the importance of Christian faith in the life and the presidency of George W. Bush, Gergen and Gaddy were correct in suggesting that Bush felt he was a man called by God to complete an important mission. But that mission was not to lead a religious revival in America, nor to Christianize the Middle East. It was instead more personal and ultimately psychological. *He wanted to defeat his father's greatest enemy and thereby restore Midland.* His beloved father's greatest enemy was Saddam Hussein, the "guy that tried to kill my dad at one time." Midland represented the childhood paradise that George W. Bush reconstructed and imagined as the first chapter of his redemptive life narrative. Midland represented so much that was fundamentally good for this deeply conservative narrator—security, innocence, freedom, fidelity, opportunity, small-town neighborliness. As he made clear in *A Charge to Keep*, Midland values are natural, God-given, universal values. They go beyond Christianity and the American way of life per se.

In the grand redemptive narrative that George W. Bush developed for his own life and then audaciously projected onto the world, Midland is how all people everywhere should live. It is the conservative Eden where the canopy of benevolent authority protects God's people and provides them with freedom, hope, and opportunity. What drives us out of Eden? Evil tyrants who oppress their people drive us out. Terrorism threatens to destroy Eden. But we can also keep ourselves out of paradise, when we indulge our basest instincts and live selfishly, without discipline, focus, and generativity. We keep ourselves out when we fall prey to the addictions of everyday life, the short-term fixes that divert us from our callings. Imagine a world without God. What do you see?

George W. Bush saw chaos. He saw tall towers crashing to the ground and monsters killing his father. He saw rampant crime in the streets. He saw infidelity and drug abuse, tearing families apart. He saw lives wasted by alcohol.

But it is very unlikely that President George W. Bush ever spent much time consciously imagining a world without God, or even imagining a world in which God was not on his side. Nightmares of chaos and destruction did not wake President Bush up in the wee hours of the morning. His redemptive life story succeeded in casting out fears and resolving any uncertainties that might trouble other men, even as the bombs fell in Baghdad and American troops poured in. The redemptive dream reinforced this narrator's supreme confidence and willpower. It kept him steadfast in his resolve to redeem, even as the war dragged on and on. With God's help, the protagonist in this story turned his life around at age 40 years. With God's help, America would turn it all around in the wake of 9/11 and in the face of threats posed by the evil tyrants of the world.

Why did George W. Bush invade Iraq? His decision was driven by an array of mutually-reinforcing psychological factors that managed to come together and achieve activation at a singular moment in history. As we saw in Chapter 1, the dispositional traits of sky-high extraversion and rock-bottom openness to experience set this particular actor up to perform boldly on the world stage. Energetic, restless, socially dominant, supremely confident, narrowly focused on a few key ideas, unwilling to entertain many dissenting points of view, he was dispositionally primed to do *something like* an Iraq invasion. The 9/11 attacks gave him the opportunity.

As we saw in Chapter 2, long-developing motivational goals helped to direct his energy toward Iraq. Saddam was his father's most hated enemy. When it came to his beloved father's enemies, George W. Bush took no prisoners. He wanted them dead and gone. The desire to defeat Saddam dovetailed beautifully with the neoconservative ideology, championed by Paul Wolfowitz and other highly influential advisors to President Bush, who aimed to remake the Middle East into a land flowing with milk, honey, and freedom. As we saw in Chapter 3, the neoconservatism that George W. Bush learned in the late 1990s fit well with the evangelically-inspired compassionate conservatism that he articulated in the 2000 presidential campaign. Both of these ideological positions, furthermore, resonated deeply with George W. Bush's redemptive dream for his own life—a narrative identity that affirmed the restoration of goodness through self-discipline.

In his self-defining life narrative, George W. Bush was the gifted protagonist who squandered much of his youth only to find focus and generativity in his middle years, with the consolidation of a stable marriage, renewal of his Christian faith, and commitment to lifelong sobriety. The midlife hero is called to a redemptive mission that cannot fail. He will turn sorrow into joy, chaos into Eden. (Let us not forget, after all, that he turned his mother's tears into laughter after Robin died.) For better and for worse, George W. Bush projected his personal redemptive story onto America and the world. He knew deep in his bones that the story must end happily. He was convinced that the mission would be accomplished, victory would be assured, and Midland would be restored. He knew this all because that is how his own life story had worked out.

FIVE

An American Story

Americans love redemptive stories. Consider those iconic Hollywood movies like *It's a Wonderful Life* and *The Wizard of Oz*. Or recall last night's episode of your favorite TV drama. The hero struggles, confronts dangers, takes on daunting challenges, endures tremendous suffering, and then—a happy ending perhaps, a lesson learned or insight gained, a glimmer of hope, a tearful moment of understanding or anticipation in the final scene. Think about the sermons that millions of American Christians hear every Sunday. Think about high-school commencement speeches and inspirational testimonials from successful athletes, celebrities, politicians, entrepreneurs, and other heroes who have "made it" in American society. It's all about overcoming adversity to achieve the big goal, staying true to yourself even when society tries to distract you, living the purpose-driven life in a difficult world, pulling yourself up by the bootstraps, putting the past behind you when necessary and moving forward in life with confidence and hope. Think about Oprah, her life and her message. Consider the American Dream.

"There is no public narrative more potent today—or through-out American history—than the one about redemption," wrote Michiko Kakutani, in a *New York Times* review of American fiction and autobiography.[1] In its most general sense, redemption is a deliverance from suffering to a better world. The protagonist of a redemptive narrative endures a negative state of some sort—be it sin, loss, poverty, shame, imprisonment, sickness, abuse, defeat, or some other unenviable situation. But the protagonist eventu-ally emerges from the negative state to experience something exceptionally positive, like salvation, love, riches, freedom, health, happiness, insight, or victory. Redemptive stories are told the world over.[2] But as a function of their unique history and heritage, Americans have traditionally expressed an especially rich assort-ment of redemptive tales. Americans celebrate the hopeful mes-sage of redemption in literature and in lives, in private stories of individual struggle and in public rhetoric about the story of the nation.[3]

Psychological research shows that American adults who see their own lives as tales of redemption tend to enjoy higher levels of well-being and greater commitment to making a positive con-tribution to society, compared to American adults who tend to see few redemptive themes in their lives.[4] In the terms introduced in Chapter 4, constructing a narrative identity that features the power of redemption appears to bring with it certain psychological and social benefits in life, at least among Americans. It is not hard to see why. When adult life throws its inevitable disappointments and frustrations at you, it is really helpful to have a story that tells you things will likely work out in the end. Your story says you have weathered the storm before, even flourished as a result of bad times, so you should be able to do it again. Redemptive stories affirm hope for the future.

Not only do Americans revel in their own redemptive narratives, but they also admire redemptive stories in their leaders. And at some level, their leaders (and their handlers) seem to know this. In recent years, many American politicians have celebrated their own redemptive journeys: Ronald Reagan rose from a dysfunctional family; Bill Clinton (nicknamed the "Comeback Kid") recovered from childhood poverty (as well as many self-inflicted wounds); George W. Bush turned his life around in his early 40s, after years of drinking and drifting. President Barack Obama's personal story has its own redemptive moments, and the larger arc of a black man's rise to the presidency actualizes one of the most powerful redemptive dreams in American history.

In constructing a redemptive narrative for his own life at midlife, George W. Bush drew upon a number of quintessentially American traditions for redemptive storytelling. The clearest source for George W. Bush's story is arguably America's oldest— the redemptive discourse of religious atonement. When the Puritans settled New England in the early seventeenth century, they brought along a way of living and a way of making narrative sense of life that were without precedent in the New World. On board the flagship *Arbella*, Governor John Winthrop urged his fellow Puritans to bind themselves together into a loving community so that they might do God's redeeming work. "We shall be as a city on a hill," Winthrop proclaimed, "and the eyes of all people shall be upon us."[5] The colonists believed that the whole world was watching them, for they had indeed embarked on a mission of cosmic significance. Their New World settlement was to be like a new Israel. Persecuted for their religious beliefs in England, the Puritans had finally escaped their tormentors, as the Israelites escaped the Egyptians. The Massachusetts forests would be the land flowing with milk and honey, long promised by their God to the chosen children of Abraham. With respect to the Christian church, the Puritans hoped (and expected) that their move to America would prove a victory of reform. Their city on a hill would serve as a model for all of Christendom—a model of a redemptive community made up redemptive souls working together to redeem the world.[6]

As the Puritans saw it, each man or woman was *called* to do the good work that God deemed necessary for the establishment, maintenance, and continuity of the good society. As that work contributed to the progressive good of the external community, the internal work of spiritual growth and development should move along at the same steady pace. Winthrop spelled out the awesome symmetry, and the deep generativity, of it all:

> "The end [of our mission on earth] is to improve our lives, to do more service to the Lord, the comfort and increase of the body of Christ whereof we are members, that our selves and our posterity may be the better preserved from the common corruptions of this evil world, to serve the Lord and work out our salvation under the power and purity of his holy ordinances."[7]

Like evangelical Christians today, the Puritans delighted in telling their stories of personal conversion and public service to each other, and in writing them down as spiritual autobiographies.[8] Whether the changes they described in their own lives were sudden or gradual, the story followed a familiar redemptive course. The protagonist must depart from an old and bad life— full of sin, filth, indifference, selfishness, and so on—and move toward a good, purified, engaged, and generative life reflecting God's grace. The climax of the story would be the point of full repentance of sin and full acceptance of God's plan for one's life.[9]

Like millions of Americans, George W. Bush followed instructions from the old Puritan playbook in formulating his own life story at midlife. Of course, the book has been edited and updated over the centuries. The Puritans might have found strange and off-putting the prospect of a traveling evangelist's winning souls for Jesus in a Holiday Inn coffee shop. Given their belief that God pre-ordains the elect, they would have objected to the very idea of persuasive evangelizing. But the Puritans surely would have recognized the redemptive message of atonement that George W. Bush accepted when, on April 3, 1984, he repeated the lines of Arthur Blessitt's prayer:

> "Have mercy on me a sinner. . . . I want to follow You. Cleanse me from my sins, and come into my life as my Savior and Lord. . . . fill me with Your Holy Spirit and give me love for all people. Lead me to care for the needs of others. Make my home in heaven, and write my name in Your book in heaven. I accept the Lord Jesus Christ as my Savior and desire to be a true believer in and follower of Jesus. Thank You, God, for hearing my prayer."

Like millions of Americans, George W. Bush came to see his own life as the manifestation of a *calling*—a self-determined mission to do good work in the world. People who feel that they are doing something especially authentic in their lives, who feel that the work they do and the kind of person they are happen to share a deep and satisfying connection, may often describe their activities as conforming to a calling or a mission in life. "I am doing what I was meant to do," they may say. The precise answer to the question of who or what "meant" them to do it may remain vague—perhaps God meant it; or maybe fate, some cosmic plan, my genetic endowment, whatever. On this score, Bush followed the Puritan model closely. As he moved into his 40s, he increasingly saw his own life as subject to the care and guidance of God. By the late 1990s, he really did believe that God was calling him to be president of the United States. The belief was not the product of narcissistic delusion, at least not any more so than any American's deep belief that God may have a plan for his or her life. Many American Christians talk about their lives this way, and they believe what they say. Of course, they can be flexible about it. If things don't happen to go as originally hoped, they may admit they were wrong about the original claim. "It appears to me now that God has a different plan for my life." God's will, after all, can sometimes be difficult to discern. Had George W. Bush lost the 2000 election, it is unlikely that he would have continued to believe God was calling him to be president of the United States.

In the story that George W. Bush began to author for his own life at midlife, the language of Christian atonement and calling dovetails nicely with a second characteristically American way of expressing redemption—the language of *recovery*. Like many substance abusers enrolled in 12-step recovery programs, George W. Bush believed that his ability to resist alcohol after age 40 years was a direct function of his faith in God. The first step forward in Alcoholics Anonymous (AA) is to submit to a higher source of control. The recovering alcoholic must first admit this: "I am not God. I cannot recover on my own. But with the help of a Higher Power and the support of a caring community, I can regain the sobriety, the goodness, and the freedom I knew long ago, before the substance took control of my life, before the chaos that ensued, once upon a time." AA and other 12-step programs express a discourse of recovery that has become pervasive in American society over the past half century. Expressed in self-help books, motivational speeches, and the testimonials of men and women who have been to hell and back, recovery narratives tell how a good and gifted protagonist became corrupted in the world—by alcohol, drugs, addiction, abuse, social conformity—and how that protagonist now seeks to recover the goodness and the gift that were stripped away. The essential redemptive move is from sickness, addiction, or abuse to the actualization of a good inner self.

The classic American source for recovery narratives is the nineteenth century intellectual Ralph Waldo Emerson. Were he living today, Emerson (1803–1882) might be running workshops on personal growth and self-fulfillment. After his wife died in 1831, this grief-stricken Unitarian minister lost his conventional faith and came to believe that God was to be found nowhere else but inside a person's heart and mind—an inner light of the self. Rather than look to history and society to find God, Emerson argued, men and women need to look within, to the mysterious, transcendent realm of human *intuition*. With his transcendentalist friends like Henry David Thoreau, Emerson drew from different religious traditions and blended them with European Romanticism and an unbridled American optimism to produce a way of thinking about life—indeed a way of living—that exalted the good inner self above all else. Distrustful of society and social norms, Emerson counseled American men and women to live in a *self-reliant* manner. To be self-reliant is to follow the "transcendent destiny" inside of you.[10] You have a gift inside. Find it and live it. Don't worry about what society says, for society will always seek to corrupt you. Each man or woman must have the courage to follow the inner light, embrace the inner gift, recover the good inner self and live it out to the fullest.

Among the many Americans who tell Emersonian stories about their lives today is one especially notable African American woman, who always carries a particular quotation from Emerson in her purse. The quote is this: "What lies behind us and what lies before us are tiny matters compared to what lies within us." The purse belongs to Oprah Winfrey. Oprah has often said that she believes her work obeys a higher calling. She has been chosen to make a positive difference in the world, to help people take charge of their lives and change for the better. Oprah believes in the deep, good, true inner self. In a 2001 *Newsweek* interview, she said: "What I teach is that if you are strong enough and bold enough to follow your dreams, then you will be led in the path that is best for you." Recover the redemptive dream within. Do not let other people dissuade you from following your own destiny. Resist society's norms and conventions if you feel they are keeping you from getting back to the gift within: "The voice of the world will drown out the voice of God and your intuition if you let it." Oprah's own redemptive life journey draws heavily on the language of recovery. As evidenced in her own recovery from childhood sexual abuse, people can survive traumatic experiences and come out even stronger: "Your holiest moments, most sacred moments, are often the ones that are most painful."[11]

After years of pain and personal chaos, George W. Bush sought to recover two positive states of being through the redemptive narrative he began to author in his midlife years. The first, of course, was sobriety. As we saw in Chapters 3 and 4, the second was a more diffuse sense of what a good life is, or might be, when people are sober, responsible, safe, and ultimately free. The object of his redemptive dream was Midland, Texas—the Midland of his childhood as he reconstructed and romanticized it in midlife. Midland was George W. Bush's city on a hill. People are safe in Midland.

People believe in God. Children play and adults work. People know their neighbors and look out for each other. Authority is benevolent and wise, dispensing tough love to produce responsible citizens. Midland values are hard work, self-determination, discipline, social responsibility, and freedom. Under the protective canopy of Midland values, the inhabitants of Midland are free to pursue their own goals and aspirations. They are drug-free. They are free from abuse and addiction. They are liberated from those negative forces (both from the outside and within) that might conceivably block them from actualizing their better, nobler, inner selves. God's greatest gift to humankind is freedom, George W. Bush believed. "Freedom is the design of our Maker and the longing of every soul," the president proclaimed, at a 2006 conference in Prague.[12] There is no freer or better place than the Midland of his redemptive dream.

America is the land of the free, according to its national anthem and identity. It should come as no surprise, therefore, that one of the most powerful redemptive languages for Americans is the language of *liberation*. In this kind of story, the essential redemptive move is from slavery to freedom. Among the most evocative stories of liberation in American history are the *slave narratives*, written by African-American slaves who, in the 1840s and 1850s, managed to escape their captivity. An especially influential slave narrative was written by Frederick Douglass and published in 1845. Like many of the other narratives written in this genre, Douglass identified himself and his fellow slaves as akin to the Old Testament Israelites—a chosen people destined to break the chains of their captors. To rally white Americans to the abolitionist cause, Douglass provided gripping accounts of slavery's horrors while casting his own improbable escape as a first act in a grand saga of American redemption. Over a century and a half later, American readers are still moved by the slave narratives. Literary scholars, furthermore, have shown how these stories have historically provided a source for imagery and motifs reworked in African-American fiction and biography.[13] The general idea of redemption through liberation has inspired Americans of all colors and persuasions and has come to characterize how many Americans make narrative sense of the women's movement, civil rights, and recent efforts to assure rights and privileges for gays and lesbians.

Throughout his life, George W. Bush had a strong emotional attachment to the idea of liberation. The very word "liberate" was one of his favorites. Joking with a police officer who was about to arrest him for disorderly conduct, young George claimed that he and his college fraternity brothers were trying to "liberate" the hotel Christmas wreath and bring it back safely to the DKE house. During his years in the oil business, he searched in vain for what Bush called "the liberator," the big gusher that would assure his fortune in the business and, presumably, liberate him from the Bush family's expectations regarding financial success.[14] In November 2003, 17 Iraqi women visited the White House. They told stories of the brutality of Saddam Hussein's regime. Upon meeting the president, one of the women greeted him with the word, "Muharrir." What does that mean? Bush asked the interpreter. "Liberator," she translated. The president broke down in tears.[15]

For his second inaugural address, President George W. Bush instructed his chief speechwriter to set one idea in bold relief: The security and the future of America depend on the spread of liberty.[16] Delivered on January 20, 2005, the address used the words "freedom" or "liberty"—or variations such as "free" or "liberate"—a total of 44 times, nine of them in the last two paragraphs.

Now that Saddam had been ousted but no weapons of mass destruction had been found, the president justified the Iraq War as part of a broad national doctrine of liberation. "It is [now] the policy of the United States to seek and support the growth of democratic movements and institutions in every nation and every culture, with the ultimate goal of ending tyranny in our world."

Although many conservatives objected to Bush's grandiose aims, his Freedom Agenda, as it came to be called, was simpatico with the neoconservative vision for foreign policy that he learned from Paul Wolfowitz and other mentors in the years leading up to his first presidential term. When journalist Bob Woodward asked Bush if America's efforts to bring freedom to Iraq and the world might be seen as "dangerously paternalistic," the president replied tartly that such might be the case "unless you're the person that happens to be liberated." "It probably looks paternalistic to some elites, but it certainly is not paternalistic to those we free."[17] Bush never hid his desire to be a liberator. Toward the end of *A Charge to Keep*, he wrote: "We have an individual responsibility to our families and our communities, and a collective responsibility as citizens of the greatest and freest nation in the world. America must not retreat within its borders. Our greatest export is freedom, and we have a moral obligation to champion it throughout the world."[18]

***

In *Leading Minds: An Anatomy of Leadership*, Harvard psychologist Howard Gardner writes: "Leaders achieve their effectiveness chiefly through the stories they relate."[19] Leaders express stories in the ways they live their own lives, and they aim to evoke stories in the lives of those they lead. "The artful creation and articulation of stories constitutes a fundamental part of the leadership vocation,"

Gardner claims. Further, "it is *stories of identity*—narratives that help individuals think about and feel who they are, where they come from, and where they are headed—that constitute the single most powerful weapon in the leader's literary arsenal."[20]

As a leader, George W. Bush was extraordinarily effective in expressing and evoking the redemptive stories Americans love. The personal narrative he began to construct for his own life around the age of 40 years eventually became part of the public perception of Bush. Many Americans recognized themselves in the president's earlier struggles with alcohol, his search for a sustaining religious faith, and his redemption from personal chaos through self-discipline. They knew that old story about the long, redemptive journey to psychological maturity—how a young man's sins sometimes give way to fidelity, commitment, and generativity in his later years. They recognized the born-again epiphany and the resolve to lead a better life. They picked up on the themes of atonement and recovery, for these are redemptive themes that play out in millions of American lives every day.

Many Americans also found comfort and inspiration in the redemptive story Bush projected onto America as a nation. America was once a great nation, he suggested, but she had lost her way. Although the Clinton years were a time of prosperity, they also witnessed the moral failings of a president unable to control his own impulses. Bush would restore order and dignity to the White House, he promised. He would focus the nation on the Midland values that once made her great. When that same great nation was devastated by the 9/11 attacks, Bush vowed to assuage her grief and strike back against the evil foe. In Bush's mind, the War on Terror was always much more than an effort in self-defense and retribution. It was a moral campaign against tyranny. In his

National Cathedral speech on September 14, 2001, the president identified America as "freedom's home and defender," and he asserted that defending freedom was "the commitment of our fathers" and "the calling of our time."

The same commitment to freedom and liberty was behind the American invasion of Iraq, the president argued. America was to be a liberator for the world, just as she had been in World War II. Let us recall what President Bush told the American people in a televised address on the night of September 11: "None of us will forget this day. Yet we go forward to defend freedom and all that is good and just in the world." *That same night* he dictated this for his personal diary: "The Pearl Harbor of the 21st century took place today."[21]

From the beginning, George W. Bush imagined America as the liberating hero. Just as she did after the Japanese bombing of Pearl Harbor, America would respond to the 9/11 attacks by summoning forth her boundless energy and self-discipline to strike back against the forces of oppression. If the airplanes hijacked by Al Qaeda operatives on 9/11 were akin to the Japanese bombers 60 years before, then Saddam Hussein was the parallel to Adolph Hitler. Hitler's oppression was not the direct impetus for America's declaration of war on December 7, 1941, after all, but Nazi Germany quickly became a prime enemy. In a similar vein, Hussein was connected to Al Qaeda as an enemy of America, even if Hussein was not directly involved in the 9/11 attacks. In this view of world events, Hussein became Hitler—a madman, a bloody tyrant, an evil foe who threatened the Middle East, just as Hitler had threatened Europe in the 1930s and 1940s. He must not be appeased! No less a moral authority than Elie Wiesel, the celebrated holocaust survivor and Nobel laureate, urged President Bush to invade Iraq to defend freedom and liberate the

Iraqi people. If the West had intervened in Europe to stop Hitler in 1938, Wiesel said, World War II and the holocaust could have been prevented. "It's a moral issue. In the name of morality, how can we not intervene?"[22]

America *would* intervene. And just as American troops liberated the oppressed people of Europe in 1945, so too would American soldiers march triumphantly through Baghdad. And grateful Iraqi citizens would pour into the streets to cheer them as liberators. And, well, . . . that was *the story*.

From an individual's perspective, a redemptive life narrative may sustain mental health and motivate generativity. From the perspective of the collective, a redemptive story of the nation may inspire idealism, patriotism, and a commitment to the common good. Going back to Lincoln's *Gettysburg Address*, American leaders have repeatedly used redemptive imagery to rally citizens around a common cause. "We have come to dedicate a portion [of the Gettysburg battlefield], as a final resting place for those who here *gave their lives that the nation might live*," Lincoln said. We "resolve that these dead shall not have died in vain—that this nation, under God, shall have a new birth of freedom."[23]

Woodrow Wilson hoped that World War I would be a "war to end all wars." He imagined a redemptive story wherein the horrible conflagration would eventually give way to a peaceful union and a new League of Nations. John F. Kennedy told a redemptive story about getting America moving again, after what he and his fellow Democrats portrayed as a long period of stagnation during the Eisenhower years. In initiating the Peace Corps, embarking on a race to the moon, and challenging Americans to ask themselves what they might do for their country, Kennedy inspired idealism and purpose. Ronald Reagan had the same impact, although with a rather different kind of redemptive dream. Reagan encouraged

Americans to feel good about themselves again, after what he and his fellow Republicans depicted as a long period of doubt and malaise during the Carter years. His redemptive message was captured perfectly in a 1984 campaign ad: "It's morning again in America."

Psychologically and culturally, there is much to like in redemptive stories. But redemptive stories can also bring trouble. No story, be it a person's life story or a story invoked to inspire a nation, is perfect for all time, for all people, and for all places and contexts. In the redemptive story that George W. Bush formulated for his own life and then projected onto the nation, at least three potential dangers may be identified. All three suggest possible limitations in his own understanding of himself and his place in the world. All three, moreover, play out in what many observers would conclude are troublesome ways with respect to his decision to invade Iraq.

PROBLEM #1: KNOWING FOR SURE THAT YOU ARE THE CHOSEN ONE

In many redemptive stories, the protagonist feels that he or she has been chosen for a special destiny. I am blessed in some way, and the world needs me. Because I am blessed, favored, gifted, or special, it should be my mission in life—my *calling*—to make the world a better place. I have been chosen to redeem. Out of gratitude, noblesse oblige, moral urgency, or some other manifestation of my having been chosen, I must take up the generative challenge—as a parent, teacher, activist, leader, or through some other generative social role. For the individual person, a psychological sense of being called for a good and generative destiny may promote positive generative behaviors. But it can also produce an arguably narrow sense of righteous entitlement, or narcissism. When a group of people or a nation as a whole come to believe that they are the chosen instruments of a favored destiny, the results can be disastrous, as the world saw with Nazi Germany. But one need not focus on such an extreme example. Going back hundreds of years, Americans have not been shy about proclaiming their special, chosen status in world affairs. John Winthrop may have gotten it all going when he told his fellow Puritans: "We shall be as a city on a hill, and the eyes of all people shall be upon us." Historians have given the name *American exceptionalism* to this strain of hubristic self-attribution in American history. In this pattern of thinking, Americans are the *exception* to all the rules—the special case, the singular nation, the self-proclaimed chosen people, as Herman Melville observed in a passage published in 1850:

> We Americans are the peculiar, chosen people—the Israel of our time; we bear the ark of the liberties of the world. Seventy years ago we escaped from thrall; and, besides our first birth-right—embracing one continent of earth—God has given to us, for a future inheritance, the broad domains of political pagans, that shall yet come and lie down under the shade of our ark, without bloody hands being lifted. God has predestinated, mankind expects, great things from our race; and great things we feel in our souls.[24]

In repeatedly describing the United States as a beacon of freedom and a force for good in the world, George W. Bush was following in the rhetorical footsteps of many American presidents before him. But his attachment to these general ideas and the certitude he expressed, both in public and private, that America was firmly and unambiguously on the right side of history were so strong and salient as to become iconic features of his public persona. The strength and the centrality of Bush's belief that America is history's favored nation may stem from the redemptive story he formulated for his own personal life. He knew deep in his bones that God had chosen *him* for a good and noble destiny. I Ie knew that if *he* stayed self-disciplined and true to God's calling, things would work out for the good in *his* own life. His psychological proof was his own redemption from chaos through self-discipline, which enabled him to restore the goodness and the freedom of his Midland youth and take on the generative commitments of father, governor, and president. So, too, he believed, America could redeem herself, and the world. By staying true to her identity as the chosen nation, Bush's story told him, America would surely summon forth the self-discipline and resolve needed to defeat terrorism, liberate the Iraqi people, and bring Midland to the Middle East.

Because they trace the move from a negative situation to a positive one, redemptive stories often feature a good character or force that is responsible for the positive transformation. In redemptive stories of atonement, that positive force may be God. In redemptive stories of recovery, the positive force may be an original state of goodness or a good inner self that the flawed or victimized protagonist now seeks to restore. The rhetorical temptation in these stories, of course, is to set up a simplistic battle between the forces of (pure) good and (pure) evil. This appears to be exactly what George W. Bush did, at least with respect to the broad redemptive narrative he projected onto America and the world. From the countless statements he made throughout his presidency regarding good and evil, let us settle on this representative passage from January 30, 2002, for a group in Winston-Salem, North Carolina:

> You know, you've heard me talk about this probably, but I really, truly view this [the war on terror, the eventual showdown with Iraq] as a conflict between good and evil. And there really isn't much middle ground—like none. The people we fight are evil people . . . Either you're with us or you're against us. Either you're on the side of freedom and justice or you aren't.[25]

In this passage and many others, President Bush expresses a decidedly Manichean view of the world. A movement founded in the third century AD by the Persian prophet Manes, the Manicheans believed that the entire world could be neatly divided between the forces of God (good) and the forces of Satan (evil). A devotee of Manicheanism in his youth, St. Augustine eventually came to condemn it as anathema to a Christian perspective on life. As a mature man of faith, Augustine concluded that seeing evil forces as the source of all that is bad in the world was merely a way of masking one's own failings. Nonetheless, the Manichean way of interpreting world history survived in various lines of Christian thinking over the centuries. After the Reformation, it appeared prominently in certain Protestant sects, who eventually transported the idea to America. Writing at the time the United States was entering World War I, the commentator and critic Walter Lippmann called the idea of a war between the forces of good and the forces of evil "one of the great American traditions."[26] As the Princeton University philosopher Peter Singer concludes, George W. Bush's "readiness to see America as pure and good, and its enemies as wholly evil, has its roots in an American-Manichean tradition."[27]

It is clear that Bush's own evangelical brand of Christianity and the religious beliefs of the many fundamentalist Christians who advised the Bush administration are consistent with a Manichean view of world events. In addition, Manicheanism came naturally to him by virtue of his personality traits. As we saw in Chapter 1, George W. Bush's low openness to experience predisposed him to favor simple dichotomies and moral absolutes in making sense of the world. One way in which Bush expressed this tendency was to size people up in broad terms upon a first meeting. After meeting with the Russian leader Vladimir Putin, President Bush famously claimed to have looked into Putin's "soul" and determined that he was a good and trustworthy person. After meeting with British Prime Minister Tony Blair, Bush announced to Blair's aides, "Your man has got *cojones*," using the colloquial Spanish for "balls."[28] His former press secretary Scott McClellan wrote that President Bush "often speaks about the people he likes in terms of their inner character—a good man, a decent man—rather than in terms of their concrete behaviors or actions." He often "simply assessed the hidden qualities of the man, as if these outweighed his actions and erased their negative consequences."[29]

Like many people who score low on measures of openness to experience, Bush regularly practiced a form of what psychologists call *cognitive essentialism*. He would reduce a complex phenomenon—such as another person's personality and behavior—to a single *essence* or quality. Putin is *good*. Tony Blair has *balls*. And Saddam Hussein is *bad*. Cognitive essentialism boils potentially complex realities down to simple categories and stereotypes. Although this may sometimes be useful in everyday conversation, cognitive essentialism can be dangerously limiting when it comes to a nation's foreign policy.

Writing in *Newsweek* on how President Bush justified going to war with Iraq, Howard Fineman observed, "He decided that Saddam was evil, and everything flowed from that."[30] Months after American troops invaded Iraq and as it was becoming clear that no weapons of mass destruction were to be found, journalist Bob Woodward asked Bush to justify the initial invasion. The president conceded that no weapons had *yet* been found, but noted Saddam had produced weapons in the past (in the 1980s and early 1990s), so therefore "a weapon could come very quickly." He added: "How could you not act on Saddam Hussein, *given his nature.*" Later in the same interview, the president concluded that the key to the Iraq War was "to understand the *nature* of Saddam Hussein, his history, his potential harm to America."[31] What the president was essentially saying is that it didn't really matter if there were weapons of mass destruction to be found in Iraq in the year 2003. Saddam had produced them before, and he is the kind of person who *would* produce weapons of mass destruction, by his very nature. He is, by nature, essentially evil—always has been, always will be, plain and simple.

The Manichean strains in Bush's redemptive narrative for America pit the chosen people against their enemies. By their very nature, the chosen people are good, and their enemies are evil. These stark moral categories work well in fundamentalist Christian sermons, television westerns from the 1960s, the *Star Wars* movies, and many other heroic tales that Americans love. But as a guide for national policy, this kind of redemptive narrative leaves little room for compromise, nuance, diplomacy, and the like. The leader of the chosen people is boxed in by the redemptive narrative that he and his people have embraced. There can be no flexibility.

If Americans really are the chosen people, destined to redeem the world, then they have absolutely no choice but to take on the forces of evil. The story demands it.

PROBLEM #2: JUSTIFYING VIOLENCE IN THE NAME OF REDEMPTION

In literature and life, redemptive narratives often portray deeply committed protagonists who move relentlessly forward, upward, and onward. Redemptive narratives tend to be linear and progressive. Over time, bad gives way to good, sin to salvation, slavery to freedom, sickness to recovery, rags to riches. Over time, there is progress, advancement. Things get better over time, and all (or much) is good in the end.

Whether serving as a narrative identity for an individual person or a self-defining story for a nation, a redemptive narrative can encourage people to believe that even if current circumstances are not so great, the situation will surely improve in the future. Redemptive stories instill hope. They make people feel that they are part of something bigger than themselves, something that is headed in a positive direction, moving forward, getting better over time. From the Puritan days onward, Americans have often perceived themselves as a people on the move, driving relentlessly forward or upward or westward, and in the process driving history to conform to their own redemptive destiny. When obstacles get in their way, Americans must overcome the obstacles. When those obstacles are competing people and competing cultures, the competition must be quashed.

For example, Americans used the language of redemption to justify the displacement of millions of indigenous people from their native North American lands. Historian Richard Slotkin analyzed how White Americans, between 1600 and 1860, came to understand their own relentless and ultimately successful campaigns to tame the wilderness, defeat the Indians, and expand their domain to encompass the vast land that is today the United States.[32] He argues that White Americans justified these acts of violence in terms of *regeneration*. To generate something new and good, we needed to destroy the old. We purged the land of its original inhabitants. We stole the land from others who claimed it was theirs. We glorified the violent heroes who were so instrumental in helping us win this ongoing war: the hunters, pioneers, cowboys, and Indian fighters.

Violence in the name of regeneration, Slotkin asserts, is the most striking theme of the American story:

> The first colonists saw in America an opportunity to regenerate their fortunes, their spirits, and the power of their church and nation; but the means to that generation ultimately became the means of violence, and the myth of regeneration through violence became the structuring metaphor of the American experience.[33]

"The land was ours before we were the land's," wrote Robert Frost.[34] The process by which we came to feel an emotional tie to the land, claims Slotkin, "was many deeds of war."[35] War in the name of regeneration and redemption—war aimed at wiping out the old so that we can start fresh anew, or war aimed at rescuing *them* from their own badness, to make them *good*, like us.

In the 1840s, the journalist John L. O'Sullivan coined the term *manifest destiny* to justify the westward expansion of the United States. O'Sullivan shamelessly asserted that it was part of a natural, God-given plan for the United States to expand its civilization and institutions across the breadth of North America. Expansion meant the spread of democratic ideals and economic opportunity. But it also meant ruthless territorial aggrandizement. The concept of manifest destiny was originally applied to the annexation of Texas, and was later taken up by those wishing to secure the Oregon Territory, California, Mexican land in the Southwest, and even Cuba. By the end of the nineteenth century, manifest destiny had come to assume explicitly racist and social Darwinian connotations. The chosen people were Anglo-Saxon American Christians. The cultural imperialism and political hegemony might readily be justified as a brutal "survival of the fittest."

The historian James Morone suggests that ever since the Puritan days, Americans have been subject to a moral fervor that reinforces the twin urges of reforming others as we redeem ourselves.[36] The drive to reform and redeem typically requires violence—the necessary means to the redemptive end. Violence in the name of redemption may be imagined as a crusade: "Onward Christian soldiers, marching as to war, with the cross of Jesus going on before." The crusader theme is central to Ernest Lee Tuveson's classic study of American destiny, *Redeemer Nation*. Tuveson describes America's redemptive mission: "Providence, or history, has put as a special responsibility on the American people to spread the blessing of liberty, democracy, and equality to others throughout the earth, and to defeat, if necessary, the sinister powers of darkness."[37]

It was never lost on his critics, indeed not on anybody, that in the days just after 9/11, President Bush characterized America's response to terrorism as a "crusade." "George sees this as a religious war," one Bush family member told biographers. "He doesn't have a p.c. [politically correct] view of this war. His view of this is that they are trying to kill the Christians. And we the Christians will strike back with more force and more ferocity than they will ever know."[38]

Whether or not this observation is correct, it was surely true that many American Christians, especially those of an evangelical persuasion, found inspiration in the starkly redemptive way President Bush framed the initial response to the 9/11 attacks and the later invasion of Iraq. On the eve of the Iraq War, there were well over 80 million adult evangelical Christians in the United States, about 38% of the adult population.[39] Although evangelicals hold a wide range of religious and political views, one strong narrative line within this tradition suggests that God works through history to affect the ultimate triumph of Christ. As portrayed in the wildly popular "Left Behind" novels authored by Tim LaHaye and Jerry B. Jenkins, an apocalyptic Christian view has it that human beings are now living in the "end times." Jesus will soon return to earth, and a series of momentous world events will follow, as described in the Book of Revelation. Israel (God's chosen people from the Old Testament) and the United States may play key roles in this drama. In that tyrants like Saddam Hussein threaten Israel and the United States, the defeat of these evil forces and the transformation of the entire Middle East may pave the way for the second coming of Christ.

It seems unlikely that President Bush invaded Iraq to speed up Christ's return to planet earth. Nevertheless, the strong support he enjoyed for the Iraq War among many evangelical American Christians may have been partly motivated by this kind of apocalyptic and ultimately redemptive Christian narrative. The enthusiastic backing American evangelical Christians have shown for the state of Israel, in recent years, stems in part from a particularly apocalyptic Christian reading of the Bible.[40] The neoconservative agenda to spread freedom and democracy to Middle Eastern countries beyond

Israel, furthermore, resonated with this particular Christian reading. What tied the two together for the case of Iraq was a broadly redemptive understanding of world history and America's role in it, an understanding that condoned, even encouraged, violence in the name of redemption. With this perspective in mind, the political analyst Craig Unger offers a searing indictment of Bush's decision to invade Iraq. In Unger's words, President George W. Bush was "a radical evangelical poised to enact a vision of American exceptionalism shared by the Christian right, who saw American destiny as ordained by God, and by neoconservative ideologues, who believed that American 'greatness' was founded on 'universal principles' that applied to all men and all nations—and gave America the right to change the world."[41]

PROBLEM #3: ASSUMING THAT ALL BAD THINGS CAN, IN FACT, BE REDEEMED

Redemptive narratives promise a deliverance from suffering. The basic redemptive move is from a negative situation or state to something better. Typically, the "something better" is so good that the preceding negative state loses its sting. In salvation, sins are washed away. In stories of upward social mobility, riches replace rags. Of course, many redemptive stories leave room for the lingering effects of negativity. A divorced man may conclude that he learned something very valuable about himself from the breakup of his first marriage, but the pain of the breakup may linger. Abraham Lincoln's redemptive interpretation of the American Civil War did not wipe away any of the casualties. Nonetheless, Lincoln's redemptive message gave meaning to the war, just as, on a much smaller level, a divorced man may find redemptive meaning in a failed first marriage. Redemptive narratives are a psychological and cultural tool for meaning-making. They help to ward off the possibility that life is random and that nothing we do really matters.

That said, it is sometimes extremely difficult to find hope and meaning in the wake of life's most brutal and seemingly senseless setbacks. What about a child's death? What about a profound disability? In the wake of the most devastating events, people struggle to find meaning and purpose. They will often look for silver linings and life lessons. But should we be surprised when they sometimes do not find them? Is it realistic to expect that all suffering will lead to redemption? Indeed, is it even morally *right* to expect it? To take the most extreme examples from the twentieth century, what redemptive meaning might we find in the extermination of six million Jews or in the atrocities of Stalin and Pol Pot? In an article entitled "Against Redemption," James Young observes that many post-holocaust writers in Europe are careful not to represent the last century's most horrific events in redemptive terms.[42] Even to suggest that something good might have come out of the systematic murder of so many people is to insult the dead, their families, and perhaps even the cosmos. In making sense of that which is grotesquely senseless, we must find forms of expression that go beyond redemption, Young suggests. We have to use different kinds of stories, more complex stories that do justice to the lived experience of the event and to suffering so intense and pervasive that to hope for redemption in its wake is to trivialize the suffering itself.

Many psychotherapists help their patients develop more redemptive understandings of their lives, to promote psychological well-being and meaningful participation in society. For the most part, this is good. But some mental health experts argue that the emphasis on redemption may be too strong, especially among American counselors and therapists. For example, the Israeli psychologists Nahi Alon and Haim Omer suggest that therapists need to help their clients understand the role of ambiguity, chance, and contingency in human life.[43] Sometimes there are no right answers or clear solutions for life's challenges. Sometimes things happen for what seem to be random and senseless reasons. Sometimes events are driven by luck, chance, and trivial coincidences. After all, good people do not always flourish; sometimes the bad guy wins. Things do not always get better; negative events sometimes lead to more negative events. Redemption is not inevitable.

Alon and Omer are not claiming that life is without meaning. They do not wish to undermine moral purpose and redemptive dreams. Instead, they seek to sensitize people to the potentially *tragic* features of human existence. In classic Greek or Shakespearian tragedy, characters suffer fates that they cannot avoid and for which they are not completely responsible. The tragic hero learns that suffering is an essential part of life, even when the suffering has no ultimate meaning, benefit, or human cause. Some suffering must simply be endured, rather than redeemed. Tragedy gives fuller expression to the ambivalence and complexity of human lives than do many other narrative forms. In underscoring human frailty and the role of contingency and chance in life events, tragedy can open people up to each other and sometimes bring them closer together. Tragedy looks with skepticism upon the ideological certitude celebrated in many redemptive stories. Surely, it is good for people to live according to strong moral principles. But perhaps those principles should be flexible and open to change as the world changes. The tragic hero anguishes over the moral complexities in the world. He does not settle for simple truths and pat answers. For him, there can be no "chosen people" and no "axis of evil."

In his critical analysis of the Bush presidency, Jacob Weisberg draws parallels between George W. Bush and the tragic hero of Shakespeare's *Henry V*. Despite the similarities between the two, Weisberg asserts, Bush showed throughout his life—before the presidency and during his years in office—that he was "lacking a tragic sense."[44] There is more psychological wisdom in this remark than perhaps even the author knew. Weisberg argues that Bush's failure to "consider the costs of his choices" showed that he never really understood the potentially tragic results of human behavior.[45] But there is more to it than that. Even if President Bush did perform his own cost-benefit analysis in weighing the decision to invade Iraq, this supremely optimistic and confident decision-maker never seemed to be able, or willing, to consider the tragic possibility that *life itself sometimes defies redemption*. His triumphant personal story, generalized now to the American people as a whole, would not permit him to do so. In the redemptive dream that George W. Bush projected onto America and the world, the deaths of 9/11 simply *had to be* redeemed, the evil dictator *had to be* overthrown, and America *had to* emerge victorious in the end. These imperatives were not merely statements of political expediency, designed to show the American electorate that President Bush was strong and steadfast. They were, in addition, the only authentic statements that his redemptive story for life would allow him to make. Lacking a tragic sense, President Bush could imagine no other story for himself, or for America.

***

I have argued in this book that psychological factors played an important role in President George W. Bush's decision to invade Iraq in the spring of 2003. I have focused on factors that arise from the makeup of the president's personality. Personality is a complex product of genes, family experience, and culture. As a foundation for personality, broad dispositional traits begin to develop early in life, strongly driven by inherited genetic tendencies that interact with environmental inputs. A second layer of personality begins to emerge in mid-childhood, as personal goals and values spell out what a person wants and how he or she plans to get it. Goals, values, specific strategies, and plans are strongly shaped by family experiences, friends, peer groups, and other interpersonal and social relationships. Finally, a third layer of personal narrative—the stories we live by—begins to take form in the early-adult years. Stories strongly reflect cultural influences. In sum, dispositional traits describe the person as an *actor* on a social stage; goals depict the person as a motivated *agent*; and life stories speak to how the person functions as an autobiographical *author*. Along with traits (the person as actor) and goals (the person as agent), stories (the person as author) continue to develop across the human life course. Genes, family experience, and culture continue to exert their effects on the development of personality from beginning to end. Genes appear to be especially influential in the shaping of traits; family experiences may have their strongest impacts on goals and values; and culture provides the narrative patterns and templates out of which we make our lives into meaningful stories.

In tracing the development of traits, goals, and stories in the life of George W. Bush, I have focused my analysis on how these features of his personality came together to influence his decision to invade Iraq. In Chapter 1, I suggested that strong dispositional traits of *high* extraversion and *low* openness to experience predisposed the president to approach the problem of Iraq as a highly energized, optimistic, and confident actor on the world stage. His traits made it likely that he would act in a swift and supremely self-assured manner. He would be bold and aggressive, and he would never doubt that the decision he made was the right one.

In Chapter 2, I suggested that after 9/11 the president found a straightforward way to channel his boundless energy and confidence into the realization of one of his most cherished life goals—to defeat his beloved father's greatest enemies. By overthrowing Saddam Hussein, the president could protect America and her allies from weapons of mass destruction (the president was convinced Saddam had them) while simultaneously accomplishing a personal motivational agenda. Invading Iraq to overthrow Hussein found ideological justification in the peculiar brand of conservatism that George W. Bush developed over the course of his life, as suggested in Chapter 3. Combining the evangelical spirit of compassionate conservatism with the neoconservative vision of democracy and freedom for the Middle East, invading Iraq represented much more than merely defending America (and his father) against a terrible foe. In George W. Bush's mind, it was just as much a noble war of liberation.

The president's action traits and agential goals ultimately dovetailed perfectly with the story he authored for his own life. In Chapter 4, I suggested that George W. Bush struggled throughout his 20s and 30s to develop a satisfying and meaningful story for his life, a narrative identity that would provide him with a sense of unity and purpose. He finally succeeded sometime in his late 30s and early 40s, after settling into a series of generative commitments in life, experiencing a religious transformation, and pledging to give up alcohol for good. The redemptive story he formulated for his life at midlife was a tale of atonement and recovery through self-discipline. Reflecting the time-honored conservative tendency to reclaim a glorious past, his redemptive story depicts a prodigal son who recaptures the sobriety, goodness, security, and freedom that he enjoyed long ago, once upon a time, in a remembered and imagined paradise named Midland, Texas.

After 9/11, George W. Bush projected his redemptive dream onto America. If he could recover his own goodness and freedom through self-discipline (and with God's help), so too would America (God's chosen nation) recover from the devastation of 9/11 through self-discipline, and in the process export goodness and freedom (Midland values) to the world. In Chapter 5, I have shown how the particular redemptive story that George W. Bush authored for his life and projected onto the nation was itself a profoundly *American* tale. Drawing unconsciously on deep cultural themes that may be traced all the way back to the Massachusetts Bay Puritans and forward to Oprah, George W. Bush crafted, personified, and projected a redemptive story as American as apple pie and the Super Bowl.

I believe that all of these psychological factors—high levels of extraversion and low levels of openness to experience, the personal goal to avenge his father, his unique brand of conservative ideology, and the redemptive narrative he developed for his life and then projected onto the nation—came together in the twinkling of history's eye to inform his decision to invade Iraq. Of course, the decision was also informed by many factors that were not themselves psychological. Political, economic, and world-historical factors all played important roles. The 9/11 attacks and the subsequent anthrax scare created an overwhelming sense of threat among Americans, which increased a sense of patriotism and the desire to strike back against America's enemies, to defend the homeland. Iraq was no random country that just happened to be controlled by a despot. It was, and is, a geo-politically crucial nation, strategically located in the Middle East. And do I need to mention that it sits upon huge reserves of oil? Or that Iraq has repeatedly threatened Israel, one of America's closest allies? There were many reasons that an American president *might* have invaded

Iraq in 2003. But there were also many reasons *not* to do it. In the case of George W. Bush, psychological factors that derived from the very makeup of his personality may have tipped the scales in the direction of "do it."

I do not believe that any single psychological factor was strong enough by itself to tip the scales. Rather, all of the factors I have identified needed to come together into an organized psychological force, a perfect psychological storm of traits (Bush the actor), goals and values (Bush the agent), and stories (Bush the author). Without the exuberance and social aggressiveness that sky-high levels of extraversion brought to the performance, President George W. Bush might not have been so predisposed to act swiftly, boldly, and with such dramatic flair on the world stage. A president with higher levels of openness to experience might have solicited a broader range of opinions on Iraq and searched more seriously for alternatives to an attack.

There is little doubt that in 2003 Saddam Hussein posed *some* threat to American interests in the Middle East. But George W. Bush's unique history with Saddam and his venerated father sensitized him to perceive the Iraqi leader as a greater threat than many other presidents might have perceived him. Rather than seeking to overcome or out-perform his father (as is commonly believed), George W. Bush had long sought to defeat his beloved father's greatest enemies. The belief that Saddam had once launched an assassination attempt on his father only fueled the fire of his motivational agenda. The evangelically-inspired neoconservative values that George W. Bush internalized in the years just before he assumed the presidency provided him with further ideological justification for invading Iraq. Without that justification, he might not have launched the military operation—an operation codenamed *Iraqi Freedom*. His redemptive life story further reinforced the president's motivation and justification for the attack. In psychological terms, the story put it all together: *The chosen hero, bold and decisive, must discipline himself to overcome the forces of chaos to recover—for himself, for America, and for the world—the security, goodness, and freedom that God has made available to all His people.* The story, or pieces of it, resonated with many Americans who initially supported the invasion, largely because it captured a redemptive dream that was so deeply American in its themes and cadences.

As the war dragged on, President Bush never wavered in his conviction that his original decision to invade Iraq was good and right. Even as American casualties piled up and countless Iraqis lost their lives in sectarian violence, the president insisted that America must stay the course. By the time he left office in January 2009, there remained approximately 150,000 American troops in Iraq. From the beginning, international support for America's invasion of Iraq was pitifully slim, and it shrank further as the years went by. Among citizens of the United States, support for the war plummeted. By 2009, a large majority of Americans considered the Iraq War to be a mistake. Yet throughout his difficult second term in the White House, President Bush never seemed to lose faith. In public appearances, he continued to exude optimism and steadfast resolve regarding the war. People who met with the president in private noted that he appeared unfazed by the problems of the war, nearly oblivious even as the political situation in Iraq deteriorated and the violence skyrocketed. He reported that he slept well at night.[46]

In the early days of the Iraq conflict, President Bush's optimism and resolve served to keep criticism of the war at bay. In Bob Woodward's *State of Denial*, the journalist reports many incidents in which top advisors found it nearly impossible to convey negative news to the president about the war. Because the president was so gung ho on the Iraq War, his advisors often kept their doubts to themselves. As public sentiment regarding the conflict began to sour, however, more contrarian views within the administration started to surface. President Bush ignored them, or deflected their effect by cheering the team on to victory. Woodward describes a typical scene from 2004, as the war continued to go badly and the president's advisors met to discuss plans to hold elections in Iraq:

> [The Chairman of the Joint Chiefs of Staff, General Richard] Myers could feel that when any doubt started to creep into the small, windowless Situation Room, the president almost always stomped it out. Whether it was alarming casualties, bad news, the current decision on the timing of the Iraqi elections, some other problem or just a whiff of one of the uncertainties that accompany war, the president would try to set them all straight.
>
> "Hold it," Bush said once. "We know we're doing the right thing. We're on the right track here. We're doing the right thing for ourselves, for our own interest and for the world. And don't forget it. Come on, guys."[47]

George W. Bush's redemptive dream for America, derived from his own life story, provided the strongest psychological source for the resolve and certitude he showed as the Iraq War dragged on and on, year after year. The only acceptable plot for America's story was the same plot that characterized his own: the recovery of goodness, security, and freedom through self-discipline. The only acceptable ending was America's victory, as God's liberating champion. To narrate the war in any other way was to engage in what psychologists call a *heretical counterfactual*.[48] In George W. Bush's mind, negative ideas about the war were counter to (what he viewed as) the fundamental *fact* that America was doing the right thing. To think otherwise was blatant *heresy*.

Psychological research shows that powerful narratives in people's lives make it nearly impossible, in many cases, to consider ideas, opinions, possibilities, and facts that run counter to the story. The redemptive dream sucked any contrarian air out of the Situation Room. The power of President Bush's redemptive story for America and for Iraq set clear limits on what the president's advisors could say about the war and how the administration could imagine its future course. These constraints were at the top of Treasury Secretary Paul O'Neill's mind when, after being forced out of the Bush administration for his contrarian views, he came to this astute conclusion: "I realized that it's very hard for an organization or an institution to achieve more than the leader can imagine."[49]

In regard to America's War on Terror, George W. Bush once said this to his close political advisor, Karl Rove: "I'm here for a reason, and this is going to be how we're going to be judged."[50] When asked why he did not consult at greater length with his own father regarding the war in Iraq, he famously said, "You know he is the wrong father to appeal to in terms of strength. There is a higher father I appeal to."[51]

In George W. Bush's redemptive story for America, he was chosen to lead the struggle against evil tyranny, so as to restore God's good gift of security and freedom, both for America and for Iraq. It is with respect to this redemptive story, he believed, that he and his presidency would ultimately be judged. "What matters [most] is the emergence of a free society where people realize their lives are better off," he told Bob Woodward. "And where they work through their traumas so they can seize the moment. . . . It is *the story of the 21ˢᵗ century.*"[52]

President Bush's response to Woodward captures perfectly the basic narrative arc of the redemptive dream. People need to "work through their traumas so they can seize the moment," just as George W. Bush himself worked through his own difficulties in life, before he seized the moment, around the age of 40 years. The result of the redemptive move is the "emergence of a free society where people realize their lives are better off." What matters is the restoration of Midland, with its God-given values of security, freedom, and self-determination. It is "the story of the 21ˢᵗ century," the story of our time.

As George W. Bush imagined it, the story of our time began on September 11, 2001, when terrorists attacked the United States. In his farewell address to the nation in January 2009, President Bush remarked: "As the years passed, most Americans were able to return to life much as it had been before 9/11. But I never did."[53] George W. Bush never looked back after 9/11. And he never looked back after that pivotal morning before his 40ᵗʰ birthday, when The Decider made the big decision to give up drinking for good. He never looked back after deciding to invade Iraq. George W. Bush kept his eyes stubbornly focused on the redemptive dream. As he saw it, the story of our time was and is *his* story—the only story, he believed, that could provide the happy ending we all want.

Notes

INTRODUCTION: WHY DID PRESIDENT GEORGE W. BUSH INVADE IRAQ?

1. Frank, J. A. (2007). *Bush on the couch: Inside the mind of the president.* New York: Harper, p. 14.
2. Woodward, B. (2004). *Plan of attack.* New York: Simon & Schuster, p. 379.
3. Woodward (2004), p. 149, reports Scowcroft's words from a Sunday morning talk show. Scowcroft made the same argument in an important opinion piece in *The Wall Street Journal:* Scowcroft, B. (2002, August 15). Don't attack Saddam. *The Wall Street Journal.*
4. McAdams, D. P., & Pals, J. L. (2006). A new Big Five: Fundamental principles for an integrative science of personality. *American Psychologist, 61,* 204–217.
   See also:
   Hooker, K. S., & McAdams, D. P. (2003). Personality reconsidered: A new agenda for aging research. *Journal of Gerontology: Psychological Sciences, 58B,* P296–P304.
   McAdams, D. P. (1994). Can personality change? Levels of stability and growth in personality across the lifespan. In T. F. Heatherton and J. L. Weinberger (Eds.), *Can personality change?* (pp. 299–314). Washington, DC: American Psychological Association Press.
   McAdams, D. P. (1995). What do we know when we know a person? *Journal of Personality, 63,* 365–396.
   McAdams, D. P. (1996). Personality, modernity, and the storied self: A contemporary framework for studying persons. *Psychological Inquiry, 7,* 295–321.
   McAdams, D. P. (1997). The case for unity in the (post)modern self: A modest proposal. In R. Ashmore and L. Jussim (Eds.), *Self and identity: Fundamental issues* (pp. 46–78). New York: Oxford University Press.

McAdams, D. P., & Adler, J. M. (2006). How does personality develop? In D. K. Mroczek and T. Little (Eds.), *Handbook of personality development* (pp. 469–492). Mahwah, NJ: Erlbaum.

McAdams, D. P., & Cox, K. S. (2010). Self and identity across the lifespan. In R. Lerner, A. Freund, and M. Lamb (Eds.), *Handbook of lifespan development* (Vol. 2, pp. 158-207). New York: Wiley.

McAdams, D. P., & Olson, B. D. (2010). Personality development: Continuity and change over the life course. In S. E. Fiske, A. E. Kazdin, and D. L. Schacter (Eds.), *Annual review of psychology* (Vol. 61, pp. 517-542). Palo Alto, CA: Annual Reviews, Inc.

CHAPTER I: THE ACTOR'S TRAITS

1. Bush, G. H. W. (1999). *All the best: My life in letters and other writings*. New York: Touchstone, p. 64.

   His father's mention of little Georgie's "sentences disjointed" might be seen as an early indication of a developing language or speech deficit. Much has been made of the mangled syntax and the multiple malapropisms that have found their way into George W. Bush's public speeches. Some observers have labeled him as dyslexic. Even if the labels have diagnostic validity, however, I do not see how any of this has much bearing on his performance as president, except to make him an easy target for late-night comedy. For this book, I basically ignore the dyslexia issue, for it seems irrelevant to my central question: Why did President Bush invade Iraq? But see Frank (2007) and:

   Weisberg, J. (2001). *George W. Bushisms: The Slate book of the accidental wit and wisdom of our 43rd President*. New York: Simon & Schuster.

2. Schweizer, P., & Schweizer, R. (2004). *The Bushes: Portrait of a dynasty*. New York: Doubleday, p. 371.

3. From Shakespeare's *As You Like It* (Act II, Scene VII, lines 139–166):

   All the world's a stage,

   And all the men and women merely players;

   They have their exits and their entrances;

   And one man in his time plays many parts,

   His acts being seven ages. At first the infant,

   Mewling and puking in the nurse's arms.

   And then the whining school-boy, with his satchel

And shining morning face, creeping like snail
Unwillingly to school. And then the lover,
Sighing like furnace, with a woeful ballad
Made to his mistress' eyebrow. Then a soldier,
Full of strange oaths, and bearded like the pard,
Jealous in honour, sudden and quick in quarrel,
Seeking the bubble reputation
Even in the cannon's mouth. And then the justice,
In fair round belly with good capon lined,
With eyes severe and beard of formal cut,
Full of wise saws and modern instances;
And so he plays his part. The sixth age shifts
Into the lean and slippper'd pantaloon,
With spectacles on nose and pouch on side,
His youthful hose, well saved, a world too wide
For his shrunk shank; and his big manly voice,
Turning again toward childish treble, pipes
And whistles in his sound. Last scene of all,
That ends this strange eventful history,
Is second childishness and mere oblivion,
Sans teeth, sans eyes, sans taste, sans everything.

4. Psychological research suggests that young children do not conceive of themselves as independent, agentic selves until around the age of 2 years. It is around this time that they begin to recognize themselves in mirrors and to show certain self-conscious emotions, such as pride and shame, indicating that they now have some sense of themselves as conscious actors on a social stage. Around the age of four years, most children develop a folk theory of their own and others' minds, realizing now that they have desires and beliefs in their own heads (as do other people) and that they (and others) act upon those desires and beliefs. See especially:
Povinelli, D. J. (2001). The self: Elevated in consciousness and extended in time. In C. Moore and K. Lemmon (Eds.), *The self in time: Developmental perspectives* (pp. 75–95). Mahwah, NJ: Erlbaum.

Rochat, P. (2003). Five levels of self-awareness as they unfold early in life. *Consciousness and Cognition, 12*, 717–731.

5. Schweizer & Schweizer (2004), p. 132.

6. Bush, G. W. (1999). *A charge to keep: My journey to the White House.* New York: Harper, pp. 80–81. In spelling out these personality traits in this passage, George W. is expressly contrasting himself to his wife Laura.

7. Suskind, R. (2004). *The price of loyalty: George W. Bush, the White House, and the education of Paul O'Neill.* New York: Simon & Schuster, p. 160.

8. G. W. Bush (1999), p. 14.

9. G. H. W. Bush (1999), p. 70.

10. Andersen, C. (2002). *George and Laura: Portrait of an American marriage.* New York: William Morrow, p. 41.

11. Andersen (2002), p. 43.

12. Andersen (2002), p. 47. Other good sources for material on George W. Bush's childhood include G. W. Bush (1999), Schweizer & Schweizer (2004), and these:

   Aikman, D. (2004). *A man of faith: The spiritual journey of George W. Bush.* Nashville, TN: Thomas Nelson.

   Bush, B. (1994). *Barbra Bush: A memoir.* New York: Charles Scribner's Sons.

   Draper, R. (2007). *Dead certain: The presidency of George W. Bush.* New York: The Free Press.

   Minutaglio, B. (1999). *First son: George W. Bush and the Bush dynasty.* New York: Times Books.

   Renshon, S. A. (2004). *In his father's shadow: The transformations of George W. Bush.* New York: Palgrave Macmillan.

13. Draper (2007), p. 29.

14. For an accessible and wide-ranging overview of contemporary personality research and theory see:

   McAdams, D. P. (2009). *The person: An introduction to the science of personality psychology* (5th ed.). New York: Wiley.

   For a more technical treatment, see:

   John, O. P., Robins, R. W., & Pervin, L. A. (Eds.). (2008). *Handbook of personality: Theory and research* (3rd ed.). New York: Guilford Press.

15. I have adopted McCrae and Costa's popular version of the Big Five trait scheme. There are other versions. In addition, not everybody agrees to the number five. Some approaches boil everything down to only two or three basic traits; others argue for six or slightly more. The disagreements reflect differences in statistical preferences and other fairly esoteric issues.

Most everybody agrees, however, that basic traits can be grouped into *a small number* of fundamental categories—that is, *approximately five* (plus or minus two or three). See McAdams (2009). Also, see:

Ashton, M. C., Lee, K., Perguini, M., et al. (2004). A six-factor structure of personality descriptive adjectives: Solutions from psycholexical studies in seven languages. *Journal of Personality and Social Psychology, 86, 356–366.*

Clark, L. A., & Watson, D. (2008). Temperament: An organizing paradigm for trait psychology. In O. P. John, R. W. Robins, and L. A. Pervin (Eds.), *Handbook of personality: Theory and research* (3rd ed., pp. 265-286). New York: Guilford Press.

De Young, C. G. (2006). Higher-order factors of the Big Five in a multi-informant sample. *Journal of Personality and Social Psychology, 91,* 1138–1151.

Goldberg, L. R. (1993). The structure of phenotypic personality traits. *American Psychologist, 48,* 26–34.

John, O. P., Naumann, L. P., & Soto, C. J. (2008). Paradigm shift to the integrative Big Five trait taxonomy. In O. P. John, R. W. Robins, and L. A. Pervin (Eds.), *Handbook of personality: Theory and research* (3rd ed., pp. 114–158). New York: Guilford Press.

McCrae, R. R., & Costa, Jr., P. T. (1997). Personality trait structure as a human universal. *American Psychologist, 52,* 509–516.

16. Long before the computer age would make such a task easy, two intrepid researchers went to an unabridged English dictionary containing 550,000 entries and identified all of the words denoting personality traits. They came up with about 18,000 words referring to psychological states, traits, and evaluations. Of these, about 4,500 reflected, in their judgment, relatively stable and enduring personality traits. Interestingly (perhaps), this list became the basis for a decades-long series of statistical studies that ultimately led to the establishment of the Big Five taxonomy of personality traits, as described in McAdams (2009). For the original study: Allport, G. W., & Odbert, H. S. (1936). Trait-names: A psychological study. *Psychological Monographs, 47* (1, Whole No. 211).

17. Friedman, H. S., Tucker, J. S., Tomlinson-Keasy, C., et al. (1993). Does childhood personality predict longevity? *Journal of Personality and Social Psychology, 65,* 176–185.

18. For evidence on the importance of personality traits in predicting consequential social behavior and life's most important outcomes: Ozer, D. J., & Benet-Martinez, V. (2006). Personality and the prediction of consequential outcomes. In S. T. Fiske, A. E. Kazdin, and

D. L. Schacter (Eds.), *Annual review of psychology* (Vol. 57, pp. 401–421). Palo Alto, CA: Annual Reviews, Inc.

Roberts, B. W., Kuncel, N. R., Shiner, R., et al. (2007). The power of personality: The comparative validity of personality traits, socioeconomic status, and cognitive ability for predicting important life outcomes. *Perspectives in Psychological Science, 2,* 313–345.

19. On childhood origins of adult personality traits, see:

Caspi, A., Roberts, B. W., & Shiner, R. (2005). Personality development: Stability and change. In S. E. Fiske, A. E. Kazdin, and D. L. Schacter (Eds.), *Annual review of psychology* (Vol. 56, pp. 453–484). Palo Alto, CA: Annual Reviews, Inc.

20. Longitudinal studies documenting stability (as well as developmental change) in dispositional traits are too numerous to list. But see:

McAdams & Olson (2010).

Roberts, B. W., & Delvecchio, W. (2000). The rank-order consistency of personality from childhood to old age: A quantitative review of longitudinal studies. *Psychological Bulletin, 126,* 3–25.

Roberts, B. W., Walton, K. E., & Viechtbauer, W. (2006). Patterns of mean-level change in personality traits across the life course: A meta-analysis of longitudinal studies. *Psychological Bulletin, 132,* 1–25.

21. Behavior genetic studies do show that environments matter in the making of traits. But environmental effects are complex and often contingent on the nature of one's genotype. Furthermore, the kinds of environments that seem to matter most are those that are unique to a person (called "nonshared environmental effects"), making him or her different from biological siblings, as opposed to those broad environmental influences that siblings share within a family, such as the overall family atmosphere, neighborhood, social class, common family activities, general parenting practices, and so on (called "shared environmental effects"). See McAdams (2009), chap. 6, for an accessible overview. For a more technical and authoritative source, see:

Krueger, R. F., & Johnson, W. (2008). Behavior genetics and personality: A new look at the integration of nature and nurture. In O. P. John, R. W. Robins, and L. A. Pervin (Eds.), *Handbook of personality: Theory and research* (3rd ed., pp. 287–310). New York: Guilford Press.

22. However, some trait dimensions show higher self/observer correlations than do others. Because extraversion, for example, involves very public kinds of behaviors (being outgoing, sociable, enthusiastic, etc.) self-ratings and peer-ratings on extraversion tend to be relatively higher than many other traits. Lower self/observer correlations typically show up for neuroticism, which may involve more internal kinds of experiences

(e.g., feelings of sadness, anxiety) that are not typically directly observable by others. Still, self/observer correlations on neuroticism are not small. See:

Funder, D. (1995). On the accuracy of personality judgment: A realistic approach. *Psychological Review, 102*, 652–670.

23. Rubenzer, S. J., & Faschingbauer, T. R. (2004). *Personality, character, and leadership in the White House: Psychologists assess the presidents.* Washington, DC: Brassey's Inc.

The researchers asked historians and other experts to complete well-validated personality scales as they would apply to each U.S. president. They aggregated and statistically analyzed the data in such a way as to arrive at trait scores for each president. They correlated the scores with various other indices of presidential performance (such as historians' ratings of "presidential greatness.") Because George W. Bush had been in office for a relatively short period of time when the project was ongoing, the researchers obtained less data on him than on the other presidents. Therefore, they supplemented what they got with their own ratings of Bush, based largely on their reading of biographies and other published sources.

24. On extraversion and the Behaviorial Approach System, see McAdams (2009), chap. 5, and:

Smillie, L. D., Pickering, A. D., & Jackson, C. J. (2006). The new reinforcement sensitivity theory: Implications for personality measurement. *Personality and Social Psychology Review, 10*, 320–335.

25. On happiness and extraversion, see McAdams (2009), chap. 5, and:

Lucas, R. E., & Diener, E. (2001). Understanding extraverts' enjoyment of social situations: The importance of pleasantness. *Journal of Personality and Social Psychology, 81*, 343–356.

26. Fredrickson, B. L. (2001). The role of positive emotions in positive psychology: The broaden-and-build theory of positive emotions. *American Psychologist, 56*, 218–226.

27. Costa, Jr., P. T., & Widiger, T. A. (Eds.). (1994). *Personality disorders and the five-factor model of personality.* Washington, DC: American Psychological Association Press.

28. Harmon-Jones, E., & Allen, J. J. B. (1998). Anger and frontal brain activity: EEG asymmetry consistent with approach motivation despite negative affective valence. *Journal of Personality and Social Psychology, 74*, 1310–1316.

29. Pearce-McCall, D., & Newman, J. P. (1986). Expectation of success following noncontingent punishment in introverts and extraverts. *Journal of Personality and Social Psychology, 50*, 439–446.

30. Andersen (2002), p. 105.

31. Unger, C. (2007). *The fall of the house of Bush.* New York: Scribner, p. 250.

32. On the Bullock incident, see: Andersen (2002), p. 190, and Weisberg (2008), p. 126.
33. Simonton, D. K. (2006). Presidential IQ, openness, intellectual brilliance, and leadership: Estimates and correlations for 42 U.S. chief executives. *Political Psychology, 27,* 511–526.
34. McClellan, S. (2008). *What happened: Inside the Bush White House and Washington's culture of deception.* New York: Public Affairs, p. 145.
35. Bruni, F. (2002). *Ambling into history: The unlikely odyssey of George W. Bush.* New York: Harper Collins.
36. Quoted in Weisberg (2008), p. 67.
37. Unger (2007), p. 154.
38. Woodward, B. (2006). *State of denial.* New York: Simon & Schuster, p. 419.
39. McClellan (2008), p. 145.
40. Singer, P. (2004). *The president of good and evil: The ethics of George W. Bush.* New York: Dutton, p. 211.
41. Andersen (2002), p. 56.
42. The exact relationship between openness to experience on the one hand and intelligence on the other remains somewhat contested in empirical psychology. The two are clearly different constructs in principle, but are they positively related to each other in practice? Most research suggests a statistically significant but moderate positive association between the two, meaning that people who tend to score high on self-report measures of openness tend also to score somewhat high on measures of intelligence. But the statistical tendency is not strong, and there are many exceptions to the rule. Openness to experience is also positively associated with number of years of education. See McAdams (2009), chap. 5, and:
    McCrae, R. R., & Costa, Jr., P. T. (1997). Conceptions and correlates of openness to experience. In R. Hogan, J. Johnson, and S. Briggs (Eds.), *Handbook of personality psychology* (pp. 825–847). San Diego, CA: Academic Press.
43. Rubenzer & Faschingbauer (2004). See also Simonton (2006).
44. Draper (2007), p. 88. See also Suskind (2004), p. 189.
45. Draper (2007), p. 88.
46. Quoted in Unger (2007), p. 198.
47. On integrative complexity, see McAdams (2009), chap. 8, and:
    Suedfeld, P., Tetlock, P. E., & Streufert, S. (1992). Conceptual/integrative complexity. In C. P. Smith (Ed.), *Motivation and personality: Handbook of thematic content analysis* (pp. 376–382). New York: Cambridge University Press.

48. Porter, C. A., & Suedfeld, P. (1981). Integrative complexity in the correspondence of literary figures: Effects of personal and social stress. *Journal of Personality and Social Psychology, 40,* 321–330.

49. See Simonton (2006) and:
    Suedfeld, P., & Leighton, D. C. (2002). Early communications in the war against terrorism: An integrative complexity analysis. *Political Psychology, 23,* 585–599.

50. Tetlock, P. E., Peterson, R. S., & Berry, J. M. (1993). Flattering and unflattering personality portraits of integratively simple and complex managers. *Journal of Personality and Social Psychology, 64,* 500–511.

51. Tetlock, P. E., Armor, D., & Peterson, R. S. (1994). The slavery debate in antebellum America: Cognitive style, value conflict, and the limits of compromise. *Journal of Personality and Social Psychology, 66,* 115–126.

52. Frum, D. (2003). *The right man: The surprise presidency of George W. Bush.* New York: Random House, pp. 91–92.

53. Woodward (2006), p. 155.

54. McClellan (2008), p. 127.

55. G. W. Bush (1999), p. 79.

56. Woodward (2006), p. 490.

57. Woodward, B. (2002). *Bush at war.* New York: Simon & Schuster, pp. 15–18.

58. Woodward (2002), p. 39. In an interview with Bob Woodward, President Bush acknowledged that bin Laden had not been the focus of his national security team before 9/11: "There was a significant difference in my attitude after September 11. I was not on point, but I knew he was a menace, and I knew he was a problem. I knew he was responsible, or we felt he was responsible, for the [previous] bombings that killed Americans. I was prepared to look at a plan that would be a thoughtful plan that would bring him to justice, and would have given the order to do that. I have no hesitancy about going after him. But I didn't feel that sense of urgency, and *my blood was not nearly as boiling.*" (Italics added.)

59. Woodward (2002), p. 168. The remarks were made to King Abdullah of Jordan, on September 28.

60. Woodward (2002), p. 45. The remarks were made to reporters on September 12.

61. Woodward (2002), p. 108.

62. Woodward (2002), p. 109.

63. My characterization of Bush's performance as commander-in-chief in the months immediately following 9/11 owes much to Woodward (2002), who enjoyed unparalleled access to war planning during this time. Woodward describes his book as "an account of President George W. Bush

at war during the first 100 days after the September 11, 2001, terrorist attacks." He writes: "The information I obtained for this book includes contemporaneous notes taken during more than 50 National Security Council and other meetings where the most important decisions were discussed and made. Many direct quotations of the president and the war cabinet members come from these notes. Other personal notes, memos, calendars, written internal chronologies, transcripts and other documents also were the basis for direct quotations and other parts of the story." (Woodward, 2002, p. xi). In addition, Woodward interviewed more than 100 people involved in the execution of the war. Most of the interviews were tape-recorded. He interviewed President Bush on the record twice— once for 90 minutes in the fall of 2001, and a second time for 2 ½ hours on August 20, 2002, at the president's ranch in Crawford, Texas.

CHAPTER 2: FATHERS AND SONS

1. Stone, O. (Director), & Weiser, S. (Writer). (2008). *W.* [Motion Picture]. United States: Lionsgate.
2. Minutaglio (1999), p. 148.
3. The relationship between George W. Bush and his father (George H. W. Bush) appears to be the central animating theme in Minutaglio (1999), Renshon (2004), Unger (2007), and Weisberg (2008). More broadly, family dynamics in the Bush clan are at the heart of Frank's (2007) psychoanalytic speculations about George W. Bush, Schweizer & Schweizer's (2004) generally sympathetic history of the Bush family, and these two popular sources:

    Kelley, K. (2004). *The family: The real story of the Bush dynasty.* New York: Anchor Books. A very readable but highly controversial account of the Bush family, going back generations.

    Phillips, K. (2004). *American dynasty: Aristocracy, fortune, and the politics of deceit in the house of Bush.* New York: Penguin. Here, the title says it all.
4. Freud's classic accounts of the Oedipus complex include:

    Freud, S. (1913/1958). Totem and taboo. In J. Strachey (Ed.), *The standard edition of the complete psychological works of Sigmund Freud* (Vol. 13). London: Hogarth.

    Freud, S. (1923/1961). The ego and the id. In J. Strachey (Ed.), *The standard edition* (Vol. 19). London: Hogarth.

    Freud, S. (1933/1964). New introductory lectures on psychoanalysis. In J. Strachey (Ed.), *The standard edition* (Vol. 21). London: Hogarth. See especially Lecture 31.

For a clinical/literary application of the Oedipus myth to the life (and death) of a famous person, see:

McAdams, D. P. (1985). Fantasy and reality in the death of Yukio Mishima. *Biography: An Interdisciplinary Quarterly, 8*, 292–317.

See also Chapter 11 in McAdams (2009).

5. But see Freud (1933/1964). Lecture 33.

6. Technically speaking, theory of mind involves two cognitive achievements in early childhood. First, the child comes to understand that minds have desires and wants, which in turn motivate behavior. Second, the child comes to understand that minds have *beliefs* that also inform what people do. People act because they either want or believe certain things. People own their wants and beliefs, and their goal-directed actions result from the activation of those wants and beliefs that they own. To act upon one's wants and beliefs is to exhibit personal agency. The whole idea of an autonomous, agentic, self-determining self—a bedrock assumption for mental health and maturity—is premised on the development of theory of mind. Interestingly and tragically, there is some evidence that children with severe autism do not develop theory of mind, or else develop it to a lesser extent than do most other children. Some psychologists believe that the striking social deficits that autistic children show are partly due to a compromised or dysfunctional theory of mind. See:

Baron-Cohen, S. (1995). *Mindblindness: An essay on autism and theory of mind. Cambridge*, MA: MIT Press.

Wellman, H. M. (1993). Early understanding of mind: The normal case. In S. Baron-Cohen, H. Tager-Flusberg, and D. J. Cohen (Eds.), *Understanding other minds: Perspectives from autism* (pp. 10–39). New York: Oxford University Press.

7. Long ago, the developmental psychologist Jean Piaget showed that children begin to become much more systematic and organized in their thinking around the age of 7 years, with the advent of what he called *concrete operations*. The hallmarks of concrete operations include the ability to arrange objects in linear order (seriation), to classify objects into nested hierarchies (class inclusion), and to comprehend an underling stability or consistency in the face of surface transformations of objects (conservation). Although many of the specifics of Piaget's theory of concrete operations have been challenged by subsequent research, this general idea still holds: that children's thinking becomes less egocentrically idiosyncratic and more systematic and logical with respect to the concrete world sometime in the early grade-school years. Cognitive developmental changes that take place at this time, then, help children to set up goals and plans for their behavior and enable them to structure their thinking and

their behavior in accord with systematic goal pursuit. Schooling builds on these changes, as teachers present tasks and goals in highly systematic ways and teach children how to think about various subject areas (social studies, arithmetic, science) in logical and systematic ways. On Piaget, see:

Elkind, D. (1981). *Children and adolescents: Interpretive essays on Jean Piaget.* New York: Oxford University Press.

Piaget, J. (1970). Piaget's theory. In P. H. Mussen (Ed.), *Carmichael's manual of child psychology* (Vol. 1). New York: Wiley.

8. Harter, S. (2006). Developmental and individual difference perspectives on self-esteem. In D. K. Mroczek and T. D. Little (Eds.), *Handbook of personality development* (pp. 311–334). Mahwah, NJ: Lawrence Erlbaum.

9. William James (1892) produced the first and most famous definition of self-esteem, conceiving it as the ratio of success to pretensions. Think of self-esteem as a fraction: the numerator is the success that a person perceives he or she is experiencing in the achievement of goals that are important to him, and the denominator is those goals (pretensions) that he or she most wants to achieve.

James, W. (1892/1963). *Psychology.* Greenwich, CT: Fawcett.

10. According to McAdams and Pals (2006), personality may be conceived as three layers: traits, goals, and stories. Traits begin to appear shortly after birth; goals kick in during the elementary school years; self-defining life stories (see Chapters 4 and 5) begin to form as a third layer in late adolescence and early adulthood.

See also: McAdams (2009), chap. 7; McAdams & Olson (2010).

On the importance of goals in personality, see especially:

Emmons, R. A. (1986). Personal strivings: An approach to personality and subjective well-being. *Journal of Personality and Social Psychology, 51,* 1058–1068.

Freund, A.M., & Riediger, M. (2006). Goals as building blocks of personality and development in adulthood. In D. K. Mroczek and T. D. Little (Eds.), *Handbook of personality development* (pp. 353–372). Mahwah, NJ: Lawrence Erlbaum.

Little, B. (1999). Personality and motivation: Personal action and the conative evolution. In L. A. Pervin and O. P. John (Eds.), *Handbook of personality: Theory and research* (2nd ed., pp. 501–524). New York: Guilford Press.

11. B. Bush (1994), p. 38.

12. B. Bush (1994), p. 39.

13. Andersen (2002), p. 37.

14. G. W. Bush (1999), p. 14.

15. G. W. Bush (1999), p. 15.

16. G. W. Bush (1999), p. 15.

17. Andersen (2002), p. 38.

18. B. Bush (1994), pp. 46–47.

19. Andersen (2002), p. 45.

20. G. W. Bush (1999), p. 183.

21. Schweizer & Schweizer (2004), p. 326.

22. Frum (2003), p. 40.

23. Chodorow, N. (1978). *The reproduction of mothering: Psychoanalysis and the sociology of gender.* Berkeley, CA: University of California Press.

24. Renshon, S. A. (2005). In his father's shadow: George W. Bush and the politics of personal transformation. In W. T. Schultz (Ed.), *Handbook of psychobiography* (pp. 323–343). New York: Oxford University Press.

25. G. W. Bush (1999), p. 167.

26. Minutaglio (1999), p. 24.

27. Kelly (2004) and Phillips (2004) are among the most relentless critics of the Bush family and its proclivity for using money and social connections to consolidate power.

28. Andersen (2002), p. 106.

29. Minutaglio (1999), p. 101.

30. Quoted in Renshon (2004), p. 32.

31. G. W. Bush (1999), pp. 6–7.

32. G. W. Bush (1999), p. 8.

33. Quoted in Renshon (2005), p. 327.

34. Woodward (2002), p. 16. In his first speech to the nation after the World Trade Center attacks, Bush said, "Terrorism against our nation will not stand." The phrasing echoed his father's famous "This will not stand" formulation used in 1990 after Iraq invaded Kuwait.

35. Some doubt has been expressed regarding just how serious the alleged assassination attempt was. See, for example, Weissberg (2008), pp. 183–184. The Kuwaiti government quickly convicted, but subsequently commuted the death sentences of all six co-conspirators. Nonetheless, there is little doubt that George W. Bush believed what intelligence officers told the family after the incident: that Saddam planned to kill not only his father but the other family members visiting Iraq with him, which included his mother Barbara, wife Laura, and his two youngest brothers, Neil and Marvin.

36. Among Muslims in the Middle East, an object becomes especially degraded when somebody steps on it with his shoes or feet. For this reason, the Iraqi journalist who famously threw his shoes at President George W. Bush on December 14, 2008 was not only threatening Bush with physical harm but also hurling an insult—a strong reaction of disgust and disdain.

37. Quoted in Unger (2007), p. 264.

38. McClellan (2008), p. 139.

244 Notes to pages 78–96

39. McClellan (2008), p. 141.

40. Isikoff, M., & Corn, D. (2006). *Hubris: The inside story of spin, scandal, and the selling of the Iraq War.* New York: Crown, p. 3.

41. For example, Weissberg (2008) writes: "All sons compete with their fathers. But the term *competition* doesn't begin to do justice to the Oedipal complexities of this particular relationship. George W. Bush has been driven since childhood by a need to differentiate himself from his father, to challenge, surpass, and overcome him." (p. xviii). The same author adds: "Driven by family demons, overflowing with confidence, and lacking any capacity for self-knowledge, Bush seems to me to have done precisely what we should have expected of him. My feelings follow the sympathy Sigmund Freud expresses in the study of Woodrow Wilson he wrote with the American diplomat William C. Bullitt. Freud and Bullitt argue that Wilson's inability to process aggressive feelings toward the man he called his 'incomparable father' left him increasingly messianic and detached from reality" (Weissberg, 2008), p. xxiii. For what it is worth, most Freud scholars—even those who, like me, greatly admire Freud's work—consider his book on Wilson to be an embarrassment.

42. Quoted in Renshon (2004), p. 32.

43. Paul O'Neill's account of the first National Security Council meeting, including the direct quotes, comes from Suskind (2004), pp. 70–75.

44. Clarke, R. A. (2004). *Against all enemies: Inside America's war on terror.* New York: Free Press, p. 24.

45. Clarke (2004), pp. 30–31.

46. Clarke (2004), p. 32.

47. Woodward (2004), p. 26.

48. Woodward (2004), p. 24.

49. Woodward (2004), p. 24.

50. Woodward (2002), p. 49.

51. Woodward (2004), p. 24.

52. Woodward (2004), p. 2.

53. Woodward (2004), p. 271.

54. (2005, September 8). Colin Powell on Iraq, Race, and Hurricane Relief. *ABC News, 20/20.* Retrived from: http://abcnews.go.com/2020/Politics/story?id=1105979&page=1.

55. Van Natta, Jr., D. (2009, July 6). A treasured Bush memento, once the property of a foe, may be put on display. *New York Times.* Natta writes:

> Among the thousands of gifts Mr. Bush received as president, the gun became a favorite, a reminder of the pinnacle moment of the

Iraq war, according to friends and long-time associates. . . . For many years, Mr. Bush kept the mounted, glass-encased pistol in the Oval Office or a study, showing it with pride, especially to military officials. He also let visitors in on a secret: when the pistol was recovered, it was unloaded. . . . Douglas Brinkley, an author and history professor at Rice University, said the pistol opened a psychological window into Mr. Bush's view of his presidency. "It represents this Texas notion of the white hats taking out the black hats and keeping the trophy," Mr. Brinkley said. "It's a True West magazine kind of pulp western mentality. For President Bush, this pistol represents his greatest moment of triumph, like the FBI keeping Dillinger's gun. He wants people generations from now to see the gun and say, 'He got the bad guy.'"

To add to Professor Brinkley's psychological musings, it is difficult to avoid the Freudian equation of guns with the penis. Among other things, Saddam's pistol might be said to symbolize the tyrant's aggressive masculinity. Capturing the gun is a Freudian metaphor for castrating the aggressor, an Oedipal victory for George II, in a sense. Why does the president delight in telling people that the gun was unloaded? Maybe because it symbolizes the fact that the tyrant had nothing left to shoot—his masculinity was completely depleted. What do I think of these Freudian musings? I love them. But we are walking off of the scientific reservation here, which is the prime reason to relegate this kind of speculation, as interesting as it may be, to the endnotes.

CHAPTER 3: ON BEING A CONSERVATIVE

1. In his socioanalytic theory of personality, Robert Hogan argues that human beings evolved to live in complex and highly ritualized social groups in which the needs for social acceptance (getting along) and social status (getting ahead) were strong determinants of social behavior. See:

   Hogan, R. (1982). A socioanalytic theory of personality. In M. Page (Ed.), *Nebraska symposium on motivation* (pp. 55–89). Lincoln, NE: University of Nebraska Press.

   My imagined portrayal of group life among human beings 50,000 years ago is based on many sources, including these:

   Buss, D. (2008). Human nature and individual differences: Evolution of human personality. In O. P. John, R. Robins, and L. A. Pervin (Eds.),

> *Handbook of personality: Theory and research* (3rd ed., pp. 29–60). New York: Guilford Press.

Tooby, J., & Cosmides, L. (1992). The psychological foundations of culture. In J. H. Barkow, L. Cosmides, and J. Tooby (Eds.), *The adapted mind: Evolutionary psychology and the generation of culture* (pp, 19–136). New York: Oxford University Press.

Pinker, S. (1997). *How the mind works.* New York: Norton.

Wright, R. (1994). *The moral animal.* New York: Pantheon.

2. Social identity theory states that human beings tend to: (1) categorize and define themselves in terms of the groups to which they belong, (2) identify strongly with and prefer their own groups (in-groups), and (3) compare themselves and their groups to other groups (out-groups), towards which they typically feel some antagonism or negative bias. See:

Tajfel, H. (1981). *Human groups and social categories: Studies in social psychology.* London: Cambridge University Press.

Turner, J. C. (1987). *Rediscovering the social group: A self-categorization theory.* New York: Basil Blackwell.

In-group favoritism and out-group antagonism are also at the root of prejudice and discrimination, even as they serve basic evolutionary needs. See especially:

Fishbein, H. D. (2002). *Peer prejudice and discrimination: Evolutionary, cultural, and developmental dynamics* (2nd ed.). Mahwah, NJ: Lawrence Erlbaum.

3. Research on what psychologists call *terror management theory* shows that when people are reminded of their own mortality they tend to embrace more strongly dominant religious, political, and ethical ideologies. Whether or not this is a shift to "conservatism," per se, is sometimes debated in this literature, for one can feel a strong attachment to a "liberal" ideology (e.g., socialism), which may be enhanced under threat. However, even the tendency to *conserve* what a particular society considers to be a "liberal" value system might be seen as a kind of conservatism in and of itself. In any case, the shift that tends to show up when people experience mortality reminders and other threats to their security and esteem is predominantly in the direction of traditional ideologies and frameworks that are associated with what most people see as conservative points of view. Relatedly, studies suggest that these kinds of threats enhance tendencies toward *right-wing authoritarianism*, which itself tends to be associated with political conservatism, as will be discussed later in this chapter. See:

Doty, R. M., Peterson, B. E., & Winter, D. G. (1991). Threat and authoritarianism in the United States, 1978-1987. *Journal of Personality and Social Psychology, 61,* 629–640.

Greenberg, J., & Jonas, E. (2003). Psychological motives and political orientation – The left, the right, and the rigid: Comment on Jost et al. (2003). *Psychological Bulletin, 129,* 376-382.

Hastings, B. M., & Shaffer, B. (2008). Authoritarianism: The role of threat, evolutionary psychology, and the will to power. *Theory & Psychology, 18,* 423–440.

Jost, J. T., Glaser, J., Kruglanski, A.W., et al. (2003b). Exceptions that prove the rule—Using a theory of motivated social cognition to account for ideological incongruities and political anomalies: Reply to Greenberg and Jonas (2003). *Psychological Bulletin, 129,* 383–393.

Silbey, C. G., Wilson, M. S., & Duckitt, J. (2007). Effects of dangerous and competitive worldviews on right-wing authoritarianism and social dominance orientation over a five-month period. *Political Psychology, 28,* 357–371.

Solomon, S., Greenberg, J., & Pyszczynski, T. (1991). A terror management theory of social behavior: The psychological functions of self-esteem and cultural worldviews. In M. P. Zanna (Ed.), *Advances in experimental social psychology* (Vol. 20, pp. 297–340). Hillsdale, NJ: Lawrence Erlbuam.

4. Sullivan, A. (2006). *The conservative soul: Fundamentalism, freedom, and the future of the right.* New York: Harper, pp. 9–10.

5. Sullivan (2006), p. 275.

6. Sullivan (2006), p. 232.

7. Sullivan (2006), p. 6.

8. Allit, P. (2009). *The conservatives: Ideas and personalities throughout American history.* New Haven, CT: Yale University Press, p. 2.

9. Greenwald, G. (2007). *A tragic legacy: How a good vs. evil mentality destroyed the Bush presidency.* New York: Three Rivers Press, p. 32.

10. Alford, J. R., Funk, C. L., & Hibbing, J. R. (2005). Are political orientations genetically transmitted? *American Political Science Review, 99,* 153–167.

11. Bouchard, Jr., T., Lykken, D. T., McGue, M., et al. (1999). Sources of human psychological differences. *Science, 250,* 223–228.
    Tellegen, A., Lykken, D. J., Bouchard, Jr., T. J., et al. (1988). Personality similarity in twins reared apart and together: The Minnesota study of twins reared apart. *Journal of Personality and Social Psychology, 54,* 1031–1039.

12. Block, J., & Block, J. H. (2006). Nursery school personality and political orientation two decades later. *Journal of Research in Personality, 40,* 734–749.

13. Rubenzer and Faschingbauer (2004) rate Bush as 49th percentile on neuroticism, which corresponds to the middle of the distribution on this trait for U.S. presidents. Renshon (2004, 2005) does not provide a

systematic rating, but he tends to underscore Bush's emotional stability, which would put him toward the lower end of neuroticism. My own sense is that Bush was relatively low on such features of neuroticism as tendencies toward anxiety and sadness, but that he was relatively high on neuroticism descriptors like "tense" and tending toward "anger." All in all, then, I would rate him in the middle range for neuroticism.

14. The link between political conservatism and the broad personality trait of conscientiousness is weakly but sometimes statistically significantly positive, meaning that there is a slight tendency for more conservative people to show higher levels of conscientiousness. In the one study showing the clearest evidence here, conservatism proved to be positively related to these two facets of conscientiousness: achievement striving and orderliness. See:

Jost, J. T. (2006). The end of the end of ideology. *American Psychologist, 61,* 651–670.

15. Rubenzer and Faschinbauer (2004) rate Bush as relatively low on conscientiousness, giving him especially low marks on the conscientiousness facets of dutifulness, competence, and deliberation. By contrast, Renshon (2004, 2005) highlights discipline and self-control as defining features of Bush's personality. I would split the difference here. Ratings of Bush's conscientiousness depend on which features of this broad trait a rater wishes to focus on and also depend on what point in Bush's life course one wishes to evaluate. When he was a young man, George W. Bush was impulsive and undisciplined. But his conscientiousness rose considerably as he grew older—a developmental trend that, by the way, shows up for many people. See:

Roberts et al. (2006).

16. Rubenzer & Faschingbauer (2004).

17. From Bush's farewell address at the end of his second term as president. In: Stolberg, S. G. (2009, January 16). A somber Bush says farewell to the nation. *The New York Times,* p. A19.

18. In their comprehensive review of the psychological literature, Jost et al. (2003) report a correlation of -.32 between openness to experience and conservatism, indicating a statistically significant and moderately robust negative relationship. See:

Jost, J. T., Glaser, J., Kruglanski, A. W., et al. (2003a). Political conservatism as motivated social cognition. *Psychological Bulletin, 129,* 339–375.

19. Michalski, R. L., & Schackelford, T. K. (2002). An attempted replication of the relationship between birth order and personality. *Journal of Research in Personality, 36,* 182–188.

Schooler, C. (1972). Birth order effects: Not here, not now! *Psychological Bulletin, 78,* 161–175.

20. Sulloway, F. J. (1996). *Born to rebel: Birth order, family dynamics, and creative lives.* New York: Pantheon.

21. Equivocal support for Sulloway's thesis can be found in this study:

    Paulhus, D. L., Trapnell, P. D., & Chen, D. (1999). Birth order effects on personality and achievement within families. *Psychological Science, 10*, 482–488. The findings in this interesting study also suggest that to the extent personality differences do show up as a function of birth order, they manifest themselves within families rather than as general dispositions that can be compared across people from different families.

22. G. W. Bush (1999), p. 207.

23. Jost et al. (2003a).

24. G. W. Bush (1999), p. 15.

25. G. W. Bush (1999), p. 18.

26. G. W. Bush (1999), p. 17.

27. Mansfield, S. (2003). *The faith of George W. Bush.* Lake Mary, FL: Charisma House, p. 35.

28. Minutaglio (1999), p. 180.

29. Jost (2006). See also:

    Jost, J. T., Huyadhy, O. (2005). Antecedents and consequences of system-justifying ideologies. *Current Directions in Psychological Science, 14*, 260–265.

    System-justifying beliefs may reflect a more general tendency of human beings to assume that the way things are in life are pretty much the way they should be. Eidelman, Crandall, and Pattershall (2009) call this the "existence bias." See:

    Eidelman, S., Crandall, C. S., & Pattershall, J. (2009). The existence bias. *Journal of Personality and Social Psychology, 97*, 765–775. See also:

    Kay, A. C., Gaucher, D., Peach, M. M., et al. (2009). Inequality, discrimination, and the power of the status quo: Direct evidence for a motivation to see the way things are as the way they should be. *Journal of Personality and Social Psychology, 97*, 421–434.

30. Napier, J. L., & Jost, J. T. (2008). Why are conservatives happier than liberals? *Psychological Science, 19*, 565–572.

31. Schweizer & Schweizer (2004), pp. 153–154.

32. Aikman (2004), p. 132.

33. Research on authoritarianism goes back to the 1940s, when social scientists asked why so many middle-class, law-abiding citizens of Germany could possibly support the Hitler regime. They began to suspect that a general tendency to defer to strong authority, especially under conditions of threat,

explained part of the problem. Those who were more likely to show such deference might be motivated by a particular personality syndrome. The authors of the classic book on authoritarianism—*The Authoritarian Personality* (Adorno, Frenkel-Brunswik, Levinson, et al, 1950)—listed nine cardinal features of this personality syndrome: rigid adherence to conventional values, submission to authority in the in-group, aggression toward out-groups, suspicion of art and psychology, superstition and a tendency to stereotype, preoccupation with power and toughness, cynicism and hostility, paranoid ideas about wild and dangerous things happening in the world, and an obsession with sexuality. Combining Freudian theory with a neo-Marxist political frame, the authors argued that authoritarianism had its roots in a complex web of family dynamics that typically play out under conditions of economic insecurity. In essence, a highly repressive family environment sows the seeds for the growth of authoritarianism in children. The child represses strong biological impulses because of an overly punitive environment, ultimately projecting those impulses onto others, in a defensive way. Criticism of the theory and the measure used to assess individual differences in authoritarianism (the F-Scale, "F" for "fascism") led to more modest claims and important improvements in measurement. Robert Altemeyer's (1981, 1996) development of the *Right-Wing Authoritarianism Scale* (RWA) marked a major advance in this line of research. The RWA focuses on three fairly well-established features of authoritarianism: authoritarian submission, authoritarian aggression, and conventionalism. Key sources:

Adorno, T. W., Frenkel-Brunswik, E., Levinson, D. J., et al. (1950). *The authoritarian personality*. New York: Harper & Brothers.

Altemeyer, R. A. (1981). *Right-wing authoritarianism*. Winnipeg: University of Manitoba Press.

Altemeyer, R. A. (1996). *The authoritarian specter*. Cambridge, MA: Harvard University Press.

See also:

Jost (2006).

McAdams (2009), pp. 190–192.

34. Thornhill, R., & Fincher, C. L. (2007). What is the relevance of attachment and life history to political values? *Evolution and Human Behavior, 28*, 215–222.

35. A substantial body of research suggests positive relations between authoritarianism (typically assessed via the Right-Wing Authoritarianism scale, or RWA) and a number of attitudinal variables such as socially-conservative values, anti-Semitism, distrust of outsiders, and highly punitive attitudes toward those deemed to be "deviant" in a society. Peterson, Doty,

and Winter (1993) found that authoritarians hold hostile and punitive attitudes toward people with AIDS, people who use drugs, and people who are homeless. Among Dutch students, authoritarianism strongly predicted ethnocentric prejudice, as evidenced in strong support among authoritarians for a Dutch political party that advocated the expulsion of immigrant workers (Meloen, Hagendoorn, Raaijmakers, & Visser, 1988). Authoritarianism is associated with support for the caste system among citizens of India (Hassan & Sarkar, 1975) and with nostalgia for the old Soviet regime and distrust of democratic reforms among citizens of Russia (McFarland, Ageyev, & Abalakina-Paap, 1992). Authoritarians tend to cherish the traditions of their own group but are highly distrustful of the traditions of other groups (Duckitt, 2006). Among North American college students, authoritarianism is associated with support for pro-Christian religious instructions in the public schools (Altemeyer, 1996). The same study, however, showed that authoritarian North American students were *opposed* to pro-Muslim religious instructions in public schools in Muslim countries. Sources:

Altemeyer (1996).

Duckitt, J. (2006). Differential effects of right-wing authoritarianism and social dominance orientation on out-group attitudes and their mediation by threat from and competitiveness to outgroups. *Personality and Social Psychology Bulletin, 32*, 684–696.

Hassan, M. K., & Sarkar, S. N. (1975). Attitudes toward caste system as related to certain personality and sociological factors. *Indian Journal of Psychology, 50*, 313–319.

McFarland, S. G., Ageyev, V. S., & Abalakina-Paap, M. A. (1992). Authoritarianism in the former Soviet Union. *Journal of Personality and Social Psychology, 63*, 1004–1010.

Meloen, J. D., Hagendoorn, L., Raaijmakers, Q., et al. (1988). Authoritarianism and the revival of political racism: Reassessments in the Netherlands of the reliability and validity of the concept of authoritarianism by Adorno et al. *Political Psychology, 9*, 413–429.

Peterson, B. E., Doty, R. M., & Winter, D. G. (1993). Authoritarianism and attitudes toward contemporary social issues. *Personality and Social Psychology Bulletin, 19*, 174–184.

36. Dean, J. W. (2006). *Conservatives without conscience.* New York: Viking.
37. In my own studies, correlations between RWA and self-ratings on how conservative a person is run as high as +.60. See:

McAdams, D. P., Albaugh, M., Farber, E., et al. (2008). Family metaphors and moral intuitions: How conservatives and liberals narrate their lives. *Journal of Personality and Social Psychology, 95*, 978–990.

38. Haidt, J., & Joseph, C. (2004). Intuitive ethics: How innately prepared intuitions generate culturally variable virtues. *Daedalus: Special Issue on Human Nature, 133*(4), 55–66.
    See also:
    Haidt, J. (2007, May 18). The new synthesis in moral psychology. *Science, 316*, 998–1001.
39. Graham, J., Haidt, J., & Nosek, B. A. (2009). Liberals and conservatives rely on different sets of moral foundations. *Journal of Personality and Social Psychology, 96*, 1029–1046.
40. McAdams et al. (2008), Study 2.
41. Suskind (2004).
42. Andersen (2002), pp. 276–277.
43. G. W. Bush (1999), p. 235.
44. G. W. Bush (1999), p. 235.
45. Draper (2007), p. 51.
46. (2001, October 15). The anthrax source: Is Iraq unleashing biological weapons on America? *Wall Street Journal.* Retrieved from: http://www.opinionjournal.com/editorial/feature.html?id=95001324.
47. Unger (2007), p. 254.
48. Landau, M. J., Solomon, S., Greenberg, J., et al. (2004). Deliver us from evil: The effects of mortality salience and reminders of 9/11 on support for President George W. Bush. *Personality and Social Psychology Bulletin, 30*, 1136–1150.
    See also:
    Cohen, F., Ogilvie, D. M., Solomon, S., et al. (2005). American roulette: The effect of reminders of death on support for George W. Bush in the 2004 presidential election. *Analyses of Social Issues and Public Policy, 5*, 177–187.
49. Woodward (2004), pp. 88–89.

CHAPTER 4: VARIATIONS ON A REDEMPTIVE THEME

1. Frum (2003), p. 283.
2. Minutaglio (1999), p. 91.
3. Minutaglio (1999), p. 95. Also Andersen (2002), p. 63.
4. Andersen (2002), p. 64.
5. Andersen (2002), p. 70.
6. Andersen (2002), p. 64.
7. Andersen (2002), p. 70.

8. Reports of Bush's drug usage in college and later have never been substantiated. It seems likely that George W. Bush might have tried marijuana during his college or young-adult years, as did many young people in the late 1960s and 1970s. Some Bush detractors allege he may have used cocaine. Bush himself has consistently refused to discuss speculation regarding marijuana and cocaine use. He has stated, however, that when his father became president in 1989 and required White House employees to affirm that they had not used illegal drugs for 15 years, he would have passed that test. That would take Bush back to 1974, which is still after his college years and after his stint in the Texas Air National Guard.

9. Andersen (2002), p. 106.

10. Unger (2007), p. 82.

11. G. W. Bush (1999), p. 135.

12. Andersen (2002), p. 107.

13. Minutaglio (1999), p. 135.

14. The incident is described in numerous sources, such as: Renshon (2005), p. 43; and Andersen (2002), p. 143.

15. Andersen (2002), p. 139. Bush makes reference to the same incident in his campaign autobiography: G. W. Bush (1999), p. 135.

16. Andersen (2002), pp. 145–146.

17. G. W. Bush (1999), p. 136.

18. Renshon (2004, 2005).

19. G. W. Bush (1999), p. 136.

20. Quoted in Unger (2007), pp. 79–80.

21. Unger (2007), pp. 81–84.

22. The account of Blessitt's meeting with George W. Bush on April 3, 1984 comes largely from Mansfield (2003), pp. 61–66.

23. Mansfield (2003), pp. 64–65.

24. Mansfield (2003), p. 65.

25. Unger (2007), p. 85.

26. The famous psychoanalytic theorist Erik Erikson identified *identity versus role confusion* as the key psychosocial challenge of adolescence and young adulthood. For Erikson, developing an identity involves exploring various options that society has to offer for vocation, ideology, and relationships, and then ultimately making choices and commitments to particular vocational, ideological, and relational choices. Ideally, establishing an identity should situate a person within a meaningful, satisfying, and productive niche in society and provide the person with a sense that his or her life is more-or-less unified and purposeful. See:
Erikson, E. H. (1968). *Identity: Youth and Crisis*. New York: Norton.

On particular identity problems facing contemporary youth and on the idea that identity exploration in contemporary society often extends well into the 20s and 30s, see:

Arnett, J. J. (2004). *Emerging adulthood.* New York: Oxford University Press.

In numerous articles and books, I and a growing number of my colleagues have argued that developing an identity in adulthood centrally involves constructing a meaningful story of the self, which incorporates the reconstructed past and imagined future into a broad narrative providing a person's life with some semblance of unity and purpose. See especially:

McAdams, D. P. (1985). *Power, intimacy, and the life story: Personological inquiries into identity.* New York: Guilford Press.

McAdams, D. P. (1990). Unity and purpose in human lives: The emergence of identity as a life story. In A. I. Rabin, R. A. Zucker, R. A. Emmons, et al (Eds.), *Studying person and lives* (pp. 148–200). New York: Springer.

McAdams, D. P. (1993). *The stories we live by.* New York: Guilford Press.

McAdams, D. P., Josselson, R., & Lieblich, A. (Eds.). (2006). *Identity and story: Creating self in narrative.* Washington, DC: American Psychological Association Press.

McLean, K. C., Pasupathi, M., & Pals, J. L. (2007). Selves creating stories creating selves: A process model of self-development. *Personality and Social Psychology Review, 11,* 262–278.

Singer, J. A. (2004). Narrative identity and meaning-making across the adult lifespan: An introduction. *Journal of Personality, 72,* 437–459.

27. In an unforgettable moment in the 1988 vice-presidential debate, Dan Quayle, in responding to charges that he was too young and inexperienced to be vice president, said that he had about as much experience in the Congress as did John F. Kennedy when Kennedy sought the White House. His opponent, Lloyd Bentsen, then said this: "Senator. I served with Jack Kennedy. I knew Jack Kennedy. Jack Kennedy was a friend of mine. Senator, you're no Jack Kennedy."

28. Habermas, T., & Bluck, S. (2000). Getting a life: The emergence of the life story in adolescence. *Psychological Bulletin, 126,* 748–769.

29. On the psychology of redemption, see:

McAdams, D. P. (2006). *The redemptive self: Stories Americans live by.* New York: Oxford University Press. See also:

McAdams, D. P., & Bowman, P. J. (2001). Narrating life's turning points: Redemption and contamination. In D. P. McAdams, R. Josselson, and A. Lieblich (Eds.), *Turns in the road: Narrative studies of lives in transition* (pp. 3–34). Washington, DC: American Psychological Association Press.

McAdams, D. P., Reynolds, J., Lewis, M., et al. (2001). When bad things turn good and good things turn bad: Sequences of redemption and contamination in life narrative, and their relation to psychosocial adaptation in midlife adults and in students. *Personality and Social Psychology Bulletin, 27,* 472–483.

30. Andersen (2002), p. 121.
31. Andersen (2002), p. 121.
32. G. W. Bush (1999), p. 79.
33. For example, Schweizer and Schweizer (2004), p. 262, write that George W. "saw in Laura the sort of steely discipline that he had been lacking in his life and that his parents epitomized. Family members also noticed that Laura had the ability to influence her husband, and to regulate or restrain his behavior."
34. See: Erikson, E. H. (1963). *Childhood and society* (2nd ed.). New York: Norton.
35. On generativity, see:
    McAdams, D. P. (2001). Generativity in midlife. In M. E. Lachman (Ed.), *Handbook of midlife development* (pp. 395–443). New York: Wiley.
    McAdams, D. P., & de St. Aubin, E. (Eds.). (1998). *Generativity and adult development: How and why we care for the next generation.* Washington, DC: American Psychological Association Press.
36. G. W. Bush (1999), p. 80.
37. G. W. Bush (1999), pp. 86–87.
38. Research suggests that individual differences in generativity (typically measured through self-report questionnaires) are statistically significantly and positively associated with involvement (past or current) in a religious tradition or a practice of spirituality. The statistical findings are not large in magnitude, meaning that there are many exceptions to the rule—that is, many especially generative people who do *not* characterize themselves as religious or spiritual as well as many people low in generativity who are religious or spiritual. Furthermore, the statistical association has been shown mainly in American society, a society that is more religious, overall, than almost any other modern democracy. Whether or not the same statistical association would hold in a less religious society remains an open question. See McAdams (2006),chap. 6. See also:
    Dillon, M., & Wink, P. (2004). American religion, generativity, and the therapeutic culture. In E. de St. Aubin, D. P. McAdams, and T. C. Kim (Eds.), *The generative society* (pp. 153–174). Washington, DC: American Psychological Association Press.

Hart, H. M., McAdams, D. P., Hirsch, B. J., et al. (2001). Generativity and social involvement among African American and white adults. *Journal of Research in Personality, 35*, 208–230.

Rossi, A. S. (Ed.). (2001). *Caring and doing for others*. Chicago: University of Chicago Press.

39. On themes of redemption in the life stories of highly generative adults, see:

McAdams (2006).

McAdams & Bowman (2001).

McAdams et al. (2001).

McAdams, D. P., Diamond, A., de St. Aubin, E., et al. (1997). Stories of commitment: The psychosocial construction of generative lives. *Journal of Personality and Social Psychology, 72*, 678–694.

See also:

Walker, L. J., & Frimer, J. A. (2007). Moral personality of brave and caring exemplars. *Journal of Personality and Social Psychology, 93*, 845–860.

40. The first step in Alcoholics Anonymous and other 12-step recovery programs is the realization that the addict is powerless to change on his or her own. What is needed is a surrender of personal agency to a higher force. In a brilliant analysis of how the same kind of redemptive sequence can play itself out in the lives of reformed criminals, Maruna (2001) maps out the transformative narratives that ex-criminals often construct to explain and sustain their own transformation. See:

Maruna, S. (2001). *Making good: How ex-convicts reform and rebuild their lives*. Washington, DC: American Psychological Association Press.

41. G. W. Bush (1999), p. 14.

42. G. W. Bush (1999), p. 15.

43. McAdams (2006). See also:

Colby, A., & Damon, W. (1992). *Some do care: Contemporary lives of moral commitment*. New York: The Free Press.

44. Sanger, D. E. (2001, July 25). On world stage, America's president wins mixed review. *New York Times*, p. A1.

45. The story of Mark Craig's sermon and its alleged effect on George W. Bush's decision to run for president is told in many places. Whereas Bush (1999) argued that the sermon convinced him to run for president, others have suggested that Bush's mind was made up long before he heard Craig's sermon (e.g., Weisberg, 2008). See also:

Aikman (2004), pp. 109–120.

Mansfield (2003), p. 109.

Unger (2007), p. 160.

It should also be noted that whereas Governor Bush told some family members that he felt God was calling him to run for the presidency, Laura strongly discouraged this kind of talk. See Schweiker & Schweiker (2004), p. 438.

46. Frum (2003), p. 3.

47. The Oval Office story is told in Aikman (2004), p. 157, and Mansfield (2003), p. 173. Aikman claims that he got confirmation of the incident from two independent sources.

48. Quoted in Aikman (2003), p. 157. For a searing critique of the role of faith in the Bush White House, see:

Suskind, R. (2004, October 17). Faith, certainty, and the presidency of George W. Bush. *New York Times Magazine*, pp. 44–51, 64, 102, 106.

49. McAdams (2006) pp. 28–33. See also:

Affleck, G., & Tennen, H. (1996). Construing benefits from adversity: Adaptational significance and dispositional underpinnings. *Journal of Personality, 64*, 899–922.

Pennebaker, J. W. (1997). Writing about emotional experiences as a therapeutic process. *Psychological Science, 8*, 162–166.

Tedeschi, R. G., & Calhoun, L. G. (1995). *Trauma and transformation: Growing in the aftermath of suffering.* New York: Macmillan.

50. G. W. Bush (1999), p. 1.

51. G. W. Bush (1999), p. 139.

52. McAdams, D. P., & Albaugh, M. (2008). What if there were no God? Politically conservative and liberal Christians imagine their lives without faith. *Journal of Research in Personality, 42,* 1668–1672.
See also: McAdams et al. (2008).

53. On downward counterfactuals, see:

Roese, N. J. (1997). Counterfactual thinking. *Psychological Bulletin, 121*, 133–148.

54. By contrast, the Christian liberals were more likely than their conservative counterparts to narrate life-story scenes in which authority figures taught lessons of empathy and openness toward others (McAdams et al., 2008). The findings are somewhat consistent with the characterization of conservatives and liberals made by the sociolinguist George Lakoff (2002). Lakoff argues that citizens often see government as akin to parents. As a result, citizens tend to project family metaphors onto political systems. Conservatives tend to adopt what Lakoff calls *strict father* metaphors for government. By contrast, liberals tend to see government as a *nurturant caregiver*. Lakoff's views and the study's findings are also broadly consistent with a distinction in ideological orientation made by the psychologist Silvan Tomkins (1987). Tomkins distinguished between normative (conservative) and humanistic (liberal) ideological scripts in life. For a full elaboration of Tomkins's perspective, see also de St. Aubin (1996).

de St. Aubin, E. (1996). Personal ideology polarity: Its emotional foundation and its manifestation in individual value systems, religiosity, political orientation, and assumptions concerning human nature. *Journal of Personality and Social Psychology, 71*, 152–165.

Lakoff, G. (2002). *Moral politics: How liberals and conservatives think.* (2nd ed.). Chicago: University of Chicago Press.

Tomkins, S. S. (1987). Script theory. In J. Aronoff, A. I. Rabin, and R. A. Zucker (Eds.), *The emergence of personality* (pp. 147–216). New York: Springer.

55. Quoted in Romano, L., & Lardner, Jr., G., (1999, July 29). Young Bush, a political natural, moves up to the majors. *Washington Post*, p. A1.

56. Wischnia, B., & Carrozza, P. (2003). 20 questions for President George W. Bush: A running conversation. *Runner's World* on line: http://www.runnersworld.com/footnotes/gwbush/home.html.

57. G. W. Bush (1999), pp. 53–54.

58. Renshon (2005), p. 340.

59. G. W. Bush (1999), p. 8.

60. Frum (2003), p. 55.

61. G. W. Bush (1999), p. 56.

62. Woodward (2002) writes: "At the end of the service, the congregation stood and sang 'The Battle Hymn of the Republic.' [Condoleeza] Rice felt the whole church stiffen with determination. When the presidential party walked out of the cathedral, the grayness and rain of the morning had lifted, replaced by brilliant sunshine and blue skies." (p. 67).

63. Weisberg (2008), p. 200.

64. The words are from Richard Perle. In Unger (2007), p. 290.

65. A president puts his faith in Providence. *New York Times*, "Week in Review." Also, see Phillips (2004), p. 233.

66. Religious leaders uneasy with Bush rhetoric. *Pittsburgh Post-Gazette*. Also, see Phillips (2004), p. 233.

CHAPTER 5: AN AMERICAN STORY

1. Kakutani, M. (2001, February 4). Faith base: As American as second acts and apple pie. *New York Times*, p. D1.

2. In *The Varieties of Religious Experience*, the great American psychologist and philosopher William James (1902/1958) suggested that redemption is a core idea in all of the world's major religions. He wrote that different religious traditions promise a "certain uniform deliverance" *from* an initial

"sense that there is *something wrong about us* as we naturally stand" *to* a subsequent "solution" whereby *"we are saved from the wrongness* by making proper connection with the higher powers" (p. 383, *italics* in the original). Put simply, religions tell us that things are bad at the beginning (perhaps because we are bad) but that things will get better and we will be delivered to a better place. Examples of stories that encode the sequence of early suffering followed by a (promised or actual) deliverance to a better state are legion in the Judeo-Christian tradition: Abraham and Sarah suffer infertility into old age until God sends them Isaac, their son; the Israelites suffer through Egyptian captivity and 40 years of wandering until God delivers them to the Promised Land; Christ is crucified but raised up on the third day. Today, personal stories of conversion—moving suddenly from a bad and sinful state to a good and Godly one—are a staple of many Christian communities, a traditional paragon of which is the New Testament's story of Paul's conversion on the road to Damascus. Redemption sequences are also prevalent in Islam. The Arabic term *Islam* means "surrender," as in surrendering to the ultimate will of Allah in order to be purified and redeemed. In Hinduism and Buddhism, redemption sequences take the form of liberation from perpetual reincarnation. The first and second of the Four Noble Truths of the Buddha explain how it is that human existence is *dukkha*—full of conflict, dissatisfaction, sorrow, and suffering. The third and fourth speak of the liberation and freedom for human beings that come from following the Noble Eightfold Path on the way to Nirvana. See:

James, W. (1902/1958). *The varieties of religious experience*. New York: New Academic Library.

3. For a full exposition of the role of redemptive stories in American life and culture see McAdams (2006).

4. McAdams (2006); McAdams & Bowman (2001); McAdams et al. (1997); McAdams et al. (2001).

5. Written in 1630, Winthrop's precise words were as follows: "For wee must Consider that wee shall be as a Citty upon a Hill, the eies of all people are upon us." From Winthrop's lay sermon delivered on board the *Arbella*, "A Modell of Chistian Charity," in Bellah et al. (1985), p. 26. See:

Bellah, R. N., Madsen, R., Sullivan, W. M., et al. (1985). *Habits of the heart*. Berkeley, CA: University of California Press.

6. The fact that the New England Puritans modeled themselves after the biblical Israelites has been noted and analyzed in detail by many scholars. See especially:

Bercovitch, S. (1975). *The Puritan origins of the American self*. New Haven, CT: Yale University Press.

Delbancho, A. (1999). *The real American dream: A meditation on hope.* Cambridge, MA: Harvard University Press.

Glaude, E. S., Jr. (2000). *Exodus! Religion, race, and nation in early nineteenth-century black America.* Chicago: University of Chicago Press.

Wills, G. (1990). *Under God: Religion and American politics.* New York: Simon & Schuster.

See also: McAdams (2006), chaps. 1 and 4.

7. Winthrop's precise words: "The end is to improve our lives, to doe more service to the Lord, the comforte and encrease of the body of Christ whereof wee are members, that our selves and our posterity may be the better preserved from the Common corrupcions of this evill world, to serve the Lord and worke out our Salvacion under the power and purity of his holy Ordinances." From Bellah et al. (1985), p. 25.

8. Delbancho (1999) describes the Puritans as "incessant talkers" (p. 28). Ministers held private conferences with members of the flock, in which they tried to promote their congregants' spiritual development. Two hundred years before the birth of Freud, Puritan ministers engaged in a kind of talking therapy with their congregants. Delbancho calls them "soul physicians" (p. 29), suggesting that these conversations prefigure the modern forms of individual psychotherapy with which we are familiar today. Individual members would also give public testimonials of their own struggles with faith. Unlike the Puritans who stayed behind in Europe, the New England Puritans stipulated that before an adult could become a full member of the church he or she had to give a satisfactory life narrative of his or her development in faith. Puritans would even debate the merits and limitations of different life-narrative accounts. See also:

Shea, Jr., D. B. (1968). *Spiritual autobiography in early America.* Princeton, NJ: Princeton University Press.

9. See: Cole, T. R. (1992). *The journey of life: A cultural history of aging in America.* New York: Cambridge University Press.

10. This passage captures Emerson's faith in the inner self and his inherently redemptive message:

"Trust thyself: every heart vibrates to that iron string. Accept the place the divine providence has found for you, the society of your contemporaries, the connection of events. Great men have always done so, and confided themselves childlike to the genius of their age, betraying their perception that the absolutely trustworthy was seated at their heart, working through their hands, predominating in all their being. And we are now men, and must accept in the highest mind the same transcendent destiny; and not minors and invalids in a protected corner, not cowards fleeing before a revolution, but guides, redeemers, benefactors, obeying the Almighty effort and advancing on Chaos and the Dark."

From:

Emerson, R. W. (1841/1993). *Self-reliance and other essays*. New York: Dover, p. 20.

11. Clemetson, L. (2001, January 8). The age of Oprah: Oprah on Oprah. *Newsweek*, pp. 38–48).

12. Quoted in Weisberg (2008), p. 219.

13. See for example: Gates, Jr., H. L. (Ed.). (1987). *The classic slave narratives*. New York: Penguin.

    See also: McAdams (2006), chap. 7.

14. Minutaglio (1999), p. 200.

15. Woodward (2006), p. 270.

16. Woodward (2006), p. 371.

17. Woodward (2004), p. 89.

18. G. W. Bush (1999), p. 240.

19. Gardner, H. (1995). *Leading minds: An anatomy of leadership*. New York: Basic Books, p. 9.

20. Gardner (1995), p. 43.

21. Woodward (2002), p. 37.

22. Woodward (2004), p. 320.

23. For an analysis of the redemptive imagery in Lincoln's *Gettysburg Address*, see McAdams (2006), pp. 70–72. See also:

    Wills, G. (1992). *Lincoln at Gettysburg: The words that remade America*. New York: Simon & Schuster.

24. Melville, H. (1850/1892). *White-jacket, or the world in a man-of-war.* Boston: Page, p. 144.

25. Quoted in Greenwald (2007), p. 39.

26. Quoted in Singer (2004), p. 209.

27. Singer (2004), p. 209.

28. Woodward (2004), p. 178.

29. McClellan (2008), p. 251.

30. Fineman, H. (2003, March 10). Bush and God. *Newsweek*, p. 30.

31. Woodward (2006), pp. 488–489.

32. Slotkin, R. (1973). *Regeneration through violence: The mythology of the American frontier, 1600-1860*. Middletown, CT: Wesleyan University Press.

33. Slotkin (1973), p. 5.

34. Quoted in Slotkin (1973), p. 17.
35. Slotkin (1973), p. 17.
36. Morone, J. A. (2003). *Hellfire nation: The politics of sin in American history.* New Haven, CT: Yale University Press.
37. Tuveson, E. L. (1968). *Redeemer nation: The idea of America's millennial role.* Chicago: University of Chicago Press, p. viii.
38. Schweizer & Schweizer (2004), p. 517.
39. Unger (2007), p. 19.
40. See especially Phillips (2004) and Unger (2007). See also:
    Strozier, C. B., & Swiderski, K. (2005). The psychology and theocracy of George W. Bush. *The Journal of Psychohistory, 33,* 102–116.
41. Unger (2007), p. 4.
42. Young, J. E. (2000). Against redemption: The arts of countermemory in Germany today. In P. Homans (Ed.), *Symbolic loss: The ambiguity of mourning and memory at century's end* (pp. 126–144). Charlottesville, VA: University of Virginia Press.
43. Alon, N., & Omer, H. (2004). Demonic and tragic narratives in psychotherapy. In A. Lieblich, D. P. McAdams, and R. Josselson (Eds.), *Healing plots: The narrative basis of psychotherapy* (pp. 29–48). Washington, DC: American Psychological Association Press.
44. Weisberg (2008), p. xxvii.
45. Weisberg (2008), p. xxvii.
46. Woodward (2006), p. 155.
47. Woodward (2006), p. 371.
48. Tetlock, P. E. (2003). Thinking the unthinkable: Sacred values and taboo cognitions. *Trends in Cognitive Science, 7,* 320–324.
49. Suskind (2004), p. 293.
50. Woodward (2006), p. 81.
51. Woodward (2004), p. 421.
52. Woodward (2004), p. 424.
53. Stolberg (2009).

Index

interpretive steps, redemption, 162
introvert, traits, 24, 26, 29
Iraqi Freedom (military operation),
    6, 226–27
Iraqi Intelligence Service, 77
Iraq War, 52, 77, 79, 91, 106–7, 191
    Americans' view (2009) on, 227–28
    and Bush, G.H.W., 77–78
    and Bush, G.W., 6, 79, 81, 83,
        90–91, 106–7, 193–94
    justification of, 137–38, 142–43,
        205, 214, 218
    out-group fear, 137–38
    redemptive Christian narrative
        and, 218–19
    war planning on, 85–86
Isikoff, Michael, 78
Israeli–Palestinian peace agreement,
    36, 81

Jackson, Henry ("Sccop"), 140
James, William, 242n9, 258n2
Jefferson, Thomas, 37
Jews, extermination of, 220
Johnson, Lyndon B.
    on civil rights legislation, 126
    and Graham, Billy, 152
    and Vietnam War, 4
Judeo-Christian tradition, 258–59n2

Karzai, Hamid, 5, 49
Kennedy, John F., 66, 158, 208–9,
    254n27
    redemptive story, 208–9
Kerry, John, 41, 80, 139
Kristol, Irving, 105, 140
Kuwait, 77, 243n35

"liberal" ideology, 246n3
liberalism, 105
    vs conservatism, 111–12

liberation, 178, 203, 204
    and freedom, 207
    of Iraqi people, 211
    and Iraq War, 205
    from negative forces, 203
Lincoln, Abraham, 208, 219
"Little George." *See* Bush, George W.

Mallon, Neil, 70
Manichean view, on chosen one,
    212–13
mass destruction weapons, 5, 6, 45,
    50, 85, 91, 137–38, 142–43, 190,
    214, 224
McCain, John, 38
McClellan, Scott, 37, 38, 44, 213
McCrae, Jeff, 22, 234n15
meaning-making, psychological and
    cultural tool for, 219–20
Midland, Texas, 61, 119–23, 135, 185,
    191, 192, 202–3
militant anticommunism, 105
modern society
    identity, challenge of, 155
    narrative identity, 156
moral domains, Haidt on, 130–32
moral steadfastness, 171–73

narrative identity, 156–65
    cultural expectation,
        impact of, 158
    as disciplined man, 176–77
    drunkenness and sobriety, 168–69
    fundamental feature of, 159
    parts of, 158–59
    past, imaginative
        re-interpretation of, 160
    wealth and prominence,
        disadvantages of, 157–58
National Prayer Service, 185
Nazi Germany, 207, 210